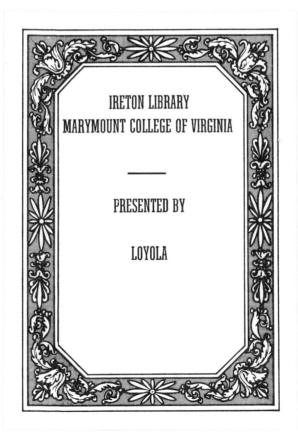

THE

AMERICAN
Short Story

before 1850

A CRITICAL HISTORY

TWAYNE'S CRITICAL HISTORY
OF THE SHORT STORY

William Peden, General Editor
University of Missouri-Columbia

The American Short Story, 1850–1900
Donald Crowley, University of Missouri-Columbia

The American Short Story, 1900–1945
Philip Stevick, Temple University

The American Short Story, 1945–1980
Gordon Weaver, Oklahoma State University

The English Short Story, 1880–1945
Joseph M. Flora, University of North Carolina-Chapel Hill

The English Short Story, 1945–1980
Dennis Vannatta, University of Arkansas-Little Rock

The Irish Short Story
James F. Kilroy, Vanderbilt University

The Latin American Short Story
Margaret Sayers Peden, University of Missouri-Columbia

The Russian Short Story
Charles Moser, George Washington University

THE

AMERICAN
Short Story

before 1850

A CRITICAL HISTORY

Eugene Current-García
Auburn University

Twayne Publishers

85814

The American Short Story
before 1850:
A Critical History

Published in 1985 by Twayne Publishers
A Division of G. K. Hall & Company
A publishing subsidiary of ITT
70 Lincoln Street, Boston, Massachusetts 02111

Printed on permanent/durable
acid-free paper and bound in
the United States of America.

First Printing

Book production by Marne Sultz

Book design by Barbara Anderson

Typeset in 11 pt. Garamond
with Perpetua display type
by Compset, Inc. of Beverly, MA

Library of Congress Cataloging in Publication Data

Current-García, Eugene.
The American short story before 1850.

(*Twayne's critical history of the short story*)
Bibliography: p. 146
Includes index.
1. Short stories, American—History and criticism.
2. American fiction—19th century—History and criticism.
I. Title. II. Series.

PS374.S5C87	1985	813'.01'09	84-28006

ISBN 0-8057-9359-3

To Walton R. Patrick,
my wise counselor and
faithful friend for forty years

Contents

Preface

This study is included in Twayne's Critical History of the Short Story, a series designed to cover the development of short fiction in America from its beginnings in the eighteenth century to the present. This volume traces the evolution of a new genre from its crude origins as an entertainment feature in the early magazines of the Revolutionary period to its achievement of a distinctive form of literary art during the first half of the nineteenth century.

Lacking fixed principles of content, composition, and form, the original pieces of short fiction published in American magazines before 1800 were often anonymous adaptations of tales or anecdotes casually lifted from British or Continental magazines without reference to their authorship or point of origin. In the course of their transfer from Europe to America, however, they soon began to acquire a faintly indigenous coloration as a result of changes in their settings, place names, ethnic characteristics, and character relationships. Native elements thus began appearing in these short tales and anecdotes, even though the basic fictions themselves were but thinly disguised carbon copies of foreign works. They showed little evidence of any effort to produce a form of literature peculiar to America, since there was as yet little national consciousness among the American people. Neither were there any established criteria or traditional standards that might be applied to the literary evaluation of these fledgling productions. They fulfilled their purpose simply by appealing to an unsophisticated reading public eager to be amused, instructed, preached to, shocked, or titillated.

In the early 1800s the artistry of Washington Irving transformed such borrowings as these into genuinely disciplined literature. Irving was fascinated by the colonial Dutch legends of his native New York, and through his fertile imagination transformed these tales into his broadly comic *Knickerbocker History*. Then, with the added experience of Germanic tales learned chiefly in translations and from Sir Walter Scott, he combined these with his American source materials to produce in *The Sketch Book* such classics as "Rip Van Winkle" and "The Legend of Sleepy Hollow."

Irving's craftsmanship, as evidenced in the creation of his jovial persona Geoffrey Crayon, Esq., thus established both a medium and an individual style for the production of a distinctive new narrative form, which he developed further in his next two volumes of short fiction, *Bracebridge Hall* and *Tales of a Traveller.*

The models that Irving set forth in these works served to inspire the literary aspirations of his two younger contemporaries Nathaniel Hawthorne and Edgar Allan Poe. With greater dramatic power than Irving possessed, together these two writers broadened, enriched, and intensified both the content and the form of American short fiction. Whereas Irving's narrative style seldom ventured beyond the visible surface of character and incident, Hawthorne skillfully employed symbols and imagery to suggest hidden depths in the motives and actions of his characters, while Poe sharpened the role of the narrator to provide both verisimilitude and extreme tension in his tales. Thus in nearly two hundred tales they produced during the 1830s and 1840s, Hawthorne and Poe demonstrated that the short-story form, based on a carefully controlled narrative framework, could be fashioned into a subtly varied yet durable literary art, capable of being read and reread with pleasure, studied and restudied, interpreted and reinterpreted, without diminishing its appeal to either the common reader's imagination or the critic's scrutiny.

The method employed in chapters 2, 3, and 4 of this study therefore seeks to show how Irving, Hawthorne, and Poe, working within the romantic tradition of the early nineteenth century, contributed in turn to the enrichment of the short-story form, bringing it to a peak of imaginative intensity by midcentury. Chapter 5, dealing with another group of romanticists led by the South Carolinian William Gilmore Simms, also seeks to show how these writers during the same period extended American short fiction into yet other areas, primarily raw frontier humor. Though less fully committed to artistic excellence than Poe and Hawthorne, such writers as Longstreet, Hooper, Harris, and Thorpe likewise contributed an important dimension to American short fiction, particularly in their occasionally realistic treatment of unsavory American types and behavior generally ignored in the more genteel literature of the period. Thus the Southwest frontier humorists also played a small but significant transitional role, that of turning the American short story toward the kind of realistic fiction that came into prominence later in the century and became increasingly dominant in our own time. That shift of emphasis is treated in the final chapter of this study.

Auburn University   Eugene Current-García

Chronology

1706 Daniel Defoe's "A True Relation of the Apparition of One Mrs. Veal," earliest influential short fiction in English.

1741 First American magazines: Andrew Bradford's *American Magazine* and Benjamin Franklin's *General Magazine, and Historical Chronicle.*

1770 Stamp Act and Boston Tea Party: prelude to American Revolution.

1775 Battles of Lexington and Concord: "the shot heard round the world."

1776 Thomas Jefferson writes the Declaration of Independence; signed 2 July.

1783 General Cornwallis surrenders at Yorktown, ending Revolutionary War.

1787 Royall Tyler's *The Contrast,* America's first significant comedy drama, opens in New York, 16 April.

1787–1789 Constitutional Convention in Philadelphia establishes federal republic of the United States; *The Federalist* papers, written by James Madison, Alexander Hamilton, and John Jay, consolidate the form of American government; George Washington takes office as first president.

1789 Beginnings of short fiction in American magazines: "Azakia: A Canadian Story" in the *American Museum* 6 (September) and "The Story of the Captain's Wife and an Aged Woman" in the *Gentleman and Lady's Town and Country Magazine* 6 (October and November).

1796 "Narrative of the Unpardonable Sin" published in the *Theological Magazine* 2 (September–October).

1797   Ludvich Tieck's "The Fair-haired Eckbert" translated into English.

1789–1801 Charles Brockden Brown, America's first significant novelist, publishes *Wieland, Edgar Huntly, Ormond, Arthur Mervyn, Clara Howard,* and *Jane Talbot.* Exerts influence on both Cooper and Poe.

1803   The Louisiana Purchase, authorized by President Jefferson, adds huge western territory to nation's land mass.

1820   The Missouri Compromise: United States laws passed to maintain political balance between southern slave states and northern nonslave ones.

1820–1824 Washington Irving's three collections of tales and sketches published in England by John Murray: *The Sketch Book, Bracebridge Hall: or, The Humorists,* and *Tales of a Traveller.*

1820–1836 Transcendentalism emerges as full-fledged movement of New England thought. Ralph Waldo Emerson's *Nature* published (1836).

1821–1850 James Fenimore Cooper's patriotic novels of land and sea published: *The Spy, The Pioneers, The Pilot, The Last of the Mohicans, The Prairie, The Red Rover, Homeward Bound, The Pathfinder, The Deerslayer, The Two Admirals, Jack Tier, The Ways of the Hour,* et al.

1830–1832 Nathaniel Hawthorne's earliest tales ("Provincial Tales" and "Seven Tales of My Native Land") published individually in the *Token, Salem Gazette,* and the *Atlantic Souvenir.*

1830–1835 Edgar Allan Poe tries unsuccessfully to publish his *Tales of the Folio Club.* His first published tale, "Metzengerstein," appears in the *Philadelphia Saturday Courier* in 1832.

1830–1856 William T. Porter edits the popular sporting weekly *Spirit of the Times.*

1833   William Gilmore Simms's first collection of stories, *The Book of My Lady,* published in Philadelphia.

1833–1835 Separate portions of Hawthorne's "The Story Teller" published piecemeal in the *New England Magazine.*

1835   Augustus B. Longstreet's collection, *Georgia Scenes,* published in Augusta, Georgia.

Alexis de Tocqueville's *Democracy in America* published in English translation; exerts lasting influence both in United States and abroad regarding philosophical principles of democratic government.

1836–1838 Poe edits the *Southern Literary Messenger;* reviews *Georgia Scenes.*

1837 Hawthorne's *Twice-Told Tales* published by American Stationers Company, Boston.

Emerson's Phi Beta Kappa address at Harvard University, "The American Scholar," acclaimed as "our Intellectual Declaration of Independence" by Oliver Wendell Holmes.

1840 Hawthorne's *Grandfather's Chair* published by Elizabeth Peabody.

Poe's *Tales of the Grotesque and Arabesque* published by Lea and Blanchard.

1841–1850 Emerson's major essays and poems published in various editions.

1842 Second edition of *Twice-Told Tales,* two volumes, published by Munroe; reviewed by Poe in *Graham's Magazine.*

1842–1847 Early anthologies of American literature published: *The Poets and Poetry of America; The Prose Writers of America.*

1843 Poe's second collection, *The Prose Romances of Edgar Allan Poe,* published by William H. Graham.

William Tappan Thompson's *Major Jones's Courtship* published in Madison, Georgia.

1845 William T. Porter's edition of *The Big Bear of Arkansas, and Other Sketches* published by Carey & Hart.

Simms's *The Wigwam and the Cabin* published; revised edition in 1856.

Poe's third collection, *Tales,* published by Wiley & Putnam.

Johnson Jones Hooper's collection, *Some Adventures of Captain Simon Suggs,* published by Carey & Hart.

1846 Hawthorne's *Mosses from an Old Manse,* two volumes, published by Ticknor & Fields; reviewed by Poe in "Tale Writing—Nathaniel Hawthorne," published in *Godey's Lady's Book* in 1847.

Thomas Bangs Thorpe's first collection, *Mysteries of the Backwoods,* published by Carey & Hart.

1847   Porter's edition of *A Quarter Race in Kentucky, and Other Sketches* published by Carey & Hart.

1850   Hawthorne's *The Scarlet Letter* published by Ticknor & Fields.

Melville's *White-Jacket* published by Harpers; his review-essay "Hawthorne and his Mosses" published in the *Literary World* (17 and 24 August).

Henry Clay Lewis's collection, *Odd Leaves from the Life of a Louisiana Swamp Doctor,* published by A. Hart of Philadelphia.

Emerson's *Representative Men: Seven Lectures* published by Samson and Company of Boston.

TYPES OF MAGAZINE SHORT FICTION BEFORE 1820

To understand the origins and development of the American short story, often referred to as our nation's unique contribution to modern literary forms, one must first know something about the history of American magazines. For the multifaceted short story of today is a creature of the magazines: its tentative beginnings during the infancy of American periodicals matched the primitive characteristics they displayed, and its growth during the past two centuries has continued to reflect their proliferation and diversity. Conversely, throughout its course of development, the short story in our land has been shaped, trimmed, remodeled, and updated by the shifting exigencies and conventions governing the success of magazine publication. Its quality and substance, notwithstanding the many creative talents that have nourished its growth, still reveal today as they did over 150 years ago the compromises and limitations imposed upon this art form by the changing tastes of a democratic, profit-oriented society. Without the magazine for an outlet, it is doubtful whether the short story would have emerged at all in the United States; lacking this outlet, it certainly could not have prospered.

Why and how did the magazine, more than any other single agency, stimulate and support the emergence of distinctively native types of short fiction in America? To what extent did the printing of short fiction contribute to the spread and continuity of the magazine itself? Although definitive answers to these questons are still being sought, studies of America's earliest literary history have repeatedly shown closely interacting forces at work between the magazine as a medium of communication and the short story as a literary form. Gradually, often haltingly, during a period of little more than fifty years following the American Revolution, as a few magazines acquired stature and sophistication, the short story achieved vigor, versatility, and distinction, especially in the works of major artists. Poe, Hawthorne, and Melville, for example, all published most of their short stories originally in magazines. But the striking difference in quality

1

between a masterpiece like Melville's "Benito Cereno," published in *Putnam's Magazine* in 1855, and an anonymous little tale entitled "Azakia: A Canadian Story," published sixty years earlier in the *Monthly Miscellany and Vermont Magazine,*[1] offers dramatic proof of the rapidity with which the American short story sprang from the humblest of origins into an art form of internationally praiseworthy dimensions.

To appreciate how the American magazine quickly became so important a means of propagating such artistic excellence, one must also be aware of certain foreign influences, chiefly English, that helped to determine the kinds of magazines that emerged in the American colonies and the variety of literary fare with which they hoped to gain public favor. Magazines began appearing in the colonies as early as 1741, and, since the proprietors of these first ventures regarded themselves as patriotic subjects of the king, they strove to emulate the most successful British periodicals such as the *Gentleman's* and the *London Magazine.* Men like Andrew Bradford and Benjamin Franklin, publishers of the first two American magazines, frankly acknowledged that they hoped to profit by emulating those models, as well as to give their own colonial society a favorable image abroad in doing so.

The latter motive became even more important after the Revolution, when social and political leaders of the United States sought every possible means for establishing the credibility and integrity of the new nation. "Shall we not then exert ourselves to appear as respectable abroad as we really are at home?" asked the editor of one of them.[2] Obviously, one of the surest ways to capture that respectability was to borrow from British magazines and to republish in the American ones the kinds of literary material that Englishmen admired. In the middle and later eighteenth century these included the essays of Addison, Steele, and Johnson; the poetry of Dryden, Pope, and Gray; and the fiction of Richardson, Sterne, and Mackensie. Accordingly, many of the earliest American magazines simply reprinted—often without bothering to acknowledge the source—both excerpts from and amateurish imitations of the works of these leading English writers. Lacking an established class of professional American writers, the magazine publishers sometimes even encouraged their own readers to try their hand at contributing some of the more popular types of short fiction, such as character sketches, sentimental tales, or oriental tales.[3]

This effort to secure original contributions provided slight opportunity for noteworthy fiction. The nation as a whole was too new and immature to produce a literature matching in scope and richness the literatures of western Europe. Scattered over a broad stretch of land extending two thousand miles from Maine to Georgia, the few small towns where an urban atmosphere would presently nourish an infant American literature represented only 3 percent of the total population. Compared to London or Paris, even the three most pretentious cities—Boston, New York, and Philadelphia—were still unfledged, lacking even the basic facilities for producing and distributing books. There were as yet no publishing houses; instead, there were only small commercial printers. If a writer wished to have his book published, he literally had to bring it out himself by negotiating privately with a printer, assuring the printer beforehand by means of a subscription list that the book's sales would cover the cost of production and provide a profit. If he actually got the book published, there were no critics or book reviewers to discuss its contents or value; and there was only the crudest advertising system for putting it into the hands of a reading public remote from his native city. The likelihood of its being widely read, even available, outside its neighboring areas was thus very slight.

Not surprisingly, although a fairly sizable number of books containing practical advice were published in the colonies—farmers' almanacs, books of sermons, legal or medical digests, and the like—the earliest full-length American novels did not appear until the 1790s, more than half a century after the great English novels of Defoe, Fielding, and Richardson. To pay for publishing a novel of one's own in that period of belletristic drought would have been too risky a venture for all but the most foolhardy to contemplate. But what is surprising is that by 1820 Americans, despite such unpromising conditions, had published about ninety novels, most of them rather shoddy imitations of British models.[4] Even more surprising is that during the same period more than a hundred magazines had come into being, flourished fitfully for a time, and then disappeared, leaving behind in their files many hundred pieces of short fiction.[5] From this mass of rudimentary fiction, much of it crude and inept by modern standards, sprang the American short story. Serving as printer, publisher, editor, bookseller, advertiser, preceptor, and encourager, the magazinist during these transitional decades provided perhaps the only feasible means of producing a new national literature, since he alone possessed the business methods and manufacturing techniques needed to overcome the many problems he confronted.

By 1800 between 400 and 500 short tales of one sort or another had appeared in American magazines, and their numbers increased proportionately during the next few decades as more and more magazines came into existence.[6] Many of these early tales were mere fragments of one or two paragraphs—sentimental character sketches of girls gone astray and comic

Indian anecdotes are typical examples cited by literary historians—and were evidently inserted both to fill space and to add spice and variety to the general contents. Many others, however, were longer narratives, running from one or two to six, eight, or more pages in length, and showing evidence of compositional skill and a concern for structure, style, and effect. Almost all of these were anonymous, or at best rounded off with initialed or cryptic Latinized pseudonyms such as *Publius* or *Sabrina;* so that unless their titles carried a byline indicating that a given story was copied or translated from a foreign source, it is almost impossible to determine which of them, if any, were original compositions written by native Americans. Nevertheless, the presence in them of a variety of native characters such as Indians and Negroes, Yankee farmers, soldiers, and backwoodsmen, French and English immigrants, as well as numerous local or regional references, strongly suggests that many of these early tales were of native American origin.

The growing numbers of these short tales, especially toward the end of the eighteenth century, clearly demonstrate the increasing popular appeal of ficton, notwithstanding its many official denouncers. The general makeup of this fiction—its themes, structure, tone, emphasis—reflected the actions, interests, and aspirations, as well as the doubts and fears, the manners and morals, of a self-conscious, democratic society adjusting to new conditions and problems and seeking its identity in the very process of dramatizing its behavior under the guise of moralistic self-examination. Ironically, therefore, the more vigorously fiction was condemned from the pulpit and public rostrum, the more it was printed and read. And the more it seemed to echo the very tones of its harshest critics!

One article taken from a London magazine and widely reprinted in American periodicals, entitled "Novel Reading a Cause of Female Depravity," warned that from such a practice "the poor deluded female imbibes erroneous principles, and from thence pursues a flagrantly vicious line of conduct."[7] Yet, while fiction was being castigated as a debaucher of young girls, giving them false ideas and hopes and turning their attention away from worthwhile tasks and obligations, the fiction they were reading consistently presented sensational types of experience involving seduction and sexual abuse. Hence the prevailing didactic tone of the stories: to meet the objections raised against fiction as a literary form per se, both their content and form were often conceived and presented as instructional aids toward exemplary conduct. To justify its existence, early American fiction was supposed to promote morality, not to mirror life; and yet, under the guise of sermonic truth-telling, many a scandalous episode or sequence of events could be luridly set forth for the reader's titillation.

Content and Method in the Early Tales

How consistently the earliest American short fiction provided both moral guidance and heightened entertainment may be seen in the kinds of subject matter as well as in the manner and methods of their presentation. By far the most prevalent themes had to do with (1) sexual incontinence—its hazards and punishments; (2) rural virtue as opposed to urban vice; and (3) the manifold risks threatening the individual's safety and peace of mind in a lawless, uncertain world. Under the first of these headings the changes were rung, with monotonous regularity and lurid variety, upon the fatal effects of seduction, rape, fornication, marital infidelity, even incest; while under the second, the gospel of work—honest daily toil and the satisfaction with one's humble station in a simple setting—was upheld as the road to salvation, the antidote to city-bred evils of luxury, idleness, and discontent, which led inevitably to perdition. Among a host of admonitory titles the following are self-explanatory: "The Exemplary Daughter," "The Merited Disappointment," "Miseries of Idleness and Affluence," "The Pangs of Repentance," "The Progress of Vice," "The Imprudent Parents," "The Extravagant Wife," "The Fatal Effects of Seduction," and "The Repentant Prostitute."[8]

With equal fervor, the third grouping dramatized most of the remaining physical or psychological dangers confronting the harried citizen in the new world: robbery, murder, kidnapping, slavery, piracy, and general violence. Like the earlier illustrative exempla in countless New England sermons, these short narratives repeatedly reinforced the Protestant ethic by showing, with whatever sensational details and dramatic skill their authors could muster, the dire results that were sure to follow when its doctrines were willfully ignored or transgressed. Scores of titles like the following, taken from the *Massachusetts Magazine,* can also be found duplicated in other magazines of the period: "The Duelist and Libertine Reclaimed" (April 1789, 205–8), "Almira and Alonzo: An Affecting Story—Founded on Fact" (June 1789, 361–64), "Treachery and Infidelity Punished" (November 1792, 659–60).

But despite the sameness of matter and the unmistakable moralistic tone prevalent in most of this early fiction, its manner of presentation varied considerably, while the methods employed by its many unknown writers in telling their tales reveal a consistent, if amateurish, groping toward the functional use of their materials. Thus, on the basis of native elements identified in them, several clearly defined types of stories have been distinguished, each manifesting a degree of local and contemporary interest, however slight. Conveniently classifying them under such rubrics as Indian stories, Negro stories, sentimental stories, ghost stories, and didactic stories, one scholar has shown that far from being merely pallid reproductions of British or Continental fiction, a great many of these early tales and sketches display a conscious, experimental effort to relate character and action to the American scene.[9]

Any such classification is necessarily arbitrary, its categories overlapping, since many an Indian story, for example, is likely also to be sentimental as well as didactic. To the student of American fiction, the more significant point is that within a quarter century of the founding of the new nation, many unknown writers were seeking to embody its current problems and characteristics in seemingly true-to-life fiction. They were seeking a usable past and a local identity so as to render the American experience—ordinary American folk grappling with ordinary, everyday concerns—in typical situations and settings. They were beginning to do what Cooper, Irving, Simms, Poe, Hawthorne, and Melville would eventually do much better; they were simply not doing it very well because they lacked the necessary artistry and techniques.

Whatever the substance of these early tales—whether violence and strife on the frontier or the woes bred of misconduct, parental tyranny, or the frustrated desires of star-crossed lovers—the basic problem confronting all their authors was that of achieving fictional validity. The fact that many a subtitle asserted that the story beneath it was based on actual events, with possibly only slight changes in the naming of characters and locale, implied a felt need for both a protective device and a means of linking together the external world of the actual and the inner world of the imagination. The writer not only wished to defend himself against the charge of falsification and distortion—of "making things up"—he also sensed the problem of establishing what Hawthorne would later call "a neutral territory, somewhere between the real world and fairyland, where the Actual and the Imaginary may meet, and each imbue itself with the nature of the other."[10]

Lacking as yet the formulae, let alone the techniques, for bringing about this transformation, these early writers had to grope for solutions to their basic problem. In organizing and setting forth their materials they had to find ways of making the story come alive, and giving it dramatic immediacy through a convincing portrayal of lifelike human beings, acting in a believable situation and place. Whether their primary aim was to teach a lesson or merely to tell an exciting tale, replete with exploits of breathtaking adventure or laced with comic mishaps, they had to learn how to suit the individual to the deed, how to master the art of character motivation, and how to relate unfolding events in a logical sequence of cause and effect. Through a process of trial and error they had to discover the most effective means of manipulating incidents and events so as to capture and hold the reader's interest throughout a series of suspenseful developments leading to an unexpected yet logical climax and an aesthetically satisfying denouement. Besides trying to achieve unity and continuity, they had finally to contend with the problem of narrative authenticity, of getting the story told in language appropriate to its tone, mood, atmosphere, and substance, as well as to its source of utterance—the problem, in short, of style and point of view.

Obviously, few of America's early fiction writers possessed the skills needed to attain all these ends or were even fully aware of the need for them. For it was not until the 1830s and 1840s, when writers like Poe, Simms, and Hawthorne began to examine critically the basis of their literary aims and specifically the distinctions between long and short fiction, that a theory of the short story gradually emerged. Practice had to precede theory; or as one scholar has noted, observing that "before 1835 the short story was usually amorphous, and was rarely thought of by either writer or critic as different from the novel in anything but length, . . ." criticism had to wait upon creation, and therefore no good analysis appeared until after the publication of Irving's *Sketch Book*. [11]

Short Fiction Models from the Past

Of course, practice in the art of prose fiction narrative, long and short, had been in vogue for centuries among European and Asiatic peoples; and long before even the age of the printing press there were famous collections of tales such as those in the Old and New Testaments of the Bible and the Apocryphal tales included in the Vulgate. Among the more famous secular collections there were also the *Thousand and One Nights,* dating from the tenth century A.D.; the *Gesta Romanorum,* probably written in the fourteenth century; the many beast fables such as Aesop's; Boccaccio's *Decameron* (1353); and Sir Thomas Malory's *Morte d'Arthur* (1485), which next to the Bible has probably exerted the strongest single influence of all these early tales upon later English short fiction. In considering the influence of these early tales upon the short story of the nineteenth and twentieth centuries, however, one must keep in mind two important characteristics—their ultimate purpose and the context in which they originally appeared. Except for the *Decameron* and the *Thousand and One Nights* (also known as the *Arabian Nights' Entertainment*), the primary motive for writing those collections, usually stated explicitly, was to instruct rather than to amuse their readers. Second, as a means of driving home the intended lesson, some overt device such as a pilgrimage, a wager or bargain, a legendary kingdom, or a protracted struggle suffered by a heroic race or nation often grouped or linked the tales together. In most of these early tales the writer's chief aim was to get the tale told; hence overt action as a vehicle for conveying the theme or meaning of the tale tends to predominate over other technical refinements such as the management of plot, incident, setting, character development, dialogue, and point of view.

This does not mean that the early tale writers created haphazardly. Rather, it is important to know that over the course of centuries, as successive generations of writers slowly developed the short tale as an art form, they gradually improved upon the methods of composition, refining little by little the techniques that enabled them to secure increasingly novel and original effects. For many centuries their progress was impeded by the lack of a large literate reading public and, until the sixteenth century, the fact that all writing was done by hand. But as printing became relatively inexpensive toward the end of the seventeenth century and readers correspondingly more numerous, newspapers and magazines soon appeared and multiplied. Competitively they brought about a vastly increased demand for short fiction, which, in turn, stimulated an artistic upsurge that led to the modern short story. By the time Poe began his career in the 1830s, scores of fiction writers were competing with one another, and hundreds of stories were being published in American and European magazines. To achieve lasting fame in the face of such competition, the fiction writer, as Poe himself recognized, had to know the techniques of his craft; he had to know how to combine his materials to produce stories that would be read with interest and appreciaton by an increasingly numerous, more sophisticated audience. In setting forth his definition of the short story, Poe unwittingly paid silent tribute to the artistry that had fashioned thousands of tales before his time. His fiction owed much to such predecessors as Boccaccio and Daniel Defoe.

British Influence: Defoe and Others

During the four centuries between the first appearance of Boccaccio's *Decameron* and Defoe's "A True Relation of the Apparition of One Mrs.

Veal," many changes had taken place in the fields of science and technology; and many new ideas concerning the nature of the universe had emerged as a result of discoveries in such areas as physics, astronomy, medicine, and geography. Although many people in the early 1700s still believed in witches and other forms of supernatural visitations (the Salem witch trials, where twenty innocent people were condemned and put to death, occurred in 1692 during Defoe's youth), belief in the literal existence of witches was no longer universally held. The spread of scientific knowledge had made thoughtful people skeptical about the reality of any phenomena that could not be explained rationally. At this point, accordingly, an interesting dichotomy arose: a continuing fascination with unexplained mysteries such as ghosts, werewolves, disembodied voices, and other such supernatural occurrences along with determined efforts either to explain these things rationally or to reject them as figments of a deranged imagination.

Defoe's "A True Relation of the Apparition of One Mrs. Veal" reflects these shifting attitudes and so marks another stage in the advancing sophistication of fiction, where it becomes the writer's deliberate effort to authenticate *within the story* the validity of his fictional illusion. Through his adroit use of a pseudojournalistic technique, Defoe shows how "to lie like the truth." There would have been no need in Boccaccio's day, or Shakespeare's, for a narrator to prove that ghosts walked the earth in human form, any more than Scheherazade would have felt obliged to prove that a genie appeared when Aladdin rubbed his magic lamp. If stories called for a ghost, the narrator supplied one, and the reader had few if any questions or doubts about it.

The whole point of Defoe's brilliant story, however, is that questions and doubts were now being raised about such phenomena. Did Mrs. Bargrave, in her own house, really see and talk for nearly two hours with Mrs. Veal on 8 September 1705—a full twenty-four hours after Mrs. Veal's death? Or did she make up the account of this visitation, either from malicious motives or the working of a deranged mind? The beauty of Defoe's story is that in dealing with these conflicting views it nails down the whole experience with such an abundance of documentary detail, set forth as plain matter of fact by a calm, persuasive, no-nonsense narrative voice, that the reader cannot help believing in Mrs. Veal's ghostly visit despite the nagging doubts that persist in his mind.

Defoe achieves this tour de force primarily through his clever management of the first-person point of view. His narrator begins by admitting that the problem is a baffling one, well worth serious inquiry, since he has known Mrs. Bargrave well for a long time and will vouch for her reputation despite the aspersions that friends of Mrs. Veal's brother have lately been casting on her character and sanity. He thus creates immediately a favorable impression of Mrs. Bargrave, which is further buttressed by the assurance that she has not grown bitter in the face of a lifetime of ill usage from both a mean father and a callous husband. Then, quickly summarizing in a flashback the long-standing friendship between Mrs. Veal and Mrs. Bargrave, the narrator describes the appearance of Mrs. Veal at a precise hour, place, and date, letting Mrs. Bargrave disclose in her own words her surprise and pleasure on seeing her old friend again after a separation of several years.

Defoe is perhaps most convincing in presenting a mass of corroborative details to support the truth of Mrs. Bargrave's testimony. His narrator, as though honor bound to secure all relevant proof of her sincerity, provides a barrage of specific data, each item of which adds a bit more to the credibility of her story. Thus, for the reader, the only logical conclusion is that Mrs. Bargrave has told the truth: she really did see and talk with the apparition of Mrs. Veal. Moreover, in its original published form (1706) Defoe prefaced "A True Relation of the Apparition" with an explanatory paragraph that accounted for the origin and present purpose of the story. It had been sent to a friend in London by someone in Kent, who had received it previously from a kinswoman living in Canterbury a few doors from Mrs. Bargrave's house. And the purpose of retelling the story once again "in the same words, as near as may be, from Mrs. Bargrave's own mouth," was avowedly didactic and utilitarian. In short, like many a lurid tale told in Puritan sermons, Mrs. Veal's ghost was to be read as an omen.

Recent scholarship has established that in 1705 there actually was a woman named Mrs. Bargrave living in Canterbury who would tell any willing listeners about her *séance à deux* with Mrs. Veal, but the extent to which Defoe reshaped both the facts and the telling of them to suit his own purposes is still a matter of conjecture. It seems clear, however, that as a writer of fiction bent on producing an entertaining ghost story, he nevertheless felt obliged to justify his craft by vigorously asserting its value as a stimulus toward piety and righteousness. Yet the story itself provides even stronger proof of his artistry, since it does convey an aura of truth that the reader is inclined to accept despite the fact that common sense prompts him to reject it. Thus, the creation of an illusion of reality based on a careful selection of details (one of Defoe's noteworthy skills) marks another stage in the development of short fiction.

Within less than fifty years after Defoe's death in 1731 fiction had become popular in the American colonies, and immediately following the American Revolution a veritable deluge of short fiction pieces appeared in the new magazines. Not surprisingly, most of these were amateurishly derivative and monotonously dull: unlike the craftmanship of Defoe's or Boccaccio's tales, technique was seldom equal to the task of combining dramatically the main elements of fiction—theme, character, action, and setting—if indeed the need for combining them was even considered. Generally speaking, the theme alone—or more specifically, the *moral,* explicitly stated first and last—*was* the story. It might be dramatized by an intervening body of reported action, involving several characters who might or might not be named; but with little apparent effort to make them seem believably lifelike, and even less to provide an appropriate milieu for them.

Narrative Purpose: Instruction versus Entertainment

But however crudely contrived, most of these tales invariably tried to reconcile the contradictory demands of moralists and fiction lovers by combining a stern moralistic tone with exciting narrative detail; the spicier and more lurid the details of the experience set forth, the more insistently did the narrator point to its obvious moral lesson. In "Calamaties of War and Effects of Unbridled Passion" (1784), for instance, an opening paragraph explaining that even at its best war breeds a reign of furies introduces the sad tale of Sophia and Martius, her husband, who was slain by her brother in battle. [12] The brother, never named, is barely prevented from suicide by Sophia, and the story concludes with the assurance that he now serves as a substitute father for her infant son. Similarly, in "Fatal Effects of Gaming" (1786), the narrator begins with a paragraph of reflections on the insidious evils of gambling. These naturally suggest to him the doleful fate of the Hargrave brothers, who fell under the influence of the dissolute Leeson, lost their patrimony, forfeited good positions, and turned highwaymen to obtain quick money for gambling. On the open road they held up their own father and shot him dead before realizing, too late, the enormity of their deed. And so the narrator concludes with two more paragraphs of moralized reflections to fill out his three pages of text. [13]

Occasionally the method might be varied, as in "Fatal Effects of Seduction" (1789), written in the then-popular epistolary style by Thomas Bellamy and copied from a British magazine. [14] The story unfolds in a frenzied letter from the "reformed Edmund" to his friend (unnamed) telling of his brother Charles's remorse and suicide, apparently because of the death of Maria, whom Charles had seduced. Ostensibly the letter is intended to dissuade his friend from a similar "destructive path" he is following, but the reader is left wondering exactly what has happened. Nearly identical in form as well as title, but three times as long, is "Melancholy Effects of Seduction" (1795), a wearily remorseful letter from Bellamon to his friend Harry, recounting the miseries of poor Fanny, a country lass he had seduced and then turned over to a worthless French couple who abandoned her. Having lost touch with Fanny, the writer tells at length of his distracted search and eventual discovery of her funeral procession. His inexorable moralizing to the bitter end—"if only every libertine felt the pangs of guilt as I do at this moment"—shows that the tear-jerking "true confession" had already begun to establish its impregnable position in American fiction.[15]

Not all first-person narratives, however, duplicated this pattern precisely, either in form or tone, notwithstanding a similarity in theme and purpose. In "Florio: A Moral History" (1786), for example, the narrator plunges at once in medias res with "You have often heard me talk of Florio." He then proceeds in a matter-of-fact tone to recount the series of troubles which, from lack of common judgment and a too easygoing wish to please his friends, led to Florio's undoing: his drunken companion assaulted a couple on the street and began fighting with the lady's escort; at this point Florio appeared and thoughtlessly killed the man, repenting too late his hasty action. Despite its subtitle, the tone rescues the story from excessive moralizing, as does that of another "affecting story" (1790), similarly titled, which tells of an upright young man who consoles an older widow in her grief and gradually becomes her lover and then the father of their illegitimate child. Horrified and remorseful, both destroy themselves in different ways: he by volunteering for sea duty and getting killed in a skirmish with privateers; she by taking poison. Of more interest to the reader, however, is the narrator's sympathetic attitude toward his characters, for instead of blaming either, he concludes that "In an ill-fated hour they were both ruined, though it is hard to tell which was the seducer or which the seduced."[16]

But even in Puritan New England the rocky road of sexual misconduct did not always require either a lugubrious fictional presentation or a disastrous end. At times the spirit of Fielding prevailed as in "The Fair Recluse" (1784), an amusing yarn about an unwanted pursuer exposed through connivance between his intended victim, Amanda, and his former lady love, Miss B——n, who hides in a closet while he tries to seduce Amanda. Thoroughly chagrined upon discovery he swears off both ladies and leaves town, but instead of moralizing over the experience the writer clearly strives for laughter through the medium of sprightly dialogue. Similar motives probably inspired numerous other tales of this sort, such as "Three

Days after Marriage," "Matrimonial Infidelity," "The Story of the Captain's Wife and an Aged Woman," and "The Child of Snow."[17] The first of these is a rollicking tale of quickly cooled conjugal felicity, wherein Ned Easy rids himself of a termagant wife three days after marrying her for her fortune of £50,000 by having his friend Pleaseall make love to her. A racy narrative style and bouncing dialogue also lighten the second, rather flat story of a rake's progress. On the subject of marital infidelity, however, the last two cited above are the most impressive by virtue of their combined use of irony, novel detail, both realistic and fantastic, and their matter-of-fact tone. "The Child of Snow" tells of a traveling merchant's wife who becomes pregnant by another man during one of her husband's long absences and, on his return, attributes her son's birth to a miraculous conception induced by a falling snowflake, inadvertently swallowed while she was leaning outside her window. There is more than a touch of the macabre in this story, as well as in "The Captain's Wife," whose anonymous author, *Ruricolla,* combines a liberal infusion of the supernatural and fresh native materials in transforming a well-worn traditional plot into a delightfully realistic fantasy.[18]

As an example of competent craftsmanship in early American short fiction, "The Captain's Wife" justifies the critical acclaim recently paid to its author for showing "that talent could and did, construct capable fiction out of fantasy, folklore, and the native scene many years before either Irving or Hawthorne developed tales from similar elements."[19] The blend here is successful because without moral preachment of any sort it objectifies in the manner of Boccaccio's framed narratives a routine social problem of the time and place—the problem of the long-absent seafaring husband and the lonely wife—and does so in terms of universal, psychologically genuine human yearning, frustration, and fulfillment. Longing for her husband's safe return, the young wife in the story miraculously achieves a reunion with him far from home, conceives his child, and miraculously returns to await his irate reappearance seven months later. Mystery and ambiguity sustain tension throughout the story; and even though the narrator makes no attempt to reconcile its realistic and its supernatural levels, his matter-of-fact tone provides the key to its disarmingly successful blending of folklore, fantasy, and common factual knowledge. Whether or not the unknown Ruricolla contributed little more than his pseudonym in reworking a standard folkloric plot of "The Resolute Wife," American short fiction would reveal no superior talent until Hawthorne's—forty years later—for presenting allegorically, yet without overt didacticism, one of the basic problems of married life.

Among the many other stories published in the early period, regardless of subject matter, motive, or methods of presentation, most would tax the patience of even a tolerant modern critic of short fiction or evoke derisive laughter from today's casual reader. Whether serious or lighthearted in manner, they were too crudely contrived to command one's respect, their intended effect being lost either through an underdevelopment of characterization, mood, setting, and atmosphere or through an overabundance of implausible, sensational details of plot and action. Yet to the perceptive scholar, the aggregate of individual touches discernible in the massive body of this early fiction signals an important, if unrecognized, contribution to the domestication of American fiction before 1800.[20] Specifically, what distinguishes the quality of many comic or sentimental stories about Indians, Negroes, and frontiersmen, as well as of the many more didactic stories published along with them, is that recognizably distinctive American character traits, attitudes, localities, and social and economic problems appear in them, often as integral parts of the story rather than simply as convenient hooks on which to hang a hackneyed, sentimental plot. With equal emphasis, the same can be said for the hundreds of comic anecdotes and shorter yarns printed in the early magazines; for these likewise exploited both the native American scene and its varied character types, together with their colloquial idioms, attitudes, social levels, and prejudices.

Questions of Origin and Authorship

Before Irving's heyday, however, very few tales employing these native materials exploited them successfully within the narrative conventions of the time; fewer still reveal even a hint of the artistry that distinguished his more memorable stories. Among these, several that deserve notice besides "The Story of the Captain's Wife" are "Azakia: A Canadian Story,"[21] the "Narrative of the Unpardonable Sin," "The Story of Constantius and Pulchera," and "Joseph and Sophia; or, The History of Juliet Johnson, as related by Herself."[22] For varying reasons, each of these can lay some claim to distinction as a respectable example of the adaptation of native elements in early American fiction, though the danger of attributing too much credit for their authorship to supposedly anonymous American writers may again be seen, as in the case of "The Captain's Wife," in that of "Azakia: A Canadian Story."

Within six pages, "Azakia" develops a fairly intricate plot turning on the problem of marital fidelity under pressure among the Huron tribe of the Canadian border country. The young squaw Azakia, aptly described as "probably the most unsentimental heroine in all early Indian fiction,"[23] remains strictly faithful to her husband, Ouabi, even though she is strongly attracted to the white French hero, St. Castins, who rescues her from sexual assault by one of his men and promptly solicits her favors as a reward for his deliverance. St. Castins respects her allegiance to the Indian code, which forbids unfaithfulness among married women while nevertheless sanctioning premarital intercourse; yet he continues to court her assiduously and, as an adopted member of the tribe, eventually succeeds in winning her for himself through a surprisingly modernistic arrangement of wife swapping. The successive events, reported throughout the story in a matter-of-fact tone, are free of romantic posturing and sentimentally inflated dialogue; consequently, both action and characters remain consistently refreshing, and the quadrangular relationship developed among them becomes convincingly alive and human, its calm denouement almost too neatly resolved with Gallic politesse: "These two marriages, so different in the form, were equally happy. Each husband, well assured that there were no competitors, forgot there had been any predecessors."[24]

Less artfully contrived than "Azakia" but perhaps equally memorable for its representation of a peculiarly American phenomenon of colonial experience, the "Narrative of the Unpardonable Sin" offers a striking, if virtually unique, instance of the use of intense religious emotion in early fiction. Though crudely told in the form of a reported case history, the story has all the earmarks of an authentic portrayal of an obsessed mind. A young man, tortured by the certainty that he has committed an unforgivable (but unnamed) transgression, asserts that his heart has become adamant and his inner torment so intense that not only can he seek no mercy for himself, but he also senses among his neighbors the same wicked fury against God that is raging in his own breast. As a victim guilty of blasphemy against the Holy Ghost, the protagonist thus emerges in this story as the ancestral prototype of a number of fiend-driven figures in nineteenth-century American fiction, notably Hawthorne's Ethan Brand, Young Goodman Brown, and the black-veiled Reverend Hooper, as well as Melville's Captain Ahab and numerous others. The story is therefore an important one, not simply because it foreshadows the more elaborate treatments of its theme worked out by these later writers (none of whom may have read it), but rather because in its own stark revelation of Puritan self-analysis it is the first fictional dramatization of a problem that had fascinated several generations of New England theologians. Rooted in the vast body of conversion literature prevailing in the region since the early seventeenth century, it is a signpost marking a shift in values and emphases while at the same time focusing upon a traditional theme.[25]

In contrast, "The Story of Constantius and Pulchera" contains little of value for the student of early American fiction, except for its elaborately contrived, sentimental plot and its occasional use of authentic native details in setting and characterization. Though evidently popular in its day, the story concocts such a mishmash of implausible action, histrionic posturing, hair-raising pursuit and escape, and remarkable coincidence, extending through seven consecutive periodical issues, that one modern scholar believes it to be a parody. But both the plot and the style of this action-packed account of young lovers, buffeted from Philadelphia to London, Paris, and back by parental disapproval, storm, shipwreck, piracy, and threatened cannibalism, resemble too closely the makeup of scores of similar tales published during the period to be regarded as mere spoofing. Despite its outlandishly inflated diction, unmotivated action, and transparent artificiality, "Constantius and Pulchera" differs from many of these in its use of details reflecting both a native setting and locale as well as Americanized customs, attitudes, ambitions, and prejudices. Although the story as a whole cannot be taken seriously by a modern reader, it is an excellent example of early American efforts to combine in fiction a realistic presentation of verifiable details and events in a plot bordering on sheer fantasy—and quite possibly lifted from a foreign source.[26]

Still another interesting effort to combine realistic elements of scene and characterization within a plot pattern of sentimentalized action is "Joseph and Sophia," one of the few early stories laid in a southern setting and thus deriving much of its impact from the conflict of social values bred by the plantation culture of South Carolina. Subtitled "The History of Juliet Johnson, as related by Herself," this story employs the device of an inside narrator, though it is primarily an account reported to her of a tragic love affair between an impoverished young girl and the scion of wealthy planters, whose objection to the match results in the young couple's destruction. As a retold scenario of young love crushed by parental pride and class discrimination, it follows a standard plot pattern of sentimental romance, recorded in typically inflated diction; yet its characters, theme, and action appear to be rooted in the social and ideological peculiarities of the regional scene.

The foregoing examples, though only a minute portion of the short fiction published in American magazines during the late eighteenth century, amply reveal that before Irving's *Sketch Book* appeared a distinctive American short-story form was emerging. However crudely contrived, they show that through its frequent employment of native elements the sheer bulk of this early magazine fiction presented a broad spectrum of life in colonial America, together with many distinctive features of the contemporary scene. And though admittedly derivative in form and manner, these sentimental and didactic tales "were domesticated by the heavy use of such native details."[27] All that was needed now was the creative imagination and artistry of someone who could seize upon these materials, both the native elements and the borrowed literary sources, and transform them into new, durable literary art. To an extent far surpassing that of his immediate predecessors, Washington Irving possessed both these qualifications and accordingly achieved lasting fame for such tales as "Rip Van Winkle" and the "Legend of Sleepy Hollow."

European Romanticism: Impact and Effects after 1800

When Irving's *Sketch Book* appeared in 1820, little that was distinctively new or aesthetically significant had yet been accomplished in the writing of American short fiction. But during the preceding two or three decades an entirely new trend of literary expression had begun to flourish in European countries and would soon become a strong influence felt in America, notably in Irving's own writing, as well as in Poe's and Hawthorne's. Eventually, that trend came to be known as romanticism or the Romantic Revolt, and it represented in effect a repudiation of established beliefs—social, political, moral—which had remained virtually unchanged for more than a century.

By the very nature of its many-sidedness, romanticism is hard to define; but it certainly implied change, flux, unrest, experimentation, a bursting apart of conventional bonds in order to seek out and explore anew the manifold mysteries of man and nature. Romantic writers and artists inevitably pursued many different paths, discovered and proclaimed many hitherto uncharted realms, and established new modes of expression. It is safe to say, for example, that the modern short story owes more to the tales written by this new generation of romanticists than it does to the entire sequence of older ones discussed earlier; for one of the major achievements of the modern short story is its freedom of form, an outgrowth of the efforts of poets and fiction writers in Germany, France, Russia, and England during the early 1800s to establish the freedom of the individual artist to seek his own form within the medium of his craft.

One of the best examples of these new trends is Ludwig Tieck's "The Fair-haired Eckbert," which strikingly reveals the force of romantic countercurrents that began drifting across Europe during the last third of the eighteenth century. Unlike such "common-sense" earlier fiction as Defoe's, Tieck's story bears the earmarks of a new age—one of introspection and revolt against tradition and social conformity. More specifically, it is also typical of the peculiar drift taken by the German romanticists, who developed in drama, poetry, and fiction the Sturm und Drang (storm and stress) movement within the larger confines of romanticism. Simply put, Sturm und Drang implied a deepseated drive to attain the unattainable and to express the inexpressible. Whatever the subject, writing in this mode was generally "characterized by fervor and enthusiasm, a restless turbulency of spirit, the portrayal of great passion, a reliance upon emotional experiences and spiritual struggles and was intensely personal."[28]

As symbolized in the famous "blue flower" of Novalis's *Heinrich von Ofterdingen,* an uncontrollable yearning *(Sehnsucht)* lay at the basis of Sturm und Drang, an agony of the individual soul or ego, seeking ways to transcend or overcome its earthly bondage. But coupled with this exhausting struggle there was also a profound despair born of the inevitable failure to reconcile the actual and the ideal. No matter how hard the artist might strive to capture and possess the beauty behind and beyond the senses, ultimately he would have to taste the bitterness of defeat—hence the strain of morbid melancholy and despondency that often flows concurrently with a sort of childlike, ecstatic wonder through much of German romanticism. It is easy to see how this dual impulse would appeal not just to Irving, but especially to Poe, Hawthorne, Melville, and many lesser nineteenth-century American writers.

Tieck's protagonist, Eckbert, is like a knight in a child's fairy tale, but with this difference: he is forty, childless, a recluse, and given to spells of silent melancholy despite having an agreeable wife, Bertha. He proposes to entertain an old friend by urging Bertha to "relate the history of her early days"; and she complies, telling a fantastic tale of childhood misery and ill usage—escape from home at the age of eight, a six-year stay with an old crone who owned a dog and a remarkable singing bird, another escape with the bird and a parcel of diamonds lifted from the old woman, her return home to find both parents dead, and finally a brief period of comfortable solitude until she met and married Eckbert. But instead of satisfying, this dolorous recital merely initiates an even wilder tale of torment and distress involving the disclosure of an incestuous relationship between husband and wife that eventually destroys them. Long after Bertha's grim demise, Eckbert, too, dies raving, the sounds of the barking dog, the screaming old woman, and the bird's reiterated song echoing in his ears.

Whatever one's reaction to this frenzied tale, it seems obvious, even in translation, that more meaning is concealed than is narrated. And even though the reader may be only vaguely aware of its different levels of meaning, without being able to distinguish precisely among them, he nevertheless feels certain that some hidden meaning is intended. An elaborately contrived allegory, perhaps? Or possibly only a loose collection of symbolic objects and acts meant to develop and enrich a study of character? In any event, the reader can see that whatever ideas may be derived from this tale, they do not resemble the clear-cut themes underlying stories like Defoe's "Apparition" or even "Azakia" or "The Captain's Wife." In fact, the contrast between Tieck's story and these earlier ones can stand as emblematic of the general shift in literary values that was taking place throughout the Western world as the eighteenth century merged into the nineteenth. In every country, leading writers, painters, and composers were now expressing the social and political ferment going on around them, a churning of ideas in many fields that heralded the breakdown of old established patterns of thought and expression and provoked a continuing quest for new ones. In the writing of short fiction, this twofold process can be seen as a primary shaping factor, bringing a greater variety than ever before to the substance and methods of stories now appearing in a rapidly expanding market.

After 1800 such European writers as Sir Walter Scott, Henri Beyle (Stendhal), Prosper Mérimée, Honoré de Balzac, Alexander Pushkin, and Nikolai Gogol were becoming increasingly concerned with the problem of the individual in their respective societies. Seeking new ways to dramatize the plight of the individual, they ransacked the past for legends and myths with which to illuminate the present and critically reexamined prevailing beliefs and accepted customs. By focusing upon crucial experiences in the lives of their characters, they tried to suggest both the inner and external forces that made the actions and reactions of these imagined persons both broadly representative and believably exciting. Increasingly, the problem of nineteenth-century fiction writers was to convey truth about life as they saw it more dramatically than had their predecessors. They were trying to create the illusion of a three-dimensional world, peopled with imaginary beings who live and breathe and whose predicaments seemed to match those of the readers themselves, notwithstanding the readers' awareness of their fictive makeup.[29]

Before Irving's day, however, very few examples of the short fiction published in American magazines approached this level of craftsmanship, although from week to week between 1800 and 1820 many more tales of the kinds described above filled the pages of such magazines as the *Balti-*

more Weekly (1800–1801), the *Boston Weekly Magazine* (1802–6), the *New England Galaxy* (1817–34), and the *Port Folio* (1801–27). These tales added little more than bulk to the fast-growing pile of sentimental sermons. After 1800 the continued story appeared more often, as well as an occasional spoof of the more lugubrious tales, rendered in the tone of lofty sincerity, along with an occasional piece of serious criticism on the comparative merits of American fiction. Under a column headed "The Novelist," for example, the *Boston Weekly* ("Devoted to Morality, Literature, Biography, History, the Fine Arts, Agriculture, &c, &c") ran a series of moralistic tales, beginning with "The Child of Misery," a typical seduction yarn in which the narrator's close friend betrays an innocent girl, Louisa Rainsforth, sending her to an early grave beneath a suitably inscribed marble headstone. Hard on its heels came "The Penitent Restored," "The Triumphs of Friendship," and many others, at least one or part of one story each week, some in straight narrative, some in letter form.[30]

Invariably syrupy, stories of this type grew so common that in 1813 a reviewer in the *Port Folio,* preparing to tackle still another of them, "Hubert and Ellen," done in verse form, observed that the sorrowful tale of seduction, seen nightly on the stage, had become trite and tiresome.[31] By that time, the *Port Folio* itself, though seldom an outlet for short fiction, had contributed its share to the rising tide of sentimental, didactic stories of misused female innocence, betrayed by ne'er-do-well husbands and lovers.[32] Thereafter, the magazine apparently discontinued this type of fiction; but late in the following year it ran an interesting short series of fictional satires entitled "Philadelphia Unroofed," in which the narrator, frankly imitating the manner of LeSage's *Diable Boiteux,* presents Satan conducting a horrified young student about the city, revealing to him the variety of scandalous misbehavior that has been going on.[33] Then, with a touch of unconscious irony, in an essay immediately following the last of this series, the *Port Folio*'s critic listed all the old familiar reasons why American literary production still lagged behind England's, alleging that the main difficulty in fiction was the lack of distinctive settings and social classes. In his view, no acceptable fiction could be written about ordinary American merchants' sons and daughters—they had no "classic Ground"—yet he recognized that American writers would achieve nothing distinctive until they stopped aping British fashions and forms.[34]

Despite encouraging its readers to send in publishable fiction, the *Port Folio* actually printed very little fiction of any sort during the next six or seven years, and only one or two pieces worth mentioning.[35] Perhaps the most noteworthy of these was the hilarious sketch by Oliver H. Prince entitled "The Militia Muster,"[36] which had appeared nearly seven years earlier in the *Baltimore Repertory of Papers on Literary and Other Topics* and which was later to be enshrined permanently among A. B. Longstreet's *Georgia Scenes,* published in 1835.[37] For the *Port Folio* this was apparently the last nod given to American fiction of any sort until 1821, when the magazine reprinted a favorable English review of Irving's *Sketch Book,* urging him enthusiastically to combine his skill and freshness in the writing of twenty more such books on America, preferably of three volumes each.[38]

Other, shorter-lived magazines of the period were equally grudging in furnishing praiseworthy native fiction and equally enthusiastic about Irving when his work appeared to end the drought. The *Boston Spectator,* a weekly that ran to sixty-one numbers, offered in each issue the usual miscellany of items on contemporary affairs, including essays, verses, notices, and chitchat; but its fictional output was restricted to two series of moralizing sketches entitled "The Confidant" and "The Writer." These were apparently designed primarily to sugar-coat some abstract idea, such as the folly of being too particular in searching for a wife or the futility of seeking happiness without virtue.[39] During the following year (1816–17), the *Boston Weekly Magazine* likewise offered the same potpourri with an occasional dash of short fiction, either obviously moralistic in tone, as in a short series entitled "Instructions to a Young Lady on the Eve of Marriage," or sentimentalized romances such as "Hierophilus and Evethes: An Egyptian Story" and "Claudine: A Swiss Tale," frankly lifted from European sources.[40] Six or seven years later, when the *Spectator* merged with the *Ladies Miscellany* to become the *Weekly Magazine and Ladies Miscellany,* short fiction appeared more regularly and in more varied forms; yet the stories copied from *Blackwood's* and other English magazines still occupied as much space as those purporting to be native American ones. In a whole year's output, the most impressive single piece, proudly noted by the editors, was Irving's "Adventure of a German Student," the horror story that had recently appeared in his *Tales of a Traveller.*[41] Clearly, Irving's mastery of the new form had now produced a variety of models with which to challenge the skill and emulation of his contemporaries.

The effect of Irving's preeminence at this point could, in fact, be seen in three ways: first, in the open admiration with which magazine editors reprinted pieces from his *Sketch Book;* second, in their parroting of favorable British reviews of his work; third, in the increasing sophistication occasionally evident in the fiction they published after 1820. Shortly after *The Sketch Book* appeared, for example, the *Belles-Lettres Repository* of New York reprinted "The Wife" and promised to follow it with other pieces in future issues because Irving was highly regarded for his "quaint humor . . . pointed wit and pungent sarcasm."[42]

Later, the same periodical reprinted several pages of extracts from laudatory reviews of Irving's work originally published in *Blackwood's,* the *London Literary Gazette,* and the *New Monthly.* It followed this with a highly complimentary critical essay on Irving, reprinted from *Poulson's American Daily Advertiser,* in which the critic noted the sharp contrast between Irving's earlier writings and those in *The Sketch Book,* which he found superior in both style and content. Similarly, the *Western Review and Miscellaneous Magazine,* a short time later, undertook a long, closely reasoned, and on the whole favorable evaluation of the book, although the critic deplored without specifying them certain of Irving's lapses into vulgarity. Taking up each sketch in turn, he described, analyzed, and illustrated its peculiar merits by means of liberal quotations; and he concluded that the book was aptly titled because "everything is painted to the life: the scenes are all presented, as it were, immediately before our view."[43] Here was one mark of Irving's superiority—the fact that his writing imparted a feeling of lifelikeness and immediacy in the most graceful piece of American writing on record, a sketch that, the critic agreed with *Blackwood's,* "well-entitled [him] to be classed with the best English writers of our day."[44]

In the development of American short fiction, *The Sketch Book* thus marked the turning point from second- and third-hand imitation toward original artistic achievement. Before its publication American critics had little to praise besides the novels of Charles Brockden Brown; but subsequently they could point to it as a touchstone, urging other aspiring American writers to savor and try to duplicate its literary virtues. Before long, stories like "The Counterfeiters" and "Peter Rugg, the Missing Man," employing some, though not all, of Irving's techniques, began finding their way into the pages of American annuals, gift books, and magazines. "The Counterfeiters," for example, like some of Irving's tales of outlawry, offered a fairly straightforward, first-person account of duplicity and divided loyalty, the narrator disclosing with apparent reluctance how he had exposed and brought to justice the leader of a band of Canadian brigands who also turned out to be a prominent citizen and the father of the narrator's fiancée.[45] True to the literary conventions of the time, the guilty man upon his unmasking praised the narrator for doing his duty and committed suicide, but except for this concession to the axiom that crime does not pay, the writer avoided both the obvious moralizing and sentimentality commonly applied to stories of antisocial behavior.

Four years later, at a time when Irving's *Tales of a Traveller* was being hailed as a "new work," William Austin's "Peter Rugg, the Missing Man," showed how the application of technical dexterity to native folklore in the Irving manner could transform a fantasy into compelling narrative on the theme of mutability.[46]

Using the letter device, Austin explores the mystery of a strange figure who has been trying for over twenty years to get to Boston, but always loses his way. The point is that, like Rip Van Winkle, Rugg is twenty years behind time and cannot recognize or catch up with the modern city of Boston. The narrator begins by saying that he met this apparition three years before while riding the stage coach from Providence—a wild-looking horseman with a child whom the stage driver called the "storm breeder" because a rain storm always pursued him. He vows to find out more about Rugg and to track him down in Boston; but although he learns a little more each time from a succession of informants, none can clear up the mystery of his endless quest. Told with unusual economy, a dry, matter-of-fact tone, and a skillful manipulation of point of view, the story of Peter Rugg matches the sophistication of Irving's best fiction in all save that "half-concealed vein of humor," which became the hallmark of his distinctive style. By 1825, Irving had cleared the path, enabling other American writers of short fiction to explore the limitless possibilities of this new literary form.

Looking back from the vantage point of the late twentieth century, we can see that stories written by even the leading writers of the late eighteenth and early nineteenth centuries often fell below the technical standards we are accustomed to in the work of present-day short-story writers. Hawthorne's characters, for example, seldom talk or act like the ordinary people we know; and the behavior of Irving's and Poe's characters, as well as the activity we encounter in the stories of their foreign contemporaries, often seems equally remote from our conception of the conduct of normal human affairs. Because we are conditioned by the more sophisticated literary techniques of our own living writers, whose artistry often discloses subtleties previously unemployed in the creation of characterization, point of view, dialogue, setting, and exposition, we attribute a degree of quaintness in the narrative methods employed by their predecessors. But, just as our Hemingways and Faulkners and O'Connors and Weltys refined the techniques of modern fiction, having profited by both the artistic achievements and the deficiencies of the past, so did their literary forebears (whom we now call the romantics) develop the art of fiction in their era by injecting into their stories greater depth and subtlety than their literary predecessors had known how to achieve.

Although many writers during the early decades of the nineteenth century kept on churning out undistinguished stories of a caliber similar to the conventional moralistic and sentimental tales appearing in the earliest magazines, the more highly skilled romanticists achieved a more permanent success because of their ability to breathe new life into their stories. However dated their methods may seem today, their best stories are still read and admired because they embody timeless values and a universal significance. We can believe in, if not actually identify with, Poe's haunted heroes, Scott's and Mérimée's proud peasants, and Gogol's humble clerks and overbearing bureaucrats because through the spell cast by their creators, we are made to feel how they felt—not simply told what they did or what happened to them. This is the sort of refinement that the great romantic writers contributed to the art of fiction. By shifting the focus of their narrative from the outside to the inside, they created an imaginary world of recognizable persons whose actions and speech, sufferings and pleasures, we can see, hear, and share emotionally and intellectually. Once drawn into their orbit, we want to know more than merely what happened to them and how their story came out; we quickly become aware in the very process of reading their story that, however it ends, the experience has given us a fresh, vivid impression of life, not just a flat, abstract "lesson" or "moral." The best stories written by the great romantic writers are thus still capable of furnishing us with a unique vision, a flash of enlightenment into the heart of reality, a "shock of recognition."

IRVING SETS THE PATTERN

Did the American short story actually begin "in 1819 with Washington Irving,"[1] as Pattee flatly asserts, or did Irving merely point the way toward its origin in the three collections of short prose narratives that made him famous in the 1820s? When he discovered with *The Sketch Book* that he "could turn out regularly books which readers were willing to buy regularly,"[2] his professional status was assured. Yet it may be argued that the urge to exploit the bonanza reaped by that book prevented him from achieving in the next two—*Bracebridge Hall* and *Tales of a Traveller*—the mastery of short-story form foreshadowed in *The Sketch Book*. He came closer to such mastery in his third collection, but, ironically, when it was severely criticized he turned his talents in directions that appeared to offer surer profits and revived popularity.

The story of Irving's unprecedented success with *The Sketch Book* is well known. Stanley T. Williams's exhaustive *Life* as well as Pochmann's and other studies long ago revealed the importance of Sir Walter Scott's influence in its genesis and swift acclaim in England;[3] more recently, William Charvat has shown how the serial publication of the same materials in the United States, in sets priced at five dollars each, brought Irving a quick net profit of nearly ten thousand dollars;[4] and a more recent study of his professional career tells how *The Sketch Book*'s rapidly mounting sales abroad led to his lucrative, lifelong connection with the prestigious publishing house of John Murray.[5] Almost overnight this modest miscellany of thirty-four loosely connected prose pieces (only three of which resemble modern short stories) catapulted Irving from obscurity to fame as Murray's most valued author; for it was certain that "Murray had rarely—if ever—published a work which pleased more and offended fewer people."[6]

Author versus Persona: Crayon as Narrator

But it is easier to document *The Sketch Book*'s immediate success than to explain its enduring appeal as a model of sprightly prose. The special charm of the book may well have been due to Irving's long apprenticeship, during which, as author of Knickerbocker's *A History of New York* and earlier whim-whams and opinions on his native city, "he had learned lucidity . . . the art of handling anecdote, and, above all, the trick of appearing under an alias."[7] In any event, the figure of Geoffrey Crayon, a clever device for binding together the disparate experiences recorded in *The Sketch Book,* stimulated Irving's imagination and sharpened his artistic skills. What seems to have caught the fancy of both his British and his American readers in the 1820s was Irving's personal warmth and congeniality, which they saw reflected in a natural, easy, limpid style. He immediately disarmed all suspicions by frankly admitting in "The Author's Account of Himself" that he had always been "fond of visiting new scenes and observing strange characters and manners." His imagination had also been stirred by books of travel and the sight of foreign ships, especially those bound for Europe, which "held forth the charms of storied and poetical associations."

And so, like an eager tourist, he had come to England with his sketch book in hand, ready to capture glimpses and memoranda of picturesque things "in nooks and corners and bye places" with which to entertain his friends. British readers were delighted to find an American writer who had not only familiarized himself with their cherished customs and traditions but could also write as charmingly about them as their own best writers did. And American readers were equally pleased to see that these sketches, written by a fellow countryman abroad, were so favorably received.

To patriotic Americans, it must have been doubly gratifying to find both English and American critics singling out for special praise the only three pieces of palpable fiction in the book—"Rip Van Winkle," "The Legend of Sleepy Hollow," and "The Spectre Bridegroom"—especially since two of these evoked vivid memories of the characters and events in old Diedrich Knickerbocker's *History*. None of the three, of course, was an original story, Irving having unearthed the skeleton of each, as he did so many of his other tales, from German folklore. But in "Rip Van Winkle" and "Sleepy Hollow" he domesticated the two German folktales and made classics of them through the magic of his transforming gloss: sharply focused specific local details, rendered with a delicacy of feeling and wit in an exquisitely modulated style. Comparison between the barebones, matter-of-fact treatment of the long-sleep motif in the German legend of Peter Klaus and the elaborately embroidered transferral of scene and characters in Irving's version quickly reveals how both his humor and his sensibility enrich the story.[8] For example, the characterization of Rip as a hen-pecked husband, eager to escape his wife's caustic putdowns as well as the work ethic, is simultaneously both funny and pathetic. Rip, the narrator tells us, in Irving's subtly cadenced diction, learned through years of matrimony that "a tart temper never mellows with age, and that a sharp tongue is the only edged tool that grows keener with constant use."

In like vein, the later climactic scene of Rip's return from his twenty-year sleep is a masterpiece of mingled humor and sadness. Finding everything changed and his own identity severely in doubt because nobody recognizes him, he cries: "Does nobody know poor Rip Van Winkle?" The reader wants to cry and laugh for and with him when his daughter Judith resolves his main problem with the news that Dame Van Winkle has recently passed on. "There was a drop of comfort, at least, in this intelligence," the narrator adds. And as Crayon winds down the story of Rip's subsequent local fame, free to go and come as he pleased "without dreading the tyranny of Dame Van Winkle," one wonders whether Irving could ever render the theme of mutability with more consummate delicacy, though he was destined to work it over and over again in later stories. Clearly, "Rip Van Winkle" deserves its reputation as America's first really great story, a classic that has perennially delighted American audiences in revived dramatic versions on stage and screen.

Irving, however, achieved much the same transformational magic with his "Legend of Sleepy Hollow." Transposing again an age-old gothic motif of the headless horseman into an American colonial setting, he gave the tale dramatic tension by developing in it the amusing rivalry between Ichabod Crane and Brom Bones for the conquest of Katrina Van Tassel. Here, too, as in "Rip Van Winkle," Irving's inimitable style turns the trick, revitalizing an ancient triangular plot device through characterization and action based on superbly effective descriptive and narrative detail. Who can ever forget the pictures of scraggly Ichabod, the New England Puritan schoolmaster, reciting epitaphs of tombstones for the amusement of country damsels, swapping witchcraft and ghost tales with the older Dutch wives, and drooling over the possibility of securing, along with the buxom Katrina, the robust livestock she would inherit for her dowry? As he jogs slowly past her father's opulent fields like a latter-day Quixote, his mind feeds on "sweet thoughts and 'sugared suppositions'": "Indian corn, with its golden ears peeping from their leafy covers, and holding out the promise of cakes and hasty pudding; and the yellow pumpkins lying beneath them, turning their fair round bellies to the sun, and giving ample prospects of the most luxurious of pies." Yet these are but a prelude to the sumptuous spread awaiting his dazzled vision at the Van Tassels' festive board. The garden and food imagery Irving lavished on these scenes builds a firm basis for the reversal of fortune he had in store for Ichabod; for the symbols of fertility inherent in these scenes strengthen one's conviction that the lusty Brom Bones and the nubile Katrina are admirably suited to each other.

In both "Rip Van Winkle" and "Sleepy Hollow" Irving's "trick of appearing under an alias" obviously contributed much to their immediate appeal because in each case he skillfully enabled his narrator, Geoffrey Crayon, to evade the responsibility of vouching for the truthfulness of the tales. Both tales, Crayon assures us, were among the unpublished papers that the late Diedrich Knickerbocker left behind; and since even Knickerbocker himself had heard the tales originally from the old Dutch wives, he had to confess some doubt regarding their credibility. Thus, with charming light irony Irving distances himself from his subject matter at three removes: through Crayon to Knickerbocker to the original yarnspinners. Then he doubles the irony of his invention by having Knickerbocker authenticate Rip's story in one postscript while casting strong doubt on Ichabod's in another.

In "The Spectre Bridegroom" Irving varied the same technique by calling it "A Traveller's Tale," which Crayon happened to hear told by "a corpulent old Swiss" in the kitchen of a small Dutch inn. The real literary source of the story, however, was probably a popular ballad by an eighteenth-century German poet, Gottfried Burger, in which the heroine, Lenore, is carried off by the ghost of her dead lover. But from the outset of Irving's tale his spoofing tone enlivens the situation and the characters so that the reader quickly succumbs to the effect of his gently ironic humor. Here is no gloomy German Gothicism like Ludwig Tieck's; for Irving is laughing at both himself and his reader, as well as at the principals involved in this absurd plot. The pompous little Baron Von Landshort; his lovely but unnamed daughter, an only child and "a miracle of accomplishments"; her two guardian aunts; the Baron's "abundance of poor relations," on hand to share alike in the festivities of his daughter's forthcoming nuptials and in his marvelous ghost stories; and finally, the young lady's gallant Spectre Bridegroom, Herman Von Starkenfaust, a surrogate for her murdered intended who spirits her away from the Castle, weds her in secret, and then brings her back to clear up the mystery—the whole fabric of the tale as Crayon retells it is delightfully, sportively gothic. In fact, it is told with such gusto that one is strongly tempted to find an ulterior motive in Irving's offhand manner of presenting the Baron's narrative proclivities: namely, to poke fun at the "wild tales and supernatural legends" that had become a popular legacy of German romanticism. For it was the

Baron, we note, who "nearly frightened some of the ladies into hysterics
with the history of the goblin horsemen that carried away the fair Leonora;
a dreadful, but true story, which has since been put into excellent verse,
and is read and believed by all the world."

It may be true that Crayon's role in *The Sketch Book* embodies Irving's
uncertainty regarding his artistic aims and function because there is ample
evidence throughout the work to confirm that most of the thirty-four
pieces in the book "are told by a man who is not altogether sure of himself"; and that they are "the author's elaborate way of talking about himself, . . . a fiction of dreams, fantasies, symbolic projections."[9] True or
not, however, Irving's success in using Crayon as his jocular persona, especially in the three tales we have just considered, suggests that he was not
all that unsure of himself. In any event, with *The Sketch Book* behind him,
a complete success both at home and abroad, he set about determinedly to
expand Crayon's role in his next book, *Bracebridge Hall*.

Bracebridge Hall: Problems of Content and Form

The urge to capitalize quickly on *The Sketch Book*'s vogue and yet turn
out an equally substantial but less miscellaneous sort of book raised a formidable problem for Irving: how to find a suitable subject reminiscent of
that work yet sufficiently different from it in form and development? Early
in May 1821 he eagerly seized Tom Moore's suggestion to extend the sequence of essays dealing with Christmas festivities at Squire Bracebridge's
ancestral hall in Yorkshire and to develop in the sequence "a slight thread
of a story on which to string remarks and sketches of human manners."[10]
Irving quickly wrote several hundred pages of the new work but soon discovered that a volume comparable to *The Sketch Book* could not easily be
built merely out of Crayon's reactions to May Day celebrations and Squire
Bracebridge's quirky predilections for ancient customs and superstitions.
The texture of his narrative, as well as his nonfiction commentary on rural
customs and life-styles at Bracebridge Hall, would have to be fleshed out
with a whole network of conventional figures and relationships revolving
around the central establishment.

Throughout the summer, as the manuscript grew under Moore's critical
eye, Irving evidently combed many bookish sources for materials to fill out
his canvas.[11] Echoes from Elizabethan and eighteenth-century writers
found their way into the volume, along with his own personal observations
and Knickerbockerish lore, to form another miscellany consisting of fifty
separate essays, sketches, and tales with individual titles like those of *The*

Sketch Book. Despite Irving's assertion that he was not trying to write a novel, his slight thread of a story in this carefully orchestrated work came closer to being a novel than either he or his contemporaries realized; for it contained both a serious upper-class romance involving the Squire's son, Guy, and "the fair Julia" and several other comic romances on lower social levels.[12] Flavored and strung out with titillating episodes, conventional practical jokes, and sentimental excursions into antiquarian lore, *Bracebridge Hall: or, The Humorists,* seemed well worth the 1,250 guineas that Murray was willing to pay for it. Less popular than *The Sketch Book, Bracebridge Hall* was well liked by both the critics and the reading public. Its idealized treatment of manor-house experiences firmly established Irving's reputation as a chronicler of that type of life and made him more than ever the darling of British high society.[13]

Irving obviously relished such favorable attention and even courted the approval of prominent English families, who opened their manor-house doors to him. His bland, seemingly sentimental acceptance of their values and prejudices probably accounts for Stanley Williams's contemptuous appraisal of *Bracebridge Hall* as an "insipid" book in which Irving's "determination to de-Americanize himself" betrayed him into rendering a romanticized idealization of English village life in a fatuously outmoded style.[14] But a more indulgent scrutiny of the text than Williams was inclined to give it casts some doubt upon his blunt charge of subserviency. Close analysis of *Bracebridge Hall,* in fact, clearly shows that Irving not only rendered it less sentimental than *The Sketch Book* but also achieved a consistently pervasive, subtly ironic tone of "quasi-satirical humor," which both his contemporary admirers and his twentieth-century detractors have failed to detect.[15] Indeed, Crayon's *Bracebridge* reflections on the various levels of English society—and on the attitudes of their representative members toward one another—attain a degree of sophistication that anticipates de Tocqueville's by more than a decade, rather than simply reflecting a nostalgic, sentimental glorification of outmoded forms.[16]

Apart from its account of persons and activities within Bracebridge itself, the book contains only four pieces of short fiction, none of which quite matches the appeal of either "Rip Van Winkle" or "The Legend of Sleepy Hollow." Yet each reveals an extension of Irving's narrative technique for achieving varied effects as well as a scarcely perceptible species of literary and social criticism, artfully insinuated into his descriptive references. Employing again the pretense of the conveniently "discovered" manuscript as in *The Sketch Book,* Irving here suits each story to the particular occasion and to the individual member of the Bracebridge ménage who allegedly tells it. Thus "The Stout Gentleman" (which opens the tale-telling sessions and is on the whole the most successful) is an amusing example of the hoax tale, related to the assemblage by "a thin, pale, weazen-faced man, extremely nervous," who turns up later as an important narrator in *Tales of a Traveller.* Behind Crayon's mask, Irving pretends to have been so favorably impressed by the story, which "has in it all the elements of currently popular mysterious and romantic narrative," that he writes it out for the reader's amusement. But the whole thing is a spoof; for with tongue in cheek Irving calls it "a stage-coach romance," knowing that the reader will be nettled at the end to find himself, along with the narrator, gazing fixedly at the still mysterious stranger's "broad disk of a pair of drab breeches."[17]

In sharp contrast to this jocular take-off of romantic fiction, the next two stories told at Bracebridge—"The Student of Salamanca" and "Annette Delarbe"—are so saturated with sentimentality as to be virtually unreadable today. Yet they too clearly fit the circumstances of the moment that inspired them: namely, Lady Lillycraft's request for a tender love story "to make the day pass pleasantly" on the first occasion, and her desire to reciprocate with another one a few days later on May Morning. They not only show Irving's versatility in working with romantic and gothic materials in novella form but also suggest his own half-concealed ironic attitude toward this type of fiction.

In "The Student of Salamanca," for example, Irving employed *two* persona devices to secure aesthetic distance. As a guest in the Bracebridge circle Crayon explains that the Squire's son, Guy, possesses "a role of blottered manuscript," written by *his* friend "Charles Lightly, of the dragoons . . . a great scribbler," who avowedly had composed the tale in Spain, "during the time that he lay ill of a wound received at Salamanca," and who passed it on to Guy just moments before expiring at the battle of Waterloo ("The Library," *BR H,* 98). Guy then proceeds to entertain the gathering by reading aloud this seemingly interminable fifty-three-page document, filled with sensational torments inflicted upon an implausible pair of Spanish lovers by a fiendish rival and his inquisitorial henchmen. But having witnessed their Hollywood rescue and reunion on the last page, Crayon remarks cryptically that "the residue of this story may readily be imagined by every one versed in this valuable kind of history" and leaves little doubt of his own ironic attitude toward it by noting that "the steady sound of the captain's voice" while reading it had put at least one member of the audience soundly to sleep (153–54). Irving again used the device of the cherished manuscript in setting forth "Annette Delarbe," another gruesome tale of a young French girl's mental breakdown over the presumed loss of her lover at sea and her miraculous recovery upon his reappearance. This time the manuscript, "daintily written on gilt-edged vellum paper, and stitched with a light blue ribbon," is allegedly the product of Lady Lillycraft's widowed parson, who, she says, "often brings me some of the sweetest pieces of poetry, all about the pleasures of melancholy, and such subjects, that make me cry so, you can't think" (204).

Irving contrived an even more elaborate framework for placing his fourth story, "Dolph Heyliger," in a climactic position within the context of *Bracebridge Hall*. Essentially an American tall tale, "Dolph Heyliger" is based on the same fund of Dutch legend he had worked up in the *Knickerbocker* and later in the *Sketch Book* tales; and in devising a suitable pretext for introducing it here, he presented Crayon as the embarrassed guest, suddenly called upon by the Squire during one of the storytelling sessions "to furnish some entertainment of the kind in my turn" (246–47). Flustered by "so unexpected a demand," Crayon begs leave to read another "manuscript tale . . . from the pen of . . . the late Mr. Diedrich Knickerbocker" (whom he again describes briefly as a prelude to Knickerbocker's tedious introduction in a chapter entitled "The Haunted House"), one of the many weird tales he had heard as a boy told in the "ancient city of the Manhattoes" (248).

This, then, is the story of Dolph Heyliger, deservedly called "the real hero of *Bracebridge Hall*."[18] For despite its structural weaknesses and cumbersome length, it is the typical rags-to-riches tale of a roguish but good-natured middle-class American boy, whose pluck and luck, good looks, and charm bring him riches and a winsome bride. Transcending the genteel pretensions of his widowed mother, Dolph abandons his role as guardian of a haunted house to follow the lure of its ghostly visitor, runs off to river and wilderness where he survives the perils of near drowning and the terrors of snakes and wild Indians, and joins the hunting expedition of a gregarious land-owner and spinner of tall tales, Anthony Vander Heyden, who turns out to be a distant relative. As a guest in the latter's Albany mansion, Dolph identifies the subject of an ancestral portrait as the ghost of the haunted house; he returns to New York, digs up a treasure buried on the property years before by his ancestor, and, having established his rightful claim to it, marries old Anthony's daughter and secures her fortune.

Dolph is a worthy successor to Rip, Ichabod Crane, and Brom Bones because he possesses energy, courage, and imagination, along with a superb talent "for making ghosts work for him." Had Irving felt confident enough to continue developing fully in his new collection the vein of fiction Dolph represented, his work might have received the acclaim he felt it deserved. For in "Dolph Heylinger," as in "Rip Van Winkle" and "Sleepy Hollow," his modified mock-heroic approach was transforming American life into legend, creating a world in which "strenuous heroism is beside the point," and reaching toward "a myth of deliverance from the Protestant ethic."[19] But with the success of *Bracebridge* assured, Irving set off in 1822 on his tour of Germany, ostensibly to gather fresh materials from the rich legendary lore of that country as a basis for what his friends expected to become his "German Sketch Book." The turmoil of a year's social distractions, however, and a second abortive love affair in Dresden, apparently scotched his plans for systematic study, sending him, forlorn and confused, back to Paris, where he composed most of the *Tales of a Traveller* the following year.

Tales of a Traveller: Craftsmanship, Versatility, and Parody

When this work appeared in 1824, it was harshly criticized by English and American reviewers alike. Finding it neither a sketchbook like Crayon's earlier offerings nor a romanticized fictional treatment of German legends, localities, manners, or customs, they condemned Irving's alleged lack of originality and seriousness as well as his slapdash methods of composition and "droll indecencies."[20] So despite the fifteen hundred guineas Murray had willingly paid him for *Tales of a Traveller,* the chorus of sarcastic reviews convinced Irving that the book was a failure,[21] even though he felt that much of it had been written "in freer and happier vein than almost any of my other writings."[22] During its early stages of composition, Irving had said that he wished to strike out on his own with a method in which "style" rather than "narrative" would enable him to avoid both "Scott's manner" and that of the commonplace "legendary and romantic tales . . . littering from the press in both England and Germany."[23] Yet now, in the face of all those hostile reviews, he had to admit resignedly that the mass of his readers—"intent more upon the story than the way in which it is told"—evidently failed to observe the very qualities in his writing that he valued most: namely, "the play of thought, and sentiments and language; the weaving in of characters, lightly yet expressively delineated; . . . and the half-concealed vein of humor that is often playing through the whole."[24]

With his emphasis upon "nicety of execution," Irving's effort to achieve a new departure in fiction brought him to the threshold of the modern concept of the short story, though he fell short of it, perhaps because the genre itself, conceived as a self-contained fictional form based on its own artistic principles, had not yet been defined. Since he was not attempting to write short stories in this sense, but rather "a series of relatively short narratives that could somehow be combined into a book," his *Tales of a Traveller* has been accurately characterized as "the work of a short-story writer who had not quite discovered his form, even though he had already, partly by chance, written two or three stories that are destined to survive."[25] Although Irving scorned the practice of writing for the magazines, had he been obliged to tailor his short fiction to the requirements of serial publication, as Poe and Hawthorne did originally, he might have succeeded as well as they in realizing the form of the short story as a self-contained, independent entity. But it is not surprising that many of Irving's contemporaries misconstrued his purpose, since even his major biographer, Stanley T. Williams, dismissed *Tales of a Traveller* as a slovenly book full of unpardonable faults, obsolete ghost stories and robber tales, and hollow mirth. "In Parts I and III," Williams wrote, "we yawn over the machinery of haunted *chateaux*, sinister storms, mysterious footsteps, and hidden panels. Spirits sigh in the darkness; portraits wink; furniture dances; and brooding, sensitive heroes woo melancholy maidens—in vain . . . nor are they effective as satire."[26]

What Williams apparently failed to appreciate in the book is the element of burlesque, spoofery, hoaxing, and lightly satiric parody—characteristics Irving's fiction shared with Poe's earliest prose writings. Nor were these the only technical similarities between them: a more important one was their awareness of what has been called "a certain fraudulent quality in fiction."[27] Both recognized that a story need not be just a straightforward narrative of actual events; that its acceptability as a story depends not on its content primarily, but on *the way it is told*—that is, upon the established authenticity of its narrator. Both accordingly stressed the value of the storyteller's style or "voice" as an important element in fiction, for both "saw that an audience will accept almost any plot or story, no matter how fantastic, if it is made convincing by being put in the mouth of someone with a reason or need for telling it."

The stories in *Tales of a Traveller* are put into a variety of different mouths, though Irving again used Crayon to serve as a controlling focus. Posing this time as "an old traveller" whose head is stuffed with a vast assortment of odds and ends, Crayon pretends that he cannot remember where he picked up most of the tales and is therefore "always at a loss to know how much to believe" of them.[28] He cannot even be sure they are amusing but is nevertheless confident that each contains a valuable moral, deftly disguised "as much as possible by sweets and spices, so that while the simple reader is listening with open mouth to a ghost or a love story, he may have a bolus of sound morality popped down his throat, and be never the wiser for the fraud" (ix). That Irving did not expect to be taken too seriously is plainly implied in these remarks and in Crayon's parting wink, assuring his reader good humoredly that if the ensuing tales "should prove to be bad, they will at least be found short; so that no one will be wearied long on the same theme" (xi).

Crayon's mocking tone thus establishes the keynote of burlesque, which is a dominant mode in most of the thirty-two separate pieces in the volume, particularly in those of its first and third parts. All but three of the tales are indeed short—some averaging fewer than ten pages each—but the collection as a whole is perhaps more interesting than the individual stories, which Irving divided into four groups: "Strange Stories by a Nervous Gentleman," "Buckthorne and His Friends," "The Italian Banditti," and "The Money Diggers."

Superficially, there appears to be little conscious design in the arrangement of these groups, since the narratives in each group seem to bear no obvious relationship to those of the other groups. Yet there may well be an orderly progression of tales that is less slovenly than Williams alleged. It is a progression wherein structural unity and tonal consistency are achieved, at least partially, through Irving's skillful evocation and manipulation of shifting narrators, each of whom tailors his story to fit his own personality. Thus, as the reader follows each group of stories consecutively, he becomes aware that Irving's effort to establish a relationship between the narrator and his tales is moving toward a conception of fiction as the revelation of character; and that the development of mood engendered in each sequence subtly progresses from whimsy and fun-poking to terror, violence, or serious introspection.

Crayon, for example, begins the nine narratives in the first group by identifying their frame narrator as "the same nervous gentleman who told me the romantic tale of the Stout Gentlemen" (15). This second narrator then takes over, describing the setting and characterizing the male participants at a dinner party he once attended "given by a worthy fox-hunting Baronet, who kept bachelor's hall in jovial style in an ancient rook-haunted family mansion" (17). Besides the host and himself, these include a merry Irish captain of dragoons, an inquisitive "hatchet-faced gentleman, with projecting eyes like a lobster" (20), a waggish elderly gentleman "with a knowing look and . . . a flexible nose" (21), and another old gentleman, one whole side of whose head "was dilapidated, and seemed like the wing of a house shut up and haunted" (22). Since the evening's dreary weather matches the Baronet's gloomy chambers, the company's after-dinner conversation naturally turns to ghosts, and the old man is urged to retell a ghost story he is reminded of. But the "Adventure of My Uncle," which he unfolds, and the following "Adventure of My Aunt," told by "the knowing gentleman with the flexible nose"—as well as "The Bold Dragoon; or The Adventure of My Grandfather," which the merry Irishman appropriately tells next in dialect—all turn out to be jokes on the inquisitive man. Instead of evoking real ghosts, they are parodies reminiscent of *Tristram Shandy*'s risqué double entendres and sly sexual innuendos. As the old man with the haunted head pointedly observes, they have "rather a burlesque tendency" (56).

At this juncture, however, a subtle turning point occurs; for the same speaker now launches into the harrowing "Adventure of the German Student," a tale that turns out to be both a hoax and yet a fearfully compelling fantasy of a psychopath, the "ghost" in this case being a revitalized female corpse who "owes her existence to the [mad] German student's desires and frustrations, both of which she personified."[29] When read in its sequential context, the story clearly suggests that Irving was not just haphazardly switching from the matter-of-fact and the ludicrous to the mysterious and the terrifying, but rather that he was deliberately doing the sort of thing that Poe would later achieve even more effectively in such tales as "Berenice" and "The Assignation": at first "inviting and laughing at stock responses and [moving] gradually toward showing what it is like to be truly possessed."[30]

In the three remaining narratives of part 1 the mood darkens perceptibly. Successively entitled "Adventure of the Mysterious Picture," "Adventure of the Mysterious Stranger," and "The Story of the Young Italian," these are a connected series of developments growing out of the climactic experiences of the "nervous gentleman." As the party breaks up and the guests prepare to retire for the night, the host jovially avows that before morning one of them will know that he has bedded in a haunted chamber. And despite a skeptical turn of mind, the "nervous gentleman" is soon convinced that his must be the room when he finds there the gruesome portrait of an agonized face. The picture awakens in his imagination "some horror of the mind" (68) so disturbing that he is compelled against his will to abandon his bed and spend the rest of the night on a sofa in the drawing room downstairs. When his frightful experience is disclosed in the morning, the Baronet cuts short the raillery of the other guests by explaining that there is indeed a fearful "picture in my house which possesses singular and mysterious influence, and with which there is connected a very mysterious story" (74).

Thereupon the host proceeds to tell of his encounter in Venice, "many years since," with a sensitive but melancholy young Italian who shared his enthusiasm for the aesthetic beauty of the Roman Catholic Lenten ritual and who mysteriously left with him a packet containing both the picture alluded to and a manuscript explaining its significance. This then becomes "The Story of the Young Italian," which the Baronet proceeds to read to his assembled guests. The longest of the pieces in part 1, and not altogether convincing because Irving fails to identify fully with his protagonist, Ottavio, it is nevertheless a compelling tale of betrayal and revenge that, unlike "The Student of Salamanca," grapples honestly with a fundamental problem and belies the stereotype of its genial author.

Basically the theme is concerned with the question of what terrifying inner forces would drive a gifted, sensitive individual to commit a crime that implants an indelibly bloody image on his conscience. In developing the life story of the young painter as a murderer capable of arousing the reader's sympathy, Irving displays a foretaste of Hawthorne's skillful probing of a soul in torment, as well as his ability to suggest through symbolic imagery the corrosive effects of violent impulse, guilt, and remorse.

Presented from his own first-person point of view, Ottavio is seen as a highly emotional young man seeking his identity in a hostile world. Left motherless in childhood and rejected by a harsh father who favors an older brother, his life becomes a recurring pattern of jealous hostility, emotional turmoil, and flight from authority; and when eventually, as apprentice and heir to a benevolent elderly painter, he attains both an inner security and the love of a beautiful young woman whose madonnalike image he had often painted, his frenzied murder of the young friend who treacherously steals her from him becomes the climactic action in a career of agony and frustration. With a touch worthy of Hawthorne, the horror of Ottavio's remorse compels him to attempt, futilely, to exorcise the tormenting phantom of his crime by committing it to canvas and then to bequeath both the picture and his confession to the sympathetic Englishman before giving himself up to justice. By contrasting the violence of the young Italian's passionate fervor and the staid Englishman's reaction to it, Irving anticipated both Hawthorne's and James's fascination for the beauty and terror of Italy. Yet his own whimsicality prevails in the end with the Baronet's disclosure to the "nervous gentleman" that he has tricked all the other guests by having them shown, one by one, not the frightful visage in the mysterious picture they begged to see, but a portrait in a different room.

In part 2 of the *Tales*—"Buckthorne and His Friends"—Irving shifted both the focus and the style of his narrative, as the ten connected pieces play variations on the theme of authorship rather in the manner of the Addisonian periodical essay than in that of the gothic tradition involving sensational actions and events. Here Irving's basic purpose was to draw a series of ironic contrasts between the aims and aspirations of the artist and the harsh realities of the practical world. Crayon's new acquaintance, Buckthorne, introduces him to the London literary scene, where he meets a motley crowd of Grub Street hacks, impoverished authors, and third-rate poets, "most of whom will neither stop chasing phantoms altogether nor find the security of accepting their third ratedness."[31]

Buckthorne, says Crayon, "was a man much to my taste; . . . he had seen the world, mingled with society, . . . [and] evidently been a little chilled by fortune, without being soured thereby" (167). Hence these initial experiences in his company induce Crayon to draw from this "practical philosopher" an account of his own youthful vicissitudes as "the Young Man of Great Expectations." Revealing his blighted hopes and humiliations as he strove futilely to achieve status in the illusory realms of poetry and the theater before a convenient inheritance enabled him to abandon the profitless drudgery of writing, this narrative serves as comic counterpart to the violent tale of Ottavio in part 1. Neither this nor the other short tales in part 2 enhance Irving's stature as a fiction writer, though they offer interesting symbolic reflections of his own doubts and fears regarding the role of the artist in "the seductive but treacherous paths of literature."[32]

But in the eight stories comprising part 3 of the *Tales*, "The Italian Banditti," he displayed perhaps his greatest versatility and boldness as both parodist and craftsman. Shifting the narrative locus once again, this time to the inn at Terracina on the highroad from Rome to Naples, Crayon fades unobtrusively into the background and lets a group of travelers tell of their hair-raising confrontations with the notorious highwaymen infesting that remote area. Irving's basic purpose is again satiric, for while the stories begin on a note of burlesque and gradually work up to a violent climax, they repeatedly undercut the allure of illicit sex as a dominant motif in much of the popular sentimental and gothic fiction of the era.

In the opening tale the comic tone is set by the arrival of a government courier from Naples who has been stripped of his "bran new" leather pants by a formidable gang of robbers. When a fluttery Venetian bride asks him whether the robbers are cruel to strangers, he leeringly raises the specter of rampant sexuality by implying that all women who fall into their hands are summarily ravished. "Holy Virgin! . . . what will become of us!" she exclaims. This exchange opens the way for all the ensuing exploits recalled or endured by others in the group, but by bringing in a skeptical English gentleman, who contemptuously dismisses these hair-raising accounts as pure humbug, Irving slyly introduces a variety of sexual innuendo through successive contrasts between innocence and experience. The naïveté of a drooping young heroine miraculously rescued in the tale of "The Belated Travellers," for example, is set off against the bawdy sophistication of an old Spanish princess who, along with her handsome nephew, is also being held captive by bandits at an isolated tavern. Gradually the accounts of these and other narrow escapes intensify the "fair Venetian's" suppressed sexual curiosity, as well as her seemingly unconscious desire to arouse an amorous response from the bland Englishman. Thus, as the stories build up to a violent climax of overt sexuality in "The Story of the Young Robber," a brutal tale of mass ravishment and ritual murder that was severely condemned by American reviewers, it seems clear that Irving was boldly carrying the vein of sensational gothic fiction as far as he dared, without, however, abandoning his parodic aim.

Irving's next tale, "The Painter's Adventure," serves as another enveloping narrative cushioning the climactic story, which a French artist in the group promises to retell—"as near as I can recollect"—in the words of the young robber who told it to him while holding him captive. "The Young Robber's Story" then becomes an agonized confession of guilt in a double murder so horrifying in its specific details that when the Frenchman finished, it made a deep impression on his listeners, Crayon reports—"particularly on the Venetian lady."(368).

At this point Irving's dexterity in rounding off the framework of his narrative sequence in a parodic vein again becomes apparent. For the "fair Venetian," Crayon adds (and the reader wonders how he managed to overhear her), muttered impatiently to her husband as they were going to bed: "I'll warrant . . . this Englishman's heart would quake at the very sight of a bandit." Returning to the level of burlesque, Irving provides in "The Adventure of the Englishman" a comic take-off of the conventional thriller in which the lady, after leaving the inn with her husband, almost gets what she seems unconsciously to have wanted all along, as bandits attack her party and are on the point of raping her when the Englishman appears in the nick of time to rescue her singlehandedly!

Finally, in part 4 of the *Tales* Irving returns again to his favorite American scenes and subject matter, presenting in the four concluding stories of "The Money Diggers" the familiar type of legendary lore that had characterized his best work in the *Knickerbocker History* and *The Sketch Book*. Here he abandoned parody and burlesque, resorting instead to the more leisurely form of the folk tale. And though the theme of the tales in part 4 remains essentially the same as that of the preceding ones—namely, the vanity and mutability of what are called "Great Expectations" in "Buckthorne" and "Golden Dreams" in "Wolfert Webber"—Irving again demonstrates his versatility by showing that in fiction the subject matter is less important than the way the story is told.

The basic story throughout the *Tales* has to do with unfulfilled promises or the disillusionment born of experience, but whereas it is told with passion and inflated gothic rhetoric in parts 1 and 3, and with philosophic dispassionateness in part 2, in these concluding pieces it is frankly set forth in the venerable guise of folk superstitions concerning the age-old quest for buried treasure—which oftener than not proves illusory in the end. Yet Irving's stylistic skills are nowhere more prominently displayed than in his handling of this ancient chestnut. His ironic tone is established in Diedrich Knickerbocker's introductory summary of some of the many legends clustering about the frenzied search for the notorious Captain Kidd's hidden booty, in all of which, he remarks drily, "the devil played a conspicuous part" (387). Irving then promptly launches into one of the most impressive of all his short narratives, "The Devil and Tom Walker," which, despite its wildly improbable plot, foreshadows the best of Hawthorne's fictional exposure of Yankee shrewdness and Puritan hypocrisy.

In developing the Faustian character of Tom Walker, his termagant wife, and their separate confrontations with the devil, Irving once more achieved not only the subtle blend of seriocomic pathos seen in "Rip Van Winkle" but also a species of much starker imagery that transforms such commonplace American activities as money lending, timber cutting, slave trading, treasure hunting, and Bible reading into grotesque emblems of spiritual deprivation, emotional sterility, hypocrisy, and lovelessness. The image of Dame Walker, for example, dashing into the forest with her "silver teapot and spoons" (398–99) for a rendezvous with the devil, who shrivels her to a crisp, is a chilling foretaste of Young Goodman Brown's symbolic discovery of the omnipresence of evil. Yet it is of a piece with numerous other descriptive touches—of Walker's spavined horse, sterile trees, forlorn house, and worthless treasure chest, his rigid religiosity and his usurious tactics—in which Irving's mastery of wordplay, alliteration, hyperbole, metaphor, and allusion bears out his claim that what he valued most in fiction was "the play of thought, sentiment, and language [that shadowed forth] a half-concealed vein of humor."

Although these values are likewise evident in the remaining stories told about Wolfert Webber, a comic Dutch colonial, the rambling manner of these narratives seems tedious beside the concentrated effect of "The Devil and Tom Walker." But Irving had already proved in that tale, as well as in various others in the volume, that he well deserved the encomiums that Poe, twenty years later, bestowed upon his artistry. If he did not actually invent the short story, he set the pattern for the artistic re-creation of common experience in short fictional form—a pattern to which the superior genius of Poe and Hawthorne alike paid an even higher compliment by imitating, extending, and refining it in the short stories they produced in the 1830s and 1840s. Yet they, too, often fared little better than he at the hands of myopic reviewers who failed to appreciate the new literary form that they had brought into being.

Early Storytelling: Genesis of *Twice-Told Tales*

In November 1851 Nathaniel Hawthorne, savoring at last the public recognition he felt had eluded his earliest published efforts, dedicated *The Snow Image and Other Twice-Told Tales,* his third major collection of short fiction, to his lifelong friend Horatio Bridge. He reminded Bridge with genuine warmth that "if anybody is responsible for my being at this day an author, it is yourself"; for Bridge had rescued him from "the depths of . . . obscurity" by bringing out the first volume of *Twice-Told Tales* nearly fifteen years before, when "not a publisher in America . . . would have thought well enough of my forgotten or never noticed stories, to risk the expense of print and paper." Now that a "transitory gleam of public favor" lighted his path, however, Hawthorne could confidently assert that the few remaining stories gathered together for this memorial collection—some among the earliest he had written and others of more recent origin—would be the last short fiction he would attempt to write. He was tired of writing stories and sketches, not only because the effort was still less remunerative in cash and literary fame than the production of longer works like *The Scarlet Letter* and *The House of the Seven Gables* but also because he recognized that his earliest stories, despite the many faults he found in them, "come so nearly up to the standard I can achieve now. The ripened autumnal fruit tastes but little better than the early windfalls."[1]

At this stage of his career Hawthorne's awareness of his achievements and limitations as a writer of short fiction reflected a long, frustrating struggle to win popularity and a livelihood as a professional author. During the preceding quarter century he had published nearly a hundred tales and sketches, many of which had appeared originally, often anonymously, in New England magazines and giftbook annuals of the 1830s. Eventually all but a dozen or so of them, which remained uncollected, were to reappear in the three collections: *Twice-Told Tales,* first issued in 1837 in a single volume containing eighteen pieces, was expanded and reissued in 1842 and again in 1851 in two volumes containing thirty-nine; *Mosses from an Old Manse,* also published in two volumes in 1846, contained twenty-five pieces, to which another story, "Feathertop," was added in the later 1854 edition; and *The Snow Image and Other Twice-Told Tales,* published in 1851, contained fifteen. Long before the first of these collections brought Hawthorne a glimpse of the public notice he sought, however, he had striven unsuccessfully to become known as a writer. Besides the short gothic novel *Fanshawe,* written shortly after his graduation from Bowdoin and published anonymously at his own expense in 1828, Hawthorne planned and partially completed in the next few years three other collections: *Seven Tales of My Native Land, Provincial Tales,* and one that critics now refer to as *The Story Teller.* None of these turned out as he had hoped, and little is known about their original contents and design, except that some if not all the stories intended for them later appeared singly, occasionally in revised form, before finding their way into the three major collections.[2]

Hawthorne publicly noted these developments, though without specific reference to his initially aborted plans, in the famous preface he wrote for the third edition of *Twice-Told Tales* in 1851. Nostalgically recalling in a lightly ironic vein that period of youthful endeavor when he was "the obscurest man of letters in America," he avowed that his stories had created little or no stir either when first published in the magazines or when issued in his first collected volume. Indeed, not only was that book "probably ignored altogether" by most of the reading public, its expanded two-volume edition published a few years later "encountered much the same sort of . . . very limited reception." Such meager reward for his time and effort, however, was scarcely less than they deserved, Hawthorne added, since they were all too pale and insubstantial to arouse a wide public response. "Instead of passion there is sentiment; and, even in what purports to be pictures of actual life, we have allegory, not always so warmly dressed in its habiliments of flesh and blood to be taken into the reader's mind without a shiver." Lacking both power and profundity, as well as depth of pathos and humor, they failed to win "an extensive popularity." But this failure was less remarkable than the "too generous praise . . . too little alloyed with censure" some of them had occasionally received. And so, he concluded, although the *Twice-Told Tales* had proved to be an imperfectly successful attempt "to open an intercourse with the world," the fact that their publication had won him many friends and no enemies afforded him much enjoyment "far better than fame."[3]

By 1851 such deprecatory self-appraisal was typical, as Hawthorne on several occasions before then had downgraded the artistic merit of his short fiction.[4] Yet it stands in marked contrast to his youthful eagerness for popular acclaim, and the strategies he pursued in seeking it. There is ample evidence that he had intended each of his first three collections of tales to represent a varied narrative package unified by some principle designed to enlighten and entertain the reading public. In *The Story Teller,* for example, he had planned to combine a group of tales involving the adventures of a young man named Oberon, who, while traveling about the New England countryside, was earning a livelihood as a storyteller. The characterization of Oberon as narrator, like that of Irving's Geoffrey Crayon, would provide the unifying element enabling Hawthorne to convert some of his own experiences as a summer excursionist into a wide range of fictions "including the comic, serious, sentimental, gothic, historical, contemporary, folksy, broad, subtle, and literary."[5]

Failing once again in 1834 to secure a publisher for *The Story Teller,* as he had failed twice before, Hawthorne continued to supply the magazines with separate single tales and sketches written during the next three years—in all, about twenty new pieces, again displaying a remarkable range of interests, types, and techniques. So, when he set about the task of assembling the first edition of *Twice-Told Tales,* he had more than forty to choose from, including "The Canterbury Pilgrims," "My Kinsman, Major Mollineux," "Roger Malvin's Burial," and "Young Goodman Brown," which critics today recognize as among the most impressive of all his short fiction. Yet he passed over all four of those stories and several other excellent early ones, selecting instead a preponderance of more recently published pieces, some of them disappointingly innocuous and undistinguished, such as "David Swan," "Sunday at Home," and "Sights from a Steeple." The question puzzling recent critics is, accordingly, why would Hawthorne deliberately overlook some of his finer works and pad the limited space in his first publishable collection with inferior ones? Since little is known regarding what convictions, if any, underlay his decision, this question apparently remains unanswerable; and Hawthorne's probable strategy in the choice and arrangement of these materials has therefore been variously interpreted.

Irving's Influence in *The Sketch Book* Selections

One scholar, for example, argues that as Hawthorne assembled his selections for *Twice-Told Tales* he sought once again to achieve a unifying principle for the book. But instead of grouping them explicitly around either a historical or a thematic center, this time he tried to secure unity, balance, and variety implicitly by means of an intricate pattern of contrasts and juxtapositions—in short, a pattern somewhat resembling that of *The Sketch Book* or *Tales of a Traveller.* Thus, by adopting Irving's strategy of varied narrative voices, he sought to establish rapport with his audience by appealing alternately to their sense of the serious and the comic, the familiar and the legendary, the near and the remote in time and space. If successful, his clusters of juxtaposed tales and sketches, ranging from New England's colonial past to the contemporary scene, and varying in mood from stern psychological analysis to light, whimsical fantasy, would provide a blend of imaginative fiction in which there was to be "something for everyone—children, delicate ladies, hardheaded businessmen."[6]

That Hawthorne did adopt some such strategy in hopes of duplicating Irving's success with *The Sketch Book* seems evident; it is now known that while preparing his materials for publication in book form, he made numerous rhetorical revisions clearly intended to enhance his public image. Now that he was about to appear as the acknowledged author of what had originally been mainly anonymous fictions, Hawthorne took great care to modify the style and tone of his writings; to eliminate from them whatever "indelicate" diction—especially in passages hinting of sexuality—he thought likely to offend the public taste of his time.[7] His care was rewarded by generally favorable reviews of *Twice-Told Tales;* yet these tended to mark him as a "coterie" writer, and far from achieving Irving's popularity, sales of the book remained dismayingly slim.[8]

This discrepancy between the reviewers' approval and the public's apathetic response has led other recent scholars to question his awareness of what the reading public could or would accept.[9] But during the five-year interim between 1837 and 1842 Hawthorne was preoccupied with many other activities that cut into the time he could devote to the writing of short fiction: his service at the Boston Custom House, his involvement in the Brook Farm Experiment, and, most significant, his courtship of Sophia Peabody and their eventual marriage in 1842. Up to that point he had published only about twenty new tales and sketches, fifteen of which were included in the twenty chosen for the contents of volume 2 of the *Twice-Told Tales.* And except for the first four historical tales, collectively entitled "Legends of the Province House," plus one or two others like "Peter Goldthwaite's Treasure" and "Endicott and the Red Cross," most of these recent pieces were clearly inferior to earlier tales such as "The Ambitious Guest," "The Haunted Mind," and "The White Old Maid" (all dating from 1835), selected for inclusion in the volume.[10] It is not surprising, therefore, that the 1842 edition of *Twice-Told Tales* aroused no greater interest among the reading public than had the 1837 edition, although it too drew mildly favorable reviews, the most famous among them by Edgar Allan Poe. For Hawthorne, still compromising his integrity, was failing to "demonstrate any real importance in the work he was doing," by trying to give the public what he thought the public wanted.[11]

Children's Stories and Other Tales: *Mosses from an Old Manse*

And yet, during the same five-year period Hawthorne obviously matured both as a social being and as a man of letters, gaining confidence in his professional ability and extending his range. Shortly after his engagement to Sophia he had begun turning out children's literature as a potentially more lucrative effort. Written in the form of biographical tales of famous people in Massachusetts history, these were published separately in four slim volumes in 1841–42 and later reissued, after the success of *The Scarlet Letter,* in a single volume entitled *True Stories from History and Biography,* the first three under the collective title *The Whole History of Grandfather's Chair.* This portion of his work has only recently received the attention it deserves, not only as marking a significant advance in Hawthorne's developing career, but also as a literary achievement in its own right.[12]

After moving to the Old Manse with his bride in the summer of 1842, however, Hawthorne was still determined to become well known as an author of fiction for adults; and he strove earnestly but futilely to support himself and his growing family with a varied assortment of short writings that drew ready acceptance but meager financial returns from the magazines. During their three-year residence at the Old Manse he published more than twenty of these pieces, most of them sketches rather than stories with plotted action, but revealing an obvious effort to shift the emphasis of his fiction away from the historical matter characterizing much of his earlier work "toward a new concern with his contemporaries."[13]

Unfortunately, despite the domestic felicity shared by the Hawthornes and the enthusiasm with which Nathaniel embraced the task of converting his interest in world affairs into marketable fiction, he quickly discovered that a new emphasis alone would not suffice. It simply would not pay the household bills. In 1841 he had written Evert Duyckinck that he knew he could no longer write the sort of material that had gone into the *Twice-Told Tales* because those stories had grown "out of the quietude and seclusion" of his early life; whereas now "the world has sucked me within its vortex, and I could not get back to my solitude again, even if I would."[14] So he began writing a different sort of fiction—pieces like "Fire Worship," "The

Hall of Fantasy," "The Celestial Rail-road," "Earth's Holocaust," and "A Virtuoso's Collection"—producing ten of these during his first year at the Old Manse (1842–43), but only eight more during his second year in residence, and only three during his third year. By this time the family's financial situation had become desperate, and Hawthorne realized that he could no longer hope to survive as a "writer of stories for the magazines— the most unprofitable business in the world."[15]

Thus, once again in the early 1840s Hawthorne agreed, reluctantly, to follow Duyckinck's suggestion about putting together a volume of short fiction pieces with hopes of making some money, though he was not sanguine about its prospects. The original idea was to make up a single brief volume of recent fictions published in the magazines after the appearance of the second edition of *Twice-Told Tales*. It was to be a volume unified by means of a "framed" device—that is, an initial essay eventually to be titled "The Old Manse"—which would show how the contents as a whole had grown out of Hawthorne's mode of life there. But during the course of negotiating this scheme, the idea for the *Mosses* book changed as Duyckinck suggested expanding it to a two-volume collection containing some of the earlier tales not included in the 1842 edition of *Twice-Told Tales*. Hawthorne agreed to "toss in a few make weights" from among his older uncollected pieces if the collection needed more bulk. By the middle of 1845 he was still thinking of the project as a unified collection in which the initial piece would point up the biographical implications tying the remaining pieces together; but he could not seem to get that opening sketch written and actually did not finish it until after he and Sophia had left the Old Manse.[16]

Mosses from an Old Manse as first published in 1846 contained twenty-three pieces, four of them "make weights" dating from as early as 1832: "Roger Malvin's Burial," "Young Goodman Brown," "Mrs. Bullfrog," and "Monsieur du Miroir." The remaining nineteen included thirteen he had mentioned in his first proposed list, plus six more written while he was still living at the Old Manse. Obviously the *Mosses* was now no longer the unified collection that Hawthorne had originally conceived, but neither would he give up the idea of including in it the autobiographical "Old Manse" sketch, which clearly shows how his attitude toward his role as a professional author—that is, his "aesthetic caste of mind"—had changed and how "he had moved toward a new way of dealing with reality."[17]

There is probably no way of knowing what motivated Hawthorne's decision in the selection of early tales chosen as "make weights." He may again have passed over stronger works like "My Kinsman, Major Molineux," "Wives of the Dead," and "The Man of Adamant" in favor of the light-comic spoofery of "Mrs. Bullfrog" and "Monsieur du Miroir" because he wanted to avoid overloading the collection with too much seemingly pessimistic, "dark" material. This is apparently the consensus among Hawthorne scholars today, who argue that Hawthorne was still trying to achieve a popular "mix" of juxtaposed light and serious materials but not succeeding very well.[18] Still, they tend to agree that "The Old Manse," ironically the last piece to be written yet intended to serve as introduction to the collection, is the most interesting work of all in the *Mosses*.

Similarly, one critic argues that the *Mosses* as a whole is inferior to *Twice-Told Tales* because most of the pieces in the collection—except those like "Young Goodman Brown" and "Roger Malvin's Burial," which belong to Hawthorne's earlier period—are by now either forgotten or ignored.[19] But this judgment may be challenged by the reminder that at least six or seven tales in the collection dating from the 1840s still reappear frequently in anthologies, while several like "Rappaccini's Daughter," "The Birthmark," and "The Artist of the Beautiful" continue to evoke controversial critical reinterpretations in scholarly journals concerned with nineteenth-century American fiction.[20] Moreover, it should be remembered that the *Mosses* collection, though still not a best-seller by any means, aroused considerable commentary, generally favorable, among prominent critics in Hawthorne's lifetime, though several of them apparently failed to grasp what he was up to in tales like "Young Goodman Brown" and "The Birthmark." The tendency among Hawthorne's contemporaries was to praise his light, humorous sketches, the very ones that critics today either disparage or ignore. Ironically, however, the collection also brought forth from Edgar Allan Poe and Herman Melville what have been rightly called "two of the most memorable statements in nineteenth-century American literary criticism."[21]

Critical Reception of *Mosses:* Genesis of *Snow Image* Collection

Both Poe and Melville addressed themselves to the central paradox involving Hawthorne's continuing unpopularity with the reading public despite his recognizably formidable literary genius. But whereas Poe, in reevaluating Hawthorne's entire fictional career, now attributed his lack of popularity to a disappointing failure of originality, Melville argued on the contrary that it was precisely Hawthorne's originality and depth of intellect that the average reader failed to appreciate because "it is the least part of genius that attracts admiration."[22] Poe contended that Hawthorne's fictions suffered from not only a monotonously allegorical uniformity but also a repellent tendency toward the didactic, thus violating in a double sense his own basic aesthetic principle of "unity of effect." For Melville, on the other hand, Hawthorne's allegorical efforts to grapple with such towering ideas as "Original Sin" or the problem of evil in human affairs unequivocally placed him in the company of "Shakespeare and other masters of the great Art of Telling the Truth." He was not simply the pleasant, harmless sort of writer that most readers seemed to take him for; there was also the dark side of his soul, "shrouded in a blackness, ten times black"; and it was this blackness of darkness that, in a story like "Young Goodman Brown," showed him to be as "deep as Dante."[23]

Oddly enough, with the passing of time it became clear that the judgments of both critics could be reconciled. Not only did Melville modify his extravagant praise of the *Mosses* and observe that, notwithstanding Hawthorne's lofty genius, there was a lack of roundness and solidity in his fiction, but Hawthorne himself regretfully confessed toward the end of his career that even he had difficulty in comprehending some of his own "blasted allegories" and recognized that his writings did not "make their appeal to the popular mind" because they lacked the kind of solidity he admired in the fiction of Anthony Trollope.[24]

Nevertheless, with the highly favorable critical reception given to both *The Scarlet Letter* and *The House of the Seven Gables,* as well as their encouraging acceptance by the reading public, in the spring of 1851 Hawthorne reluctantly agreed to bring out a third collection of fifteen tales, although he had written only four new ones during his three-year residence at the Salem Custom House: "The Snow Image," "The Great Stone Face," "Main Street," and "Ethan Brand."[25] Besides the fifteen tales in this collection Hawthorne had published perhaps a dozen or more others, which, for one reason or another, he preferred not to include. Several of them, as we have noted, he did select later for the expanded 1854 edition of the *Mosses,* but as for the remainder it is uncertain whether he failed to locate them in time or felt that the ones he did unearth from their hiding places "among the dingy pages of fifteen-or-twenty-year old periodicals" fell below his required standard of excellence. Exactly how many more tales Hawthorne may have published anonymously besides those included in the Centenary Edition is still an open question. What has been definitely established, however, is that during the twenty-year span of his short fiction writing Hawthorne produced a total of ninety-three tales and sketches. These are now justly acclaimed as "a rich legacy of achieved form . . . a number of the finest stories in the language . . . [and] a set of possibilities that still continue to nourish the American literary imagination."[26]

Hawthorne's Chief Contribution: "Psychological Romance" and the Inner Life

For over a century since Hawthorne's death, writers, critics, scholars, publishers, and a steadily expanding reading public in the high schools and colleges have agreed that he produced some of the finest stories in the language. This fact, however, raises the problem of identifying precisely the nature of his contributions to the art of short fiction in America; within the makeup of his most familiar stories, what exactly are those possibilities that "still continue to nourish the American literary imagination"? Perhaps the key lies in Hawthorne's own admission in 1851 that as a creative artist (a "fiction monger") he had long been "burrowing, to his utmost ability, into the depths of our common nature, for the purposes of psychological romance."[27]

From his youth, Hawthorne wanted to become a professional writer of fiction rather than a practical man of affairs like his Puritan forebears. And yet his lifelong commitment to that aim was ambivalent. He recognized not only that those "stern and black-browed" ancestors would have scorned his choice of a vocation as "a writer of storybooks," but also that he himself, as their descendant and a representative of his own time and place, shared some of their doubts regarding the serviceability of purely literary endeavor. "It is well to remember," Terence Martin reminds us, "that a deep mistrust of the imagination was a part of Hawthorne's contemporary environment. One did not have to be descended from the Puritans to criticize fiction for being untrue to life."[28] If as a result of these tensions Hawthorne failed "to attain a sustained image of the artist in vital contact with society," he nevertheless strove consistently, especially in his best tales, to justify that role of the artist by showing how fiction, on its most sophisticated level, can dramatize and illuminate the individual's deepest yearnings and frustrations in an endless quest for self-fulfillment.

As a child of the Puritans Hawthorne also shared his ancestors' concern for the life of the spirit and for the manifold distractions and temptations that, like roadblocks on the path to redemption, thwarted that quest. This was what he meant by "burrowing . . . into the depths of our common nature"; and to reveal what he found in those depths—to give a palpable manifestation to the fruits of his burrowing—he evolved a theory of fiction and a manner of expression, "psychological romance," which he defended repeatedly as a legitimate mode of depicting the truth of the human heart.

Hawthorne's signal achievement can thus be seen, first, as a revitalization of standard narrative forms popular in his youth such as the gothic romances of Charles Brockden Brown or Scott's and Irving's tales and sketches. From the beginning of Hawthorne's career there was a crucial difference between his approach and Irving's to the same basic materials of fiction. For whereas Irving tended to accentuate the quaintness of the past—its picturesque external details, always carefully documented and often sentimentalized—Hawthorne's concern was to explore the dark, mysterious recesses of the human psyche. From his wide reading among the works of such seventeenth-century New England worthies as Cotton Mather, Bradford, Winthrop, and Sewell, as well as among those of eighteenth- and nineteenth-century English fiction writers, he derived both a large body of historic facts and a method of relating those facts to his own peculiar fascination with the intricacies and inconsistencies of human motives and with the turmoil and pain suffered in human relationships as a result of such inner conflicts.

Hawthorne's earliest tales suggest that he was repeatedly seeking not only to capture the values of the New England past but also to dramatize and question the relevancy of those values for his own time. How, for example, should a nineteenth-century audience of New Englanders respond to an account of their Puritan ancestors' persecution of the Quakers, their behavior in the Salem witchcraft trials in 1692, their resistance to British tyranny, or their attempts to establish a God-fearing community in the New England wilderness? In six or seven tales published originally in the early and middle 1830s, Hawthorne's response to questions like these was potent enough to disturb his most sophisticated readers. If they had fully grasped the psychological depths and interrelated meanings he was probing, or the subtly ambiguous effects he was creating, they might have recoiled in horror at his boldness.

"Alice Doane's Appeal," for example, a youthful experiment probably written within a year or two after Hawthorne's graduation from Bowdoin College but published anonymously in the *Token and Atlantic Souvenir* in 1835, is an extraordinary combination of popular gothic elements—witchcraft, seduction, incest, murder, secret guilt, exhumation—set in an eerily convoluted narrative frame. It is a story about the art of telling a story, which not only discloses some of the horrors of seventeenth-century New England but also implicitly associates those evils with the teller of the story himself and with the two young women to whom he tells it as the three of them pause on Gallows Hill, the site of the witchcraft executions in Salem. Hawthorne prudently excluded this tale when making up his three collections, possibly because he recognized that the central story of Leonard Doane's murder of his sister's seducer and the vision evoked of all the innocent victims of the witchcraft mania were inadequately unified.

These ingredients, at any rate, were clearly less successfully amalgamated than those of "The Gentle Boy," another grim tale of Puritan persecution published in the same magazine three years before. Nevertheless, as Hawthorne's young narrator reflectively surveys the shattering effect of his vision on his two listeners, the artist's ambiguity is achieved. Having seized both his arms, he says, the girls "were trembling; and sweeter victory still, I had reached the seldom-trodden places of their hearts, and found the well-spring of their tears. And now the past had done all it could."[29] It is easy to see here that Hawthorne was striving to create in these earliest tales a powerfully resonant effect based on a fusion of explosive psychological and historical elements.

Hawthorne achieved this resonance with remarkable consistency in about a dozen of his historical tales published before 1840, though only four of them appeared in his first collection of 1837, and three others remained uncollected until *The Snow Image* in 1851. The keynote to the underlying effectiveness in most of these tales was struck in an early sketch, "The Haunted Mind" (1835), which was not collected till the second edition of *Twice-Told Tales* in 1842. In this sketch a series of processional images composed of sorrows, dashed hopes, shame, and remorse vie in the mind of an insomniac narrator with contrastingly joyful images of wife, children, birds, ships, and dancing as he lies awake at two in the morning, thinking of the dead. And this dichotomy of joy and gloom is made to function in a variety of ways, usually associated in each of the earliest tales with questions of individual responsibility in a context of conflicting loyalties or obligations. The struggle between good and evil is paramount in each of them, and the outcome of that struggle, so far as the fate of the human beings involved in it is concerned, often remains ambiguous because of the ironic ambiguity that Hawthorne seems to sense lying at the heart of nature and human motives.

In "The Gentle Boy," "Roger Malvin's Burial," "My Kinsman, Major Molineux," "Young Goodman Brown," "The May-Pole of Merry Mount," and "The Minister's Black Veil"—all written before 1835—Hawthorne plays some astonishing variations upon themes of parental, conjugal, and filial love, and upon those of alienation, initiation, redemption, and retribution. Within the historical backgrounds of these tales there were actual conflicts between supporters of opposing religious or political or social dogmas, but the focus rests not so much on outward events as on the inward drama in the haunted mind of a single person or at most in the minds of two or three. Thus, in "The Gentle Boy," the violence and suffering engendered by Puritan persecution of the Quakers in New England in the 1650s can be seen as a product of shared fanaticism. Poor Ilbrahim, the gentle boy who dies from the vicious treatment received from his Puritan playmates, is a victim of his wild-eyed mother, Catherine's fanatic martyr complex, and perhaps of his dead father's "disordered imagination" as well.

Irony, Ambiguity, and Symbolic Imagery in the Major Tales

Hawthorne matches irony against irony in "The Gentle Boy," as he does again in "Roger Malvin's Burial," where we see worked out, as the result of an unfulfilled promise of burial to a dying man, a lifetime of festering secret guilt in the mind of the protagonist, guilt that can only find release through the sacrificial destruction of his own son. Reuben Bourne's failure not only to keep his original promise but also to reveal later that he had not kept it cannot be justified in his own consciousness, even though no overt wrong could be charged against him in a court of law. Yet his "sin" lies not merely in the unambiguous failure to keep his promise, but in a concatenation of ironic circumstances and ambiguous situations stretching backward through time to the "original sin" of human nature.[30]

Dramatic ironies of this sort are even more prominent in "My Kinsman, Major Molineux," a tale that hints vaguely of pre-Revolutionary activity in eighteenth-century Boston, but which is at bottom concerned with the initiation of a "shrewd" country boy into the rebuffs and pitfalls of adult urban life. Robin's abortive quest has been interpreted in many ways, no single one of which is entirely satisfactory because the several possible meanings of the tale are so densely interwoven. Is Robin's struggle toward maturity primarily a reflection of awakening Oedipal desires—for sexual freedom? freedom from parental authority? freedom to impose his own identity upon society? Or is it a ripening, rather disillusioning process of discovering the unpalatable evils that exist at the core of human experience, and the consequent need in adulthood to adopt stern moral choices in order to cope with them? Or is it finally a matter of finding out that the overthrow of any social system, however benevolent or tyrannical, is likely to involve painful aftereffects, even for those who only stand by to watch the fun? The beauty of this tale is that its subtly meshed pattern of colorful

symbolic imagery, plus hauntingly pervasive laughter echoing throughout, supports all these interpretations and more.[31]

But if "My Kinsman, Major Molineux" has earned deserved renown
only within recent decades, "Young Goodman Brown," another variation
on the themes of initiation, alienation, and the obliquity of evil, has long
been recognized as one of the most powerful—and most disturbing—examples of Hawthorne's short fiction. Melville was perhaps the first perceptive witness of its depth and impact, noting in his essay on the *Mosses* that
the tale "is deep as Dante . . . a strong positive illustration of the blackness
in Hawthorne";[32] and Henry James, while recognizing it as a "magnificent
little romance," was nevertheless so troubled by the implications he sensed
in Hawthorne's vision of evil that he tried to exorcise it by insisting that it
was meaningless, "for the simple reason that, if it meant anything, it
would mean too much."[33] Yet the story of Goodman Brown's symbolic
journey into the dark forest and the meaning of the shattering experience
he encountered there have engendered many a more remarkable effort to
interpret them during the last thirty years than James could have
anticipated.

What, exactly, does Brown see and hear when, despite the pleas of his
young wife, Faith, to "tarry with me this night . . . of all nights in the
year," he blithely sets off on some mysterious dark errand that, he feels,
"would kill her to think it"? That he evidently meets the devil himself
shortly after entering the woods is plain enough, but from there on the
results of this confrontation and all its visual, aural, tactile, and emotional
sequences are bathed in ambiguities. Does Brown actually discover that
even the saintliest elders of his community are polluted wretches? that even
he and his young bride, standing before an "unhallowed altar," are about
to be baptized into a cult of devil worshipers so that they might be "par-
takers of the mystery of sin, more conscious of the secret guilt of others,
both in deed and thought, than they could now be of their own"? Or has
Brown simply fallen asleep in the forest "and only dreamed a wild dream
of a witch-meeting"?[34] Whichever way the reader decides to answer this
final question raised by the narrator, it is clear that Hawthorne's main concern in this tale, as in "Alice Doane's Appeal," was with the seventeenth-
century Puritans' obsession with the problem of witchcraft. The story
dramatizes their futile efforts to distinguish the righteous from the damned
on the basis of "visible sanctity" and "specter evidence." These were key
terms that doomed the lives of twenty innocent folk in the Salem witchcraft hysteria. And the moral collapse of Goodman Brown's quest, in the
words of one of the most thoroughgoing recent discussions of the tale,

mirrors the collapse of that rigid theocratic system in 1692: it "shows us that witchcraft 'ended' the Puritan world. Its logic of evidence could not stand the test of Faith."[35]

The powerful impact of "Young Goodman Brown" is due in large measure to the symbolic imagery with which both its characters and action are imbued. Although little actually happens in the development of the plot, we are profoundly moved by metaphors and allusions that convey the force of biblical authority. We can identify with Brown and his Faith, not merely as figures in our colonial past but as mythical ancestors. This is characteristic of Hawthorne's most successful tales. Regardless of whether they deal with specific historical episodes or with imaginary situations, they are the tales in which a central character (or at most two or three closely associated characters) emerges sharply and clearly as a representative figure whose inner life is dramatized by means of a patterned texture of symbolic imagery.

Among the remaining historical tales that Hawthorne published before 1840, both "The Gray Champion" and "Endicott and the Red Cross," dealing with recorded instances of British tyranny in New England at two different periods, are less successful than "Young Goodman Brown." For although Hawthorne recreates the local scene convincingly in both tales, the central figures remain flat and shadowy despite their ringing patriotic harangues and the alleged crowd reactions to the melodramatic actions attributed to them. Governor Endicott emerges much more convincingly as a human figure in the earlier tale entitled "The May-Pole of Merry Mount," partly because Hawthorne manages the dialogue and characterization in this episode from the history of Plymouth Plantation with greater skill. Here, too, success comes from the greater subtlety with which his symbolic imagery resolves the basic conflict between stern Puritan moralism and the irresponsible gaiety represented by the traditional springtime nuptials of the Lord and Lady of the May.[36] Although Endicott, "the severest Puritan of all who laid the rock-foundation of New England," triumphantly slashes down the May-Pole and dispatches its heathen crew of celebrants to the workhouse, his heart is touched "at the spectacle of early love" embodied in the young couple; so that "with his own gauntleted hand" he tosses the wreath of roses salvaged from the ruin of the May-Pole over their heads. His prophetic gesture thus concludes one of the brightest of all Hawthorne's fictional tributes to the responsibilities—and satisfactions—of married life.[37]

In several important respects, this story may be compared with "The Canterbury Pilgrims" (1833), another of Hawthorne's earliest tales, which was not reprinted until the 1851 collection of *The Snow Image,* along with "The Man of Adamant," "The Devil in Manuscript," and "My Kinsman, Major Molineux." There is more than a slight similarity between the young Shaker lovers in "The Canterbury Pilgrims," who, "with chastened hopes, but more confiding affections, went on to mingle in an untried life," and the young couple of the May-Pole, who "went Heavenward, supporting each other along the difficult path which it was their lot to tread, and never wasted one regretful thought on the vanities of Merry Mount."[38] Hawthorne seldom neglected an opportunity to celebrate in fiction the joys of genuinely conjugal relationships.

Sexual Relations and Implications in the Major Tales

Equally effective—but much grimmer—treatments of relations between the sexes can be found in such tales as "The Minister's Black Veil," "Wakefield," "The Wedding Knell," "The White Old Maid," "The Wives of the Dead," "Egotism, or the Bosom Serpent," "The Artist of the Beautiful," "The Birth-mark," "Rappaccini's Daughter," and "Ethan Brand." But while each of these evokes ambiguities in the relationships of men and women, the most impressive among them are the several that probe most relentlessly into the mysterious problems of the self. The effort to attain self-knowledge is a pervasive motif throughout all of Hawthorne's fiction; it is often dramatized in the guise of secrets of various kinds that ordinary people keep hidden from one another, even from themselves. The struggles of all these tortured protagonists to cope with their secret motives, secret guilt, and secret penance may even reflect in some recondite way Hawthorne's own ceaseless quest to know himself.

One would hesitate to identify Hawthorne with his character the Reverend Mr. Hooper simply because by wearing a black veil, which he refuses to discard, Hooper appears to become an extraordinarily effective preacher. But does not the fact of the veil itself imply the artist's uncanny ability to probe into the secret heart of mankind without revealing his own motives, even to himself? And does not Mr. Hooper's ironclad refusal to discard the mask, even to his dying hour, suggest the artist's painful determination to maintain his own integrity notwithstanding the strongest personal claims against his doing so? "What, but the mystery which it obscurely typifies," cries the dying minister, "has made this piece of crape so awful? . . . I look around me, and, lo! on every visage a Black Veil!"[39] Hooper's agonized outburst reminds us of another doleful cry—"It gnaws me! It gnaws me!"—uttered by Roderick Elliston, the egotist whose obsession was that he harbored a snake in his bosom;[40] and it is reminiscent, too, of the stony-hearted Richard Digby, whose harsh rejection of proffered human affection turned him into the legendary Man of Adamant.[41] But both of these later tales are too obviously allegorical and essayistic in form to compare favorably with the leaner and tighter symbolic structure of "The Minister's Black Veil."

To some extent the same criticism may be leveled at four of the last, yet most famous, of Hawthorne's tales: "The Birth-mark" (1843), "The Artist of the Beautiful" (1844), "Rappaccini's Daughter" (1843), and "Ethan Brand" (1851). Although these have probably been more often anthologized than any of his other short fiction, the presence of the narrator as spokesman for the author himself tends to overshadow the persons and events. This tendency is perhaps more noticeable in the slightly pompous concluding homily of "The Birth-mark,"[42] and even more so in the self-consciously facetious introduction to "Rappaccini's Daughter,"[43] than it is in the other two tales. But all four of them, a recent critic argues, seem to reflect a puzzling discomfort or inability on Hawthorne's part to control the fiction he was trying to produce during his Manse period. The fact that all four "are characterized by an intervening, prosy narrator . . . [whose] commentary is often inadequate to and sometimes incompatible with the narrative and symbolic content of the fiction," may well be an indication of Hawthorne's discomfort in having to deal with the problem of sexuality as a prominent motif.[44]

Nevertheless, puzzling as these later tales may be to the modern critic, they are among the most fascinating and the richest textured in Hawthorne's entire canon. As such they will likely continue to evoke controversy and polite disagreement among the scholars and critics seeking to interpret them, and also to beguile many a future average reader. How can Beatrice Rappaccini be both pure in essence and physically poisonous at the same time? And what, exactly, does that poison represent—her sexuality? If so, is Hawthorne then trying to get across in "The Birth-mark" and "The Artist of the Beautiful" the notion that Aylmer, the scientist, and Owen Warland, the artist, are as terrified of female entrapment as Giovanni Guasconti is? And what of Ethan Brand's obsessive compulsion to track down the Unpardonable Sin until, having discovered it to be lodged in his own breast, he casts himself into a pit of molten lime? In his guilt-ridden background there is at least the hint of some sort of sexual violation perpetrated upon "the Esther of our tale; the very girl whom, with such cold and remorseless purpose, Ethan Brand had made the subject of a psychological experiment, and wasted, absorbed, and perhaps annihilated her soul, in the process."[45] But one would be hard put to establish that his predicament was an equivalent of either Giovanni's or Aylmer's.

If, however, there can rarely be complete agreement among the critics as to which of Hawthorne's tales deserve high repute—let alone any agreement at all regarding the precise literary merits of those that do deserve it—it seems safe to predict that efforts to achieve such agreement will not soon diminish or disappear. Naturally Hawthorne was not always successful in his attempts to connect through fiction the outer world of the senses and the inner world of the heart and mind. Oftener than not, perhaps, his tales and sketches must seem as disappointingly thin and unconvincing to contemporary eyes as he says they did to him. And yet by common acceptance he wrote at least twenty or more that continue to excite critics and students of American fiction, as well as to inspire contemporary writers such as Jorge Luis Borges or Flannery O'Connor. These are works that, whatever their weaknesses when judged by today's literary standards, still evoke controversy, speculation, reinterpretation, and reevaluation—just as they did in Hawthorne's own lifetime. This is the mark of permanence, the reason that scholars today insist that the crowning glory of Hawthorne's writing is that "it is art."[46]

POE'S SHORT FICTION

When Edgar Allan Poe died in Baltimore on 7 October 1849 he had written and published, during the preceding twenty years, between seventy and eighty tales and sketches, some of which had been republished, with certain revisions, a number of times in different magazines. Many of his tales and sketches also reappeared in three collections during the last decade of his life: *Tales of the Grotesque and Arabesque,* a two-volume collection containing twenty-five pieces, 1840; *The Prose Romances of Edgar A. Poe,* a small volume containing only "The Murders in the Rue Morge" and "The Man That Was Used Up," 1843; and *Tales,* which contained twelve pieces, published in 1845.[1]

As in the case of Hawthorne's canon, the difficulty of pinning down the precise number of tales and sketches that Poe wrote and published is due in part to uncertainty regarding some early prose writings attributed to him, which may or may not have been his work, and to the question of whether to consider some of Poe's reworked and retitled tales as separate ones or to call them simply variant versions of the same tale.[2] However one looks at this question, Poe's output remains very impressive, particularly when one recalls that he wrote all these tales and sketches, along with a mass of nonfiction prose criticism, three quite long works of fiction, a drama, and several volumes of poetry, during the eighteen-year period between 1831 and the year of his death. More impressive still is the fact that virtually all of Poe's short fiction was produced in accordance with a set of principles that were the outgrowth of a gradually developing but clearly defined theory of composition. Poe's theory established norms for the creation and the evaluation of fiction that, after more than a century, are still being argued about, even though short-story writers today do not often sanction their validity. Still, it is no exaggeration to claim that "Poe's tales are his chief contribution to the literature of the world," because they have been widely translated and "are known in practically every major language."[3] They have also strongly influenced the works of foreign writers of fiction, particularly in France, Russia, and Latin America.

Poe and Hawthorne together, therefore, share the honor of having established America's claim to leadership in the art of short fiction. With the nearly two hundred pieces they published during the same two decades they demonstrated that the short story—whether it be called a tale, sketch, fable, allegory, dream vision, parable, satire, or whatnot—could readily be wrought into a durable form of literary art, an art form capable of endless experimentation and variation.

Superficially, however, no two contemporary American writers could have been farther apart than Hawthorne and Poe in background, training, and temperament: Hawthorne, a typical offspring of a deep-rooted, stable New England Puritan heritage and with strong family ties; Poe, a rootless, erratic man, brilliant, but unstable and psychologically insecure. Whereas Hawthorne's political sympathies were frankly democratic, even in a predominantly Whig society, Poe's attitude was as blatantly anti-democratic as that of the plantation aristocrats he envied and esteemed. Whereas Hawthorne distrusted the claims of science, Poe admired, perhaps above all else, the orderly processes of rational analysis, combined, however, with a finely sensitized intuitive capability, as exemplified in the character of his famous detective, C. Auguste Dupin. Hawthorne, interested chiefly in probing the mystery of the human psyche, fashioned his art into a delicate instrument for exploring what he called "truths of the human heart," while Poe, though likewise fascinated by the quirks and oddities of human behavior, railed against didacticism and studiously devoted his talent in short fiction to the creation of novelty and variety, startling effects, and bizarre scenes and situations. In his tales, as one of his close associates observed, "the evident and most prominent aim of Mr. Poe is originality, either of idea, or the combination of ideas."[4]

In view of these basic differences, it is not surprising that the works of the two men present noteworthy contrasts, even though in several important respects their careers as short-fiction writers followed parallel lines of development. Both began to experiment with the form at approximately the same time; both underwent preparatory periods of solitary study; both endured the onus of popular neglect and the pinch of penury, despite repeated efforts to suit their product to the demands of a magazine-reading public; and both persevered, despite continuing discouragement, in their devotion to a high standard of literature. Both, finally, achieved a modicum of the fame they deserved only within the last few years of their lives.

Hoaxing and Comic Satire in Early Tales: *The Folio Club*

Poe's earliest fictions, except for a few samples of apprentice work he turned out as an undergraduate at the University of Virginia, were a number of stories written before the end of 1832 that he strove to publish as a collection to be called *Tales of the Folio Club.*[5] According to Poe's own statements there were to have been seventeen stories in this volume; but although he first proposed the venture in 1833 as a collection entitled *Eleven Tales of the Arabesque,* and again in 1835 as a collection of sixteen, his *Tales of the Folio Club* never appeared as an independent volume. Instead, like Hawthorne, he had to be satisfied to see these stories published separately, sometimes anonymously, in several low-paying magazines. Beginning in January 1832, "Metzengerstein" appeared in the *Philadelphia Saturday Courier;* the same periodical published "The Duc De L'Omelette" (March 1832), "A Tale of Jerusalem" (June 1832), "A Decided Loss" (November 1832),[6] and "The Bargain Lost" (December 1832).

Among the remaining stories planned for the Folio Club series, two of the most interesting were "Epimanes," first published in the *Southern Literary Messenger* and later republished with a new title, "Four Beasts in One," in *Tales of the Grotesque and Arabesque,* and still later in the *Broadway Journal;* and "Ms. Found in a Bottle," which earned Poe a prize of fifty dollars and was first published in the *Baltimore Saturday Visitor,* republished in the *Gift* of 1836, and a third time in the *Southern Literary Messenger.*[7] Exactly what Poe had in mind for his Folio Club tales as a completed volume is still a matter of conjecture because he not only changed the wording of his proposal several times, along with the number of club members involved, but also failed, apparently, to write part of the matter that was to have been included in it. In his first known proposal, sent to the *New England Magazine* in 1833, Poe submitted a manuscript of the tale "Epimanes" ("Four Beasts in One") and called it "one of a number of similar pieces I have contemplated publishing under the title of 'Eleven Tales of the Arabesque.' They are supposed to be read at table by the eleven members of a literary club, and are followed by the remarks of the company upon each. These remarks are intended as a burlesque upon criticism." Poe included in this prospectus an introduction in which, posing as a narrator-member, he described the makeup of the Folio Club and identified by name his fellow club members. The spoofing tone is obvious from the opening sentence, characterizing the club as "a mere Junto of Dunderhead-ism . . . [whose] members are quite as ill-looking as they are stupid." And the narrator continues in this jocularly ironic vein as he states that the club's constitution "forbade the members to be otherwise than erudite and witty" and that their "avowed objects . . . were 'the instruction of society, and the amusement of themselves.'"[8]

To fulfill these ends, accordingly, they had arranged to meet once a month at the home of one of the group, each prepared to read "'a Short Prose Tale' of his own composition," and to suffer the embarrassment of hearing it criticized and rated against all the others, since the author of the tale judged "to be the least meritorious, is bound to furnish the dinner and wine at the next similar meeting of the Society." At this point the narrator slyly explains that the number of members is limited to eleven for "many good reasons," one of them being "that on the first of April, in the year three hundred and fifty before the Deluge, there are said to have been just eleven spots upon the sun." And finally, while remaining nameless himself, he lists the other ten members, identifying all but two of them by such odd names as Mr. Snap, Mr. Convolvulus Gondola, De Rerum Natura, Esqr., Mr. Solomon Seadrift, Mr. Horrible Dictu, Mr. Blackwood Blackwood, Mr. Rouge-et-Noir, and Chonologos Chronology.[9]

The similarity between Poe's description of the Folio Club and Washington Irving's format in his *Tales of a Traveller* is readily apparent in both its spoofing tone and its structural design. Poe evidently intended setting up a series of "frame" narratives to be told by different members of a storytelling group, but also controlled by an overall narrator who accounts for the gathering together of the other members and also offers gratuitous commentary from time to time on the quality of their performances and the reactions to them. Had he succeeded in peddling his scheme for the Folio Club collection, it is possible that his unnamed narrator would have been given a name comparable to Irving's Geoffrey Crayon (since he admits having recently replaced a former member, Augustus Scratchaway), and that a definite author-narrator would have been assigned to each of the tales. But although the venture did not wholly work out, even after Poe had published fourteen stories and expanded his club idea to a membership of seventeen, it is clear that he kept on experimenting with a variety of forms designed to capture a popular audience by making fun of other writers and writings.

Among Poe's first eleven tales, at least six were obviously intended as comic and/or satiric extravaganzas, but their buffoonery and satire were couched in different forms and pointed in different directions. "The Duc De L'Omelette," for example, featuring a good deal of extravagant wordplay, poked elaborate fun at both the preciosity of his popular American rival, Nathaniel Parker Willis, and at that of the equally popular British novelist Benjamin Disraeli. "A Tale of Jerusalem," with even more high-flown language and more than a touch of scatological humor (one of the main characters in the original version is named Abel-Shittim, a name cleaned up in later versions to Abel-Phittim), is primarily a thrust at a popular historical novel by Horace Smith entitled *Zillah, A Tale of Jerusalem.* But if Poe's readers in the 1830s were unaware of the literary satire involved in it, this tale must have struck them—as it would most readers today—as a gratuitously offensive piece of anti-Semitism. Similarly, "Loss of Breath," "Bon-Bon," "Epimanes" (later entitled "Four Beasts in One"), and "Lionizing"—another smelly dig at Willis with phallic innuendos reminiscent of Sterne's *Tristram Shandy*—were pot shots of one sort or another aimed at current literary fads and figures, characters, styles, and themes. To appreciate them fully, readers would have to know, for example, that while "Loss of Breath" satirized the grisly absurdities found in popular *Blackwood's* stories, "Bon-Bon" poked scornful fun at the pompous or pretentious Germanic scholarship scattered in other popular fiction, and "Epimanes" ridiculed currently popular notions of American democracy and progress.[10]

Thus there is little doubt that Poe's strategy was an attempt to capture the magazine-reading public's attention by resorting to the use of the wildest and most sensational devices then current in popular magazine fiction both in England and on the Continent—that is, the so-called gothic fiction, designed to evoke chills and thrills and shudders. To his friends Poe admitted that his intent in writing tales of this sort was "half banter and half satire"; but even they sometimes failed to capture the full drift of his meaning, even when he seemed to be spelling it out explicitly. When "Berenice," the first of his *Messenger* tales, appeared in March 1835, his publisher, T. W. White, complained that this necrophilic tale of premature burial, grave snatching, and corpse mutilation (in the climactic final sentence the dead girl's thirty-two teeth come rattling out on the floor like so many pairs of dice!) was "far too horrible." Poe agreed apologetically. Nevertheless he defended the tale on the score that it typified "the kind of absurd Gothic tales that sells magazines" and he had written it on a bet to prove that he could do an effective job with such a wild subject provided he treated it seriously enough. And so he went on to assert confidentially that

the history of all Magazines shows plainly that those which have attained celebrity were indebted for it to articles *similar in nature—to Berenice* . . . I say similar in *nature.* You ask me in what does this nature consist? In the ludicrous heightened into the grotesque: the fearful coloured into the horrible: the witty exaggerated into the burlesque: the singular wrought out into the strange and mystical.[11]

Satiric Irony and the Grotesque in Later Tales

This raises a key question of definition: what, exactly, did Poe mean by his conflation of terms—"grotesque," "arabesque," "burlesque," "strange," "mystical"? G. R. Thompson's entire thesis concerning Poe's intent and performance in both his poetry and his fiction turns on this point. Poe's familiarity with such German writers as the brothers August and Friedrich Schlegel, E. T. A. Hoffmann, Ludvig Tieck, and others, Thompson argues, prompted him to become a "satiric ironist" whose writings often displayed the sort of "essential deception involved in literary irony [which] may be so subtle that the work becomes a hoax. . . ." There is abundant evidence in Poe's tales of an undercurrent of ironic mockery not far removed, he adds, from the practices and techniques of "twentieth-century expressionist playwrights . . . [and] practitioners of Theatre of the Absurd in their attempt to present an empty, absurd, illusory world."[12]

The ramifications of this new view of Poe, which differs radically from the older stereotype of the romantic dreamer writing sentimental poems and tales about sickly maidens and suffering lovers, are too esoteric to be unraveled in a few paragraphs here, for they are also involved in what critics Richard Wilbur, Eric Carlson, Patrick Quinn, Allen Tate, and others have designated as Poe's "cosmic myths."[13] But the important thing to recognize in Poe's defense of his "too horrible" grotesquerie is that he evidently conceived of the term *grotesque* as "a genre allied primarily with the ludicrous and the ironic, but curiously fusing these comic qualities with the sinister."[14] From this perspective, it is not too difficult to see that even in Poe's allegedly "serious" tales, e.g., "The Black Cat," "Ligeia," "The Cask of Amontillado," "The Fall of the House of Usher," and "The Pit and the Pendulum," there is likely to be an undercurrent of unexpressed mockery that is either at cross purposes with, or a counterpoint to, the apparent meaning or intent of the surface plot. As Thompson puts it, "There is often in a Poe tale a tale within a tale within a tale; and the meaning of the whole lies in the relationship of the various implied stories and their frames rather than in the explicit meaning given to the surface story by the dramatically involved narrator."[15]

If this judgment is accurate (it is hard to refute), it raises the issue of whether Poe was playing games with his readers throughout his career, as several other Poe specialists believe to be true today, or whether he is now being too carelessly labeled a hoaxer by these new critics. Was "Metzenger-stein"—brimful of fantastic horrors, feudal combat, a miraculous steed, and his fiendishly incendiary rider—really a serious effort to do a supernatural "tale in imitation of the German," as Mabbott sees it (*Works*, 2:15), or was it a deliberate burlesque, an example of what Thompson calls "flawed Gothic"—namely, "a parody of a genre in general and a hoax on those pleased by the genre"?[16] The weight of evidence Thompson adduces to support his argument is quite convincing, particularly if the tale itself is read carefully with his perspective in mind. And if one applies his methods of analysis to Poe's later, more famous tales, examining closely the contrasts between sensational content and, intermittently, a deadpan, matter-of-fact style, it does not seem farfetched to suspect that in most of them a hoaxing intent of some sort may often be subtly concealed beneath the surface. The main difference between his earliest and his latest works is that Poe becomes more and more clever at playing this game by virtue of his increasing skill in masking his real motives behind the character of his participating "I" narrator.

Besides "Metzengerstein" and "Berenice," several other early Poe tales are equally important examples of his extraordinary versatility in combining amusing and horrifying elements with seemingly matter-of-fact detail, so that one cannot be altogether sure of his basic intent. "Ms. Found in a Bottle," for instance, retells the legend of a phantom ship reminiscent of Coleridge's "Ancient Mariner," but it is difficult to determine whether the narrator's heightened rhetoric implies sheer lunacy or a concealed satiric irony. This is true also of "The Assignation," which Mabbott calls "the most romantic story Poe ever wrote" (*Works*, 2:148), for with its incongruous mixture of sensational echoes from Byron's illicit relationship with the Contessa Guiccioli in Venice and punning references to an altar of laughter and the death of Sir Thomas More (who obviously did not "die laughing"), the tale is almost certainly a parody of the romantic poet Tom Moore's flattering report of his visit to Byron. And again, "Morella," which deals with the idea of metempsychosis—one of Poe's favorite themes—tells of a dead mother's literal reappearance in her daughter's bodily form with such a pronounced rhythmic beat in the narrator's voice that one wonders whether he, too, like his counterpart in "Berenice," is either unstrung, utterly mad, or another member of Poe's expanding gallery of hoaxers.[17]

The reader's uncertainty of what Poe was up to in these early tales is further compounded, finally, by two others that also appeared in the *Messenger* in 1835—"Hans Pfaall" and "King Pest." Both of these involve highly implausible activities undertaken by highly improbable individuals; but whereas one is an obviously comic spoof, the other dredges up such grimly repugnant behavior that its underlying satiric thrust has only recently come to light. "Hans Pfaall," one of Poe's longest fictions, is similar to the fanciful tall tales told by the frontier yarnspinners: a simulated report of a Dutchman's nineteen-day voyage to the moon in a balloon, it is presented with such a mass of plagiarized scientific detail that modern science-fiction aficionados regard it as a pioneering treatment of space exploration. But since Pfaall's alleged voyage begins on April first, it is clear that Poe is also poking gentle fun in the manner of Irving's *Knickerbocker History*. On the other hand, the point of "King Pest" and its grisly account of drunken carousing among a cast of plague-ridden characters in a medieval London alehouse must have been mystifying even to readers in Poe's lifetime; so it is not surprising that the "allegory" referred to in its subtitle is only now recognized as an oblique political satire on the administration of President Andrew Jackson. [18]

Immediately following his Folio Club period, Poe turned out nine or ten new tales between 1836 and 1840. Included among them were three of his most famous "serious" tales—"Ligeia," "The Fall of the House of Usher," and "William Wilson"—plus two not so widely known, "Silence: A Fable" and "The Conversation between Eiros and Charmion." During the same period he also produced and published six more of his obviously comic spoofs: "Mystification" (burlesquing the style of another popular American writer, Theodore Fay), "The Psyche Zenobia" and "A Predicament" (later combined under the more tongue-in-cheek title "How to Write a Blackwood Article"), [19] "The Devil in the Belfry," "The Man That Was Used Up," and "Why the Little Frenchman Wears His Hand in a Sling." Thus, by the end of 1839, when he had finally secured a publisher for his first collection, Poe had by his own count produced twenty-five tales, enough to fill two small volumes. For this edition he wrote an interesting short preface defending his technique against continuing charges of gloomy Germanism. [20]

Such an accusation certainly made little sense if Poe's critics were applying it to tales like the "Blackwood Article" and "The Man That Was Used Up," for even though some horrifying details appear in both, their narrators' tone from the outset makes it clear that they are comic satires. In the former the Signora Psyche Zenobia, who tells how she learned directly from Mr. Blackwood himself the secret of writing surefire sensational articles, follows his directions so faithfully that she loses her head in the process. But the fun in her outlandish tale is doubled for the reader who can see that Poe is simultaneously ridiculing the sensationalism in popular magazine fiction and parodying his own methods of producing such tales.

In "The Man That Was Used Up" he seems to be writing much the same sort of two-pronged satire, though from a different angle and, possibly, for a different purpose. Here the dualism in his approach is evident first in his narrator's opening paragraphs, which are almost identical word for word to those of the narrator in "Ligeia" (published the preceding year and long regarded by Poe as his masterpiece), and second in the totally different prevailing tones of the two stories. In "Ligeia" the heroine's beauty is lavishly praised for having—in Sir Francis Bacon's words—"some strangeness in the proportion"; but the strangeness in the used-up man's proportions is due to his being almost wholly composed of artificial materials, a product of American technological expertise, with false, screwed-on legs, arms, shoulders, teeth, and even a glass eye and false palate. Without these accoutrements this ravaged veteran of the "late Bugaboo and Kickapoo campaign," Brevet Brigadier General A. B. C. Smith, was merely a squeaking, nondescript bundle of clothing; but when his black valet, Pompey, helps to manipulate them into place he becomes transformed into a handsome six-foot figure with "an *air distingué* pervading the whole man." A figure, indeed, Poe specialists today believe, who was meant to represent Van Buren's vice president, Richard J. Johnson.

From his critics' standpoint, however, excessive gloom or Germanism might be more appropriately leveled at "Ligeia," "The Fall of the House of Usher," and "William Wilson"—all three of which, first published in 1838–39, have deservedly received more attention than all the rest of Poe's early stories. In these three, each of them a masterpiece, Poe first demonstrated his extraordinary versatility in manipulating sensational incidents within a tightly woven plot that leads inexorably toward a shocking but ambiguous climax and denouement. In each, thanks to his skillful management of tone and point of view, he showed how states of mind, physical action, and a realistically described environment can be made to evoke startling effects that can be interpreted in either supernatural or psychological terms. Thus "Ligeia," ostensibly the tale of a woman whose powerful will overcomes death by enabling her to reappear in the form of another woman totally different from her, may be read as a study of either occultism or madness. And in "Usher" Poe fashioned an even subtler study on the problem of identity and the mind's rationality by setting up a sickly brother-sister combination, twins who share a common fate in a crumbling, haunted mansion that collapses horribly only moments after the frenzied narrator makes his escape from it. At the center of both "Ligeia" and "Usher" Poe inserted a poem ("The Conqueror Worm" and "The Haunted Palace") that allegorizes the substance of each story, but the effectiveness of this device is accentuated in "Usher" because it counterpoints rather than illustrates the narrative's development. In "Usher" everything contributes—resemblances between sights and sounds, house and inmates, pictures and books—toward a symbolic dramatization of the vulnerability of the human mind.

Taking a hint from Washington Irving, Poe again dramatized, allegorically, a similar theme in "William Wilson," though his treatment of the divided soul in this tale differed considerably from that of his source. Irving had published in the *Gift* for 1836 an article entitled "An Unwritten Drama of Lord Byron," in which a Spanish nobleman named Alfonso is said to have encountered at every turn a mysterious specter, obviously a personification of his own conscience, who thwarts his evil proclivities until at last Alfonso corners and kills him in a duel, only to find that he has destroyed himself. Irving concluded his sketch of this basic plot by observing that it might "hereafter suggest a rich theme to a poet or dramatist of the Byron school."[21] But, in picking up the challenge, Poe once more brilliantly enhanced his *donnée* by creating a first-person narrator whose recollection of his moral and social background realistically conjures up settings that Poe himself had experienced both at home and during his childhood in England. Wilson's avowed "double," who repeatedly whispers admonishments in his ear, accordingly becomes all the more vividly palpable as Wilson, the narrator, evokes his image in crucial situations and dispatches him in the end, staring at himself in the mirror. The beauty of Poe's treatment is that once again, as in "Usher" and "Ligeia," he produced an intense moral dilemma to which either a supernatural or a psychological interpretation can be readily applied. Presumably, the "self-willed" Wilson is as mad a narrator as Ligeia's lover and Roderick Usher's nameless friend.

Germanism, Gloom, and the Unity of Effect Theory

Like so much else that Poe wrote about his literary efforts and intentions, his defense of his first collection of tales suggests a good deal more than appears on the surface. For one thing, it may be seen as an opening wedge in the statement of his critical theory of "unity of effect." All the tales in these two volumes, he insists, reflect "a certain unity of design." And those critics who have accused him of "'Germanism' and gloom" because of a noticeable "prevalence of the 'Arabesque' in my serious tales" are badly mistaken. True enough, there is Germanism in some of the tales, but that is only a temporary vein: "Tomorrow I may be anything but German, as yesterday I was everything else." At this point Poe was leading up to one of his most famous—and most inscrutable—affirmations concerning the significance of Germanic terror in his fiction: ". . . the truth is that, with a single exception, there is no one of these stories in which the scholar should recognize the distinctive feature of that species of pseudo-horror which we are taught to call Germanic, for no better reason than that some of the secondary names of German literature have become identified with its folly. If in many of my productions terror has been the thesis, I maintain that terror is not of Germany, but of the soul,—that I have deduced this terror only from its legitimate sources, and urged it only to its legitimate results" (*Works*, 2:473).

Essentially, Poe was here stating that, in the makeup of his stories, form, technique, and content together present something more than meets the eye. The unity he was defending was a unity of "effect," a combination of the burlesque and the grotesque-arabesque modes. And six years later, very near the end of his life, he was still emphasizing the same sort of unity after he had produced nearly forty more tales, both "Gothic" and comic.[22] By this time Poe had fully demonstrated not only his virtuosity as an artist, but also his brilliance as a critic and theorist of the short story—he was, actually, the first American writer who had attempted to define its technical requirements. In numerous essays and reviews published during the 1830s he had gradually evolved his theory of effect based upon the principles of brevity and unity, the best-known statement of which is in his famous review of Hawthorne's *Twice-Told Tales*, first published in *Graham's Magazine* in 1842 but substantially amended five years later.[23]

Briefly, the three central ideas of his theory are these: (1) that since "unity of effect or impression" is of primary importance in any form of imaginative expression, the most effective poem or story is one that can be read at a single sitting; (2) that the short prose narrative, as exemplified by Hawthorne's tales, offers the greatest opportunity next to the poem for the exercise of artistic genius, provided the writer deliberately subordinates everything in his story—characters, incidents, style, and tone—to the development of a single, preconceived effect; (3) that the prose tale may be made the vehicle for a greater variety of these effects than even the short poem. From this précis of Poe's theory it is clear that his main concern focused sharply upon matters of design, proportion, composition; for what he meant by *effect* was primarily the impact that a work of art would make upon the reader's consciousness. Speaking of the artist's obligation and his reward for fulfilling it, Poe added:

If his very initial sentence tend not to the outbringing of this effect, then he has failed in his first step. In the whole composition there should be no word written, of which the tendency, direct or indirect, is not to the one pre-established design. And by such means, with such care and skill, a picture is at length painted which leaves in the mind of him who contemplates it with a kindred art, a sense of the fullest satisfaction.[24]

Given this dominant preoccupation with effect, one is not surprised to find Poe frankly praising Hawthorne's artistry, while at the same time apparently misconstruing altogether Hawthorne's equally significant moral purpose. As both critic and artist, Poe's interest in the short story was more often that of the craftsman than that of the moralist; but by insisting upon standards of literary excellence, calling attention repeatedly to the need for effective presentation, and demanding that the finished work of art be judged on its own merits rather thn on its author's unfulfilled intentions, he performed his greatest service to American literature generally and to the art of the short story in particular. Moreover, Poe strove to practice, as an artist, what he preached as a critic. Shortly after the publication of his *Tales of the Grotesque and Arabesque* in 1840, Poe entered his most productive period, publishing in the remaining decade of his career about forty new tales, many of which rank among the most famous of all his works.

To grasp the significance of this truly impressive record, it should perhaps be examined in successive time segments: fourteen of the new tales, for example, were published in the interval between 1840 and 1843, including such highly popular ones as "Murders in the Rue Morgue," "The Man of the Crowd," "A Descent into the Maelström," "The Oval Portrait," "The Masque of the Red Death," and "The Pit and the Pendulum." Thus, by midsummer 1842, when Poe again projected a second two-volume collection to be called *Phantasy Pieces,* the contents of this work were to have included twenty-two tales from his first collection plus the fourteen new ones.[25] This collection, however, remained unpublished; instead, as noted above, in 1843 Poe's second book of tales, *The Prose Romances of Edgar A. Poe,* contained only "Murders in the Rue Morgue" and "The Man That Was Used Up."

But within two more years Poe had written and published about twenty more new tales; so that when Evert Duyckinck selected twelve of his tales for a third collection to be published by Wiley and Putnam in June 1845, Poe already had more than enough for a second volume, which he wrote Duyckinck, "could be a far better one than the first—containing, for instance, 'Ligeia.'"[26] No second volume was issued, but along with old favorites like "Usher," "Lion-izing," and "Murders in the Rue Morgue," the volume included eight previously uncollected tales: "The Gold Bug," "The Black Cat," "Mesmeric Revelation," "A Descent into the Maelström," "The Colloquy of Monos and Una," "The Mystery of Marie Roget," "The Purloined Letter," and "The Man of the Crowd." Although no more new collections were published during the remaining four years of Poe's life, the 1845 *Tales* was reissued in several forms prior to 1849, each of them containing numerous revisions and emendations supervised by Poe himself[27] and, of course, he went on writing new tales till he died. More than a dozen of them appeared during his last three years, including some of the most powerful of all—such masterpieces as "The Imp of the Perverse," "The Facts in the Case of M. Valdemar," "The Cask of Amontillado" (regarded by many critics today as the greatest of all Poe's stories), and "Hop-Frog."[28]

Science Fiction, Horror, and Ratiocination: Later Tales

By the mid-1840s Poe had moved several times after leaving his southern base in Richmond. For a short time he lived with his young wife, Virginia, and her mother, Maria Clemm, in New York; then, for a period of five years beginning in 1838, the family lived in Philadelphia, and finally they returned to New York early in 1844. During these years he had quickly achieved notoriety (and a goodly number of literary enemies) as a severe critic while serving as editor of *Burton's Gentleman's Magazine* (1839–40) and later on the staff of *Graham's,* which succeeded *Burton's* in 1841. But besides the many reviews and tales he was publishing in these two journals, Poe was also contributing pieces to the *American Museum, Alexander's Weekly Messenger, Snowden's,* the *Ladies' Companion, Godey's,* and the *Saturday Evening Post.* And at the same time he was also striving to secure and manage a magazine of his own. The tales he published during this fertile period revealed new interests and pointed in promising new directions, notably the one he referred to as the "ratiocinative," a term that could be loosely applied in fiction to the solving of perplexing puzzles by means of logical analysis.

The most famous of Poe's ratiocinative tales, perhaps the most influential of his entire fictional canon, were the three that originated a new genre, the modern detective story: "The Murders in the Rue Morgue" (1841), "The Mystery of Marie Roget" (1843), and "The Purloined Letter" (1845). In all three the central figure is, of course, the transcendent sleuth, C. Auguste Dupin, who solves the mystery of the murders and restores the invaluable stolen document by applying his intuitive genius and acute perception to a cause-and-effect exploration of the available clues. Moreover, in what has come to be the approved detective-story pattern, he twits the bumbling police officials for their inefficiency and dazzles his slow–witted companion (as well as the reader!) with his brilliant, step-by-step explanation of the mental process employed to solve the mystery.

In "Murders in the Rue Morgue" Dupin's analytic skills appear in the opening paragraphs as he seemingly reads and then interprets his companion's unexpressed thoughts. The same alertness enables him not only to deduce quickly that a nonhuman creature destroyed the two women, stuffed their bodies up a chimney, and escaped from a sealed room, but also to apprehend the owner of the murderous ape. Dupin employs a similar process of detection in "The Mystery of Marie Roget," though in a much more complex and ambiguous fashion. In this story, one of his longest, Poe was attempting to solve and dramatize simultaneously an actual murder in New York by fictionally transposing the basic details of the case of Mary Rogers, whose body was fished from the Hudson River in July 1841, into a Parisian setting. In this case, however, Dupin and his creator failed to solve the mystery; but Poe did succeed, presumably, in saving an innocent man accused of murdering the girl.[29] And again in "The Purloined Letter," Dupin's role became even more ambiguous, despite his apparent triumph over his unprincipled adversary, the Minister D——, because the motives and actions that Poe attributes to him are scarcely more ethical than the Minister's. Beneath the surface action of the story the two men, indeed, seem to be almost identical twins—as though Poe were more slyly symbolizing, by means of the doppelgänger motif, the ineluctable duplicity of the human mind.

That Poe's own attitude toward Dupin's vaunted ratiocinative capabilities may have been ambivalent seems evident from his treatment of the same processes in other tales. For example, in both "The Oblong Box" and "Thou Art the Man," which appeared in *Godey's* in 1844, there is clearly a macabre sort of fun being poked at the analytic method of investigating a mystery and solving a crime. Like the tale of Marie Roget, "The Oblong Box" quite possibly was inspired by another sensational crime in New York—the Colt-Adams murder, in which Adams's body was packed in a box of salt and placed on a ship for transport to St. Louis (*Works*, 3:919–21). But the grotesque twist that Poe gave this item by having his nosy narrator expose his own hysterical efforts to probe the contents of a similar box aboard a wrecked ship has all the earmarks of a self-parody, unmistakably focused in his concluding paragraph. The parodic mood is even clearer in "Thou Art the Man," an amusing forerunner of the "comic detective story . . . 'in its first use of the least-likely-person theme, of the scattering of false clues by the real criminal,' and of 'the psychological third degree'" (quoted in *Works,* 3:1042). Here, the "least likely" criminal, "Old Charley Goodfellow," is trapped when the narrator, having cleverly stuffed the body of his victim into a wine box along with a jack-in-the-box contraption, springs the arrangement on Goodfellow and his assembled dinner guests with a ventriloquist's trick that causes the popped-up corpse to confront his murderer and slowly utter: "Thou art the man!" (ibid., 1057).

Poe worked out variations on the ratiocinative pattern in several other tales, combining it in some instances with the doppelgänger motif, as in "A Tale of the Ragged Mountains" (1844); in others, with an element of chance or accident that tends to undercut the validity of logical analysis, as in "The Gold Bug" (1843), "The Pit and the Pendulum" (1842), and "A Descent into the Maelström" (1841).

Like "Ligeia" and "Morella," "A Tale of the Ragged Mountains" develops another reincarnation theme, but one that involves mesmerism and a twofold mystery that rests on a punning reversal of a proper name: Bedloe-Oldeb. Whether the sickly young protagonist, Augustus Bedloe, merely dreamed while under the hypnotic influence of his physician, Dr. Templeton, that he had been transported backward in time and far eastward in space from Charlottesville, Virginia, to the city of Benares in India; or whether Templeton obsessively did him in, is left up in the air by Poe's seemingly unreliable narrator. Here again one senses a slight hint of mockery in his concluding statement. So too in "The Gold Bug," easily the most popular of Poe's tales during his lifetime, recent critics have found far subtler ambiguities embedded in its symbolism than appear in the surface tale unearthing Captain Kidd's legendary treasure by means of a tricky cryptographic analysis, plus a skull, a scarab, and a misfocused telescope. For all the elaborate intellection of his hero, William Legrand, was Poe once more showing that he could improve on one of his sources, Irving's "Wolfert Webber," by simultaneously replaying America's Midas complex and making fun of it?[30]

Poe explored another facet of the ratiocinative process in "A Descent into the Maelström" (1841) and "The Pit and the Pendulum" (1842), applying it in both tales to an escape motif in which the protagonist, striving to save his life in a seemingly hopeless predicament, is subjected to extreme mental stress. These two are among the most popular of all Poe's horror tales, partly perhaps because of their moderately "happy" endings; but in neither case does the protagonist manage to think his way to salvation. Rather, sheer chance seems to dictate that the survivor of a small boat's terrifying plunge to the bottom of a gigantic whirlpool should come out of it alive to tell his story, though much of what he has to tell about his experience emphasizes his intensely rationalistic observation of his surroundings and his technical efforts to cope with them. In somewhat the same manner the narrator of "The Pit and the Pendulum," a victim of the Spanish Inquisition, ultimately survives the most excruciating torture in his dark dungeon only through a chance, last-minute rescue from an outside source. Even more than "Maelström," "The Pit and the Pendulum" is a brilliant example of Poe's theory of fiction, in which every word from first to last must be combined with appropriate details, incidents, and tone toward the realization of a single, predesigned effect. Yet in both of these tales the effect he sought to achieve may not have been the mere shock of survival in a hostile world, but rather the futility of man's finite attempts to survive; for both "are apocalyptic in ways compatible with a failure of the rational mind to effect its own salvation."[31]

Death, Guilt, Alienation, and Revenge: Later Tales

The proliferation of Poe's tales in the 1840s, however, extended into numerous other directions and evoked other than purely horrifying or ludicrous effects, though these continued to predominate. Early in the decade he turned out several "landscape" tales, two of which—"Eleonora" (1841) and "The Island of the Fay" (1841)—are concerned with his favorite poetic theme, the death of a beautiful woman, while another, "The Landscape Garden" (1842), depicts a fabulous earthly paradise created by a newly rich multimillionaire, who seeks to rival the unspoiled perfection of God's nature by an arrangement of physical forms within a rearranged natural scene. Compared to "Ligeia," neither "Eleonora" nor "The Island of the Fay" is impressive, though there are doubtless echoes in both of Poe's attitude toward his fragile young wife, as there are indeed in "The Landscape Garden." In 1842 Mr. Ellison, the creator of this man-made Eden, succeeds with "the companionship and sympathy of a devoted wife" (*Works*, 2:712), but shortly before Virginia's death in 1847, when Poe undertook to rewrite and expand the tale as "The Domain of Arnheim," he omitted mention of the "devoted wife" and added a gloomy passage in which Ellison confesses an inability to match God's perfection at all points because of "abnormal disturbances [that were] . . . prognostic of *death*" (*Works*, 3:1274).

Death, guilt, and alienation appear to have weighed increasingly on Poe's consciousness as the 1840s progressed. Beginning with "The Man of the Crowd" (December 1840), some twenty-two of the remaining forty-odd tales he wrote turned on one or another of these three themes—now and then on all three in the same tale. "The Man of the Crowd" sets the tone for this dismal combination, even though the nameless old protagonist is nowhere specifically identified as either a criminal or a victim of malevolent forces. To the narrator scrutinizing him as he stalks about the streets of London, he does seem to represent "the type and the genius of deep crime. He refuses to be alone" (*Works*, 2:515). But the key term here is *alone*, suggesting the secret horrors locked up in man's conscience, which cannot be revealed. Like the German book that "does not permit itself to be read," the narrator confides at the beginning of the tale, "Men die nightly in their beds, wringing the hands of ghostly confessors, and looking them piteously in the eyes—die with despair of heart and convulsion of throat, on account of the hideousness of mysteries which will not *suffer themselves* to be revealed" (*ibid.*, 507).

The idea that man must carry a burden of secret guilt into the grave is given a more fanciful twist in "The Island of the Fay" and "The Colloquy of Monos and Una," both of which appeared in *Graham's* shortly after "The Man of the Crowd," "Murders in the Rue Morgue," and "Maelström." Both of these tales (especially the colloquy) support the proposition that mortal happiness is a mirage: progress, democracy, well-being, the pursuit of knowledge and art are alike futile—a disease—so that only through death and dissolution can a sense of true unity be achieved. Before the year was out Poe rang still other changes on the theme of death in "Eleonora," which he followed in 1842 with two of his most brilliant pieces: "Life in Death" (later revised as "The Oval Portrait") and "The Masque of the Red Death."

It is possible that "The Oval Portrait" was inspired by the alarming breakdown in Virginia's health a few weeks before Poe wrote the tale under its original title. But, since the central idea of transferring the vitality or soul of a living person to a work of art had been a standard concept dating far back into antiquity, it is more likely that Poe found suggestions of the motif in other writings, including, possibly, Irving's *Tales of a Traveller*. In any case, he evidently thought well enough of the subject to revise his first version extensively by pruning away obvious excrescences and thus producing in "The Oval Portrait" one of his subtlest studies of monomania, comparable in its effect to Hawthorne's "The Birth-mark." Poe's subtlety here, in fact, is such that recent critical interpretations have varied widely as to the ultimate meaning of the tale. Is it a moral allegory, dressed up with a touch of the occult, but concerned primarily with the mysterious connection between life and art? Or is it rather an ironic psychological exposé of a delirious narrator who is actually unaware of his condition?[32] It is a mark of Poe's genius that these opposing interpretations of "The Oval Portrait" have been ably supported.

But even more conflicting reactions have been evoked by "The Masque of the Red Death," which is one of the most bizarre of all his efforts to dramatize the human mind's reaction to the inescapability of death. Poe's dramatic arrangement of the seven halls in Prince Prospero's castle, with their lurid drapery, flickering lights, huge ebony clock, and other grim furnishings—plus the *danse macabre* revelers and their costumes—suggests a variety of sources ranging from *The Tempest* and *The Decameron* to the writings of his own contemporaries, N. P. Willis and Thomas Campbell. But whether he intended his tale to support the explicit moral "that one cannot run away from responsibility" or to create a supremely sardonic jest about human hysteria remains problematic.[33]

Whatever Poe may have been up to in "The Masque," he evidently decided early in 1843 that tales involving violent death would attract instant attention, particularly if they could be presented in some sort of confessional framework to dramatize a revenge motif. Five of his most powerful tales written during the last six years of his life worked out variations of this pattern—forerunners of the popular "true confessions" type of the present day. These were "The Tell-Tale Heart" (1843), "The Black Cat" (1843), "The Imp of the Perverse" (1845), "The Cask of Amontillado" (1846), and "Hop-Frog" (1849). In all but the last of these the narrator himself is the guilty criminal, and another dimension of Poe's mature artistry can be seen in the subtle gradations of insanity revealed in his characterization of these criminals.

In "The Tell-Tale Heart," for instance, the narrator's obsessive paranoia becomes immediately apparent through his distorted tone of voice in the opening paragraph:

True! —nervous—very, very dreadfully nervous I had been and am; but why *will* you say that I am mad? The disease had sharpened my senses—not destroyed— not dulled them. Above all was the sense of hearing acute. I heard all things in the heaven and in the earth. I heard many things in hell. How, then, am I mad? (*Works,* 3:792)

And his confession of having murdered and stashed away the body of a harmless old man, whom he actually loved, simply because he feared the old man's "Evil Eye," steadily accentuates the deterioration of his mind. Ironically, his madness traps him into committing a crime he did not want to commit and confessing what he could easily have concealed. Here again, as in his Dupin tales, Poe seized on literary sources dealing with actual murders and wrought out of them a superbly unified dramatic monologue.[34]

He duplicated that achievement shortly afterwards, though in a more complex, ambiguous fashion, in "The Black Cat." The two tales are similar in form and structure, but they differ in that here Poe develops the themes of perversity and self-incrimination through the confession of an apprehended murderer who, though apparently perfectly sane, tells of having mutilated and destroyed a pet cat in a drunken rage and then of having accidentally slain his wife when she tried to prevent him from destroying a second cat. What remains uncertain is whether the second cat, black and one-eyed like the first, is purely a figment of the drunken narrator's mind; or whether there actually was a second cat, which, inexorably, he walled up with his wife's body so that its howls would reveal the murder. The perversity of fate, coupled with motifs of the double, repressed guilt and self-exculpation, has rarely been so cleverly demonstrated.

Two years later Poe dealt with this subject in an even trickier manner, switching in "The Imp of the Perverse" from what seems at first to be a straightforward philosophical essay to another tale of murder committed by the narrator himself. And once again Poe cleverly varied his confessional pattern by having his narrator initiate a plausible discussion on the origin and nature of perverseness, which he defines as an "overwhelming tendency to do wrong for the wrong's sake" (*Works,* 3:1221). With an array of examples to support this thesis, the narrator pontificates more than halfway through his monologue before we realize that he is another member of the criminally insane. In his own eyes he is living proof that we perversely destroy ourselves, not because he botched the job of poisoning his victim but because an inner force compelled him to blurt out his guilt in public. His imp of the perverse, like William Wilson's, has proved to be his own conscience, the spur toward his self-destruction.

Whether or not Poe himself believed the philosophy of this narrator, there can be little question that he understood the dramatic value of demonstrating through paradox and irony the long-lasting, corrosive force of conscience. Within a few more months he again coupled this theme with a revenge motif in one of his greatest tales, "The Cask of Amontillado," a masterpiece of dramatic irony so tightly unified and coldly told that its full meaning is withheld until the final phrase. Here too, the criminal narrator, Montresor, calmly explains how he lured his victim, Fortunato, deep into the catacombs, where, at a dead end, he chained him to the wall and buried him alive—a perfect crime that has remained undetected, he says, for half a century. But to whom and why is he disclosing it now? A death-bed confessor who may at last shrive this old man's tortured conscience? "The Cask" is assuredly a superb exemplar of Poe's theory of short fiction.

Last Jests: Comic Satire, Hoaxing, and Spoofing Tales

After "The Cask" almost any other tale based on a revenge motif might seem anticlimactic, but Poe nevertheless tried again shortly before his death, producing in "Hop-Frog; or, the Eight Chained Orang-Outangs" another wildly exotic but inferior example of the genre. Still, as a typically romantic horror story, with all the bizarre gothic trappings like those in "Metzengerstein," "Hop-Frog" may well be another of Poe's sly hoaxes: a satiric poke at the popular magazine tales of violence from which hero and heroine "escape to their own country" to live happily ever after. For "Hop-Frog" is written in the form of a fairy tale. Its hero, the court jester Hop-Frog, is a hunchbacked dwarf; its heroine, Trippetta, also "very little less dwarfish than himself (although of exquisite proportions, and a marvelous dancer)" (*Works*, 3:1346); and its villain, a vicious Gargantuan king who enjoys, as a practical joke, torturing his jester by getting him drunk. But the vengeance Hop-Frog perpetrates against him for striking the girl is an elaborate masquerade that, with his own connivance, makes monkeys of him and his seven fat privy-councillors, leading them, chained, to a fiery death. It is, Hop-Frog says, as he and Trippetta escape through the roof, *"my last jest"* (*ibid.*, 1354). One strongly suspects that he was speaking also for his creator, although Poe wrote three more comic pieces before his own departure.

Thus, to the end of his life Poe kept alternating his ostensibily serious tales with comic or satiric spoofs; more than half of the thirty tales he is known to have written between November 1842 and October 1849 were spoofs. Beginning in 1843 with "Diddling Considered as One of the Exact Sciences," a comic exposé of some of the methods practiced by con-artists to defraud the gullible, Poe published seven more the next year in addition to "The Oblong Box" and "Thou Art the Man."[35] Poe's satire in these comic tales ranges in its intensity from light, good-natured parody to a grotesque and vitriolic brutality. At one extreme he can poke gentle fun at people's gullibility, at their fondness for lurid ghost stories, fantasies, and improbabilities; at the other, his attacks against what he viewed as the political follies of the day and the sharp competitive practices of the publishing media can sting with a cutting wit. As a travesty on the subject of mesmerism, for example, Poe varies the repulsiveness in "The Facts in the Case of M. Valdemar" with the genial dialogue between the narrator and the "revived" Egyptian mummy in "Some Words with a Mummy." The mummy convinces his embarrassed listeners that many vaunted American shibboleths—beliefs in progress, democracy, and technology—are not superior to the culture of ancient Egypt. And as further satire on current American technological marvels, gadgets, fashions, and ideas—cast this time in the form of an Arabian Nights tale—the heroine of "The Thousand-and-Second Tale of Scheherazade" strains the credulity of her husband, the Caliph, with her account of future developments in a land where eggs can be hatched in a steam incubator and women wear bustles to enhance their physical attractiveness.

Poe's last four hoaxes, all written in 1849, show that his fascination for science fiction as a means of dramatizing contemporary matters remained undiminished to the end. "Mellonta Tauta," another April Fool's balloon hoax, savagely satirizes the follies of nineteenth-century politicians, liberals, and idealists by means of a letter narrative written aboard the "Balloon 'Skylark'" from 1 to 8 April in the year 2848 and cast into the sea in a bottle.[36] Similarly, "Von Kempelen and His Discovery" is a hilarious hoaxing response to the gold-fever "Forty-niners," written in the form of a straight-faced scientific report verifying the discovery in Bremen of a method for transmuting lead into gold; but "X-ing a Paragrab" is a rather forced comic spoof on magazine editors' rivalry and retaliation, focused on the theft of an entire type font of O's. Finally, in "A Reviewer Reviewed," a gentle, unfinished self-parody, probably composed in the last few months of his life, Poe ridicules his own critical practices (*Works,* 3:1377–88).

Critical Reappraisal of Poe's Literary Achievement since 1950

Since at least half of all the stories Poe is known to have written are clearly comic or satiric spoofs, and since the apparent seriousness of some of the others is often questionable—as is the seriousness of some of his poetry and criticism—the problem of evaluating his career is a formidable one. To assess his extraordinary production of short fiction and to appreciate both its unity and diversity one must be able to read these tales not only in the light of Poe's developing aesthetic creed and of his response to the world he lived in, but also with a fairly substantial knowledge of many of his hoaxing allegations. Thus one can never be sure when, where, or how his fiction is to be taken seriously—if ever, simply at face value. Still, thanks to the voluminous scholarship that has been dedicated to Poe studies during the last three or four decades, and to the close scrutiny with which corps of specialists have examined the possible sources and influences behind each of Poe's individual tales, there are now available many trustworthy guides toward a balanced, intelligent appraisal of his overall achievement.[37]

The upshot of this reawakened interest in the tangled motives and influences that fed Poe's creative energies is a deepened respect not only for his craftmanship but for the aesthetic vision that is thought to have inspired it. Before the 1940s many American critics were still inclined to regard Poe as something of a charlatan, possibly because they still shared, however honestly, some of the prejudices handed down by his personal enemies and detractors, notably the malicious calumnies his literary executor, Rufus Griswold, had perpetrated against him. As Patrick Quinn wrote in 1957, "if apathy will serve to characterize the attitude of the common reader towards Poe, something more like hostility has been the usual response of American writers from Poe's time to our own . . . our critics, far from pushing Poe onto the stage of world literature [as Baudelaire, Mallarmé, and other French symbolists had done], have rather insisted that his name be retained exclusively as a minor one even in the cast of American letters."[38]

And so the popular image of Poe as a besotted dope pusher and sex freak persisted even after 1941, when Arthur Hobson Quinn's biography exposed the total falsity of Griswold's allegations. The old image of Poe, we are reminded, was that of "a creepy chap, somewhere in an attic, bats flapping about his head as he sits at his desk, writing. A candle sputters in a wine bottle, perhaps, casting shadows which magnify his size on the cobwebby walls and ceiling. A second bottle on the cluttered desk holds unwholesome-looking liquor. He drinks, coughs, cackles, and writes a line. . . ."[39] Earlier American critics, accordingly, often argued that his stories are sick, or at best little more than a tissue of cleverly wrought impressionistic effects—of horror, fear, melancholy, disgust, or analytic agility; and that his vaunted aesthetic theory is merely a means of rationalizing his own limitations as a literary artist. They would admit his skill in the manipulation of incidents, his inventiveness in plot construction, and his vivid depiction of bizarre settings and intense situations, but they professed to find little or no evidence in his stories of an imaginative power to re-create life and human feeling through characters. His characters, they insisted, are mere pawns in a game that Poe, the sleight-of-hand trickster, plays with his audience.

Today, however, Poe's stock has risen a good deal despite continuing misguided theories about him resignedly exposed in the Poe Studies Association newsletter.[40] His apologists are more inclined to accept his declaration that the terror in his tales was "not of Germany but of the soul"; they are eager to probe beneath the surface of his work for clues to the meaning of his ambiguities, since almost invariably those ambiguities appear to be ironic reflections on man's perverse fate. Seen from this viewpoint, Poe becomes a far more sophisticated artist than earlier critics recognized because the romantic fantasies and abnormalities in his stories—along with his morbid, narcissistic heroes, decaying damsels, and desperate narrators—no longer appear to be merely sensational gothic devices worked up to provide cheap, eerie thrills for adolescent minds. On the contrary, even the most extremely sensational elements in tales like "The Fall of the House of Usher" or "The Cask of Amontillado" or "William Wilson" may be shown to convey multiple meanings and genuine emotions. Ruin, perversity, and the disorientation of human life are prevailing themes in many of Poe's tales, and it is difficult to read any of them attentively and still deny that his concern for the human predicament is mirrored there, since much the same preoccupation with evil, the same "haunted mind" that troubled Hawthorne, hovers over them. Indeed, since recent studies have disclosed unsuspected levels of meaning artfully concealed beneath Poe's elaborate facades, perhaps most of his tales should be read as allegories of nightmarish, neurotic states of mind. Is it not stark paranoia that inspires the obsessive madness of William Wilson? an intolerable burden of guilt that motivates the confessional disclosures of the aged Montresor? a terrifying fear of the unknown that prompts the speaker in "The Imp of the Perverse"?

There is a growing conviction that Poe's aesthetic theories, as set forth in "The Poetic Principle" (1848) and "The Philosophy of Composition" (1846), offer a genuine rationale for the artist's role in seeking to create literature. In these two essays Poe strove to establish the purest source of literary aspiration and the proper methods for converting that aspiration into durable literary art—as he perceived it. And although he was concerned primarily with the creation of poetry, what he had to say about the artist's obligation to create beautiful effects that would give pleasure to a wide audience applied just as readily to the writing of fiction. This is particularly true of "The Philosophy of Composition," which purports to explain (surely, at least partially with tongue in cheek) precisely how Poe conceived and put together "The Raven," by all odds his most popular narrative poem.

At the beginning of the essay Poe asserts categorically that every worthwhile plot must be thought through to its denouement in the writer's mind before he ever begins to write: "it is only with the *denouement* constantly in view that we can give a plot its indispensable air of consequence, or causation, by making the incidents, and especially the tone at all points, tend to the development of the intention."[41] The intention, as Poe sees it, is necessarily tied, first, to the selection of a novel and vivid effect; second, to the best means of securing that effect through the combination and manipulation of incidents and tone "as shall best aid . . . in the construction of the effect." In scores of critical reviews, incidental commentary, occasional lectures, and other formal utterances, Poe reiterated this doctrine of craftsmanship in literary endeavor. By setting high standards and calling sharp attention to careless writing, he encountered a large measure of undeserved hostility. Yet he gave as good as he got, rarely flinching from the task of exposing frauds, favoritism, cliquism, puffery, and pious pomposity among his contemporary writers and critics. Conversely, he was quick to praise genuine literary merit where he found it, as in Hawthorne's tales and A. B. Longstreet's *Georgia Scenes*.

Moreover, as a literary artist in his own right, Poe practiced what he preached, experimenting with a broad variety of fictional modes in his short stories—mystery, terror, pseudo–science fiction, gothic horror tales, satiric hoaxes, pseudophilosophical analyses, confessional declarations—and always with the central aim of achieving unity and wholeness. The single effect was to be a consequence of hewing a straight path from the first word to the last; yet in reaching for that single effect, Poe demonstrated a mastery of new techniques in the management of point of view and the dramatization of disturbed mental states resulting from both physical violence and spiritual agony. To appreciate fully his preoccupation with grisly subjects or occult fantasies, one needs to recall that these weird phenomena were embedded in the intellectual environment in which Poe lived and worked. His contemporaries were fascinated by horror subjects; the magazines and newspapers of the era were full of fanciful speculations on scientific exploration, technological advancements, archaeological discoveries, hypnotism, life after death, and metempsychosis; and Poe, who took pride in being a "magazinist," was an avid reader of all these popular curiosities. As an enterprising magazine editor himself (of the *Southern Literary*

Messenger, Burton's, Graham's, and the *Broadway Journal*), he wanted to outdo his competitors.

As an artist in short fiction, he virtually did outdo them all—all but
Hawthorne—bequeathing a legacy of multileveled craftsmanship extolled
in France by Baudelaire and Mallarmé and admired and respected by many
other famous European and American writers down to our own day, including Henry James, Jorge Luis Borges, Vladimir Nabokov, and Eudora
Welty.

SIMMS AND THE SOUTHERN FRONTIER HUMORISTS

During the three decades (1820–50) in which the short fiction of Irving, Hawthorne, and Poe was steadily enhancing the prestige of American literature at home and abroad, a small army of other native scribblers was also bidding for attention among the burgeoning magazines of the period. Few of them, either writers or magazines, achieved lasting success: only a bare handful of the 350 American magazines that began publishing during those thirty years survived more than a single year, and the poetry and prose of all but a few of the writers appearing in them were quickly forgotten.[1] Among those who did contribute significantly to American letters, however, was a group of southern-based writers whose importance and influence, like Poe's, have received increasingly favorable attention from modern literary scholars and critics. The leading figure of this group was William Gilmore Simms. A man of prodigious energy, much personal charm, and a lifelong, serious dedication to the writer's craft, Simms strove to create on his own a literature firmly grounded in native American historical and cultural traditions and, in the several journals he also edited, to encourage other writers to do the same. By 1850 he had succeeded remarkably well in showing the way, having already published about fifty-three of the eighty-odd volumes of poetry and prose he produced during a career of nearly half a century that ended in 1870.

Like so much else that the South sacrificed in support of its "Lost Cause," however, Simms's literary reputation is still a casualty of the Civil War. Though serious efforts are now being made to revive interest in his writings, today his works, except for one or two books, are scarcely known at all.[2] And yet, during the 1830s and the early 1840s, Simms's patriotic fervor was reflected in both his writings and the public's acceptance of them. Within a two-year span (1834–36) he published four major works of fiction representing three separate approaches to the American scene that he felt to be of paramount importance in shaping the nation's destiny: its colonial past, the Revolutionary War, and contemporary life on the raw frontier. These were *Guy Rivers* (1834), the first of his border romances, "a tale of Georgia," he explained, "of a frontier and wild people, and the events are precisely such as may occur among a people and in a region of that character";[3] *The Yemassee* (1835), the first of his colonial romances, dealing with early eighteenth-century strife between Indians and white settlers in South Carolina; *The Partisan* (1835) and *Mellichampe* (1836), his first two of seven Revolutionary romances, centering upon the agonizing effects of the American Revolution on the lives of South Carolina loyalists and patriots.

Filled with violence, bloody hand-to-hand conflicts, hairbreadth escapes, and derring-do, all four of these were popular successes, bringing Simms substantial royalties and establishing his position as James Fenimore Cooper's foremost rival. Indeed, in some respects Simms's romances were superior to Cooper's; for even though he failed to create a heroic figure comparable to Hawkeye or Natty Bumppo, his Indians, backwoodsmen, and border outlaws were much more realistically portrayed than Cooper's. And though his fiction suffered from overinflated rhetoric, wooden dialogue, and many a wooden character (as did Cooper's!), Simms was the more skillful in combining the separate strands of his plotted action. But the strong regional emphasis of his fiction in the 1850s, chiefly in a gallant but futile effort to idealize the southern slave system as "an institution which has done more for philanthropy and humanity in one year than ever has been achieved by all the professional philanthropists of Europe and America in one hundred years" (*Letters,* 4:302), inevitably led to the alienation and neglect of his writings during the postwar reconstruction. By 1900 virtually all of his works were out of print, and few reprints of any of them became available until the recent revival of interest in southern literature.

From early youth Simms, like Hawthorne, was well equipped by background, experience, and temperament to become the literary spokesman for his native region. Half-orphaned at the age of two, he was reared by his grandmother, Mrs. Jacob Gates, who not only provided for his boyhood needs at her home in Charleston after his father had left to seek fortune in the Southwest but also sent him to school and nourished his early love of literature by telling him stirring eye-witness tales of her own youth during and before the Revolution in South Carolina. Despite his father's repeated urgings to join him on the frontier (of which he too had exciting stories to tell!), Simms chose to remain in Charleston, where he read voraciously, studied both medicine and law, but cared less for either than for writing and publishing locally, while still in his teens, a mass of youthful Byronic poetry. As a lad of eighteen he finally did gain firsthand experience of life on the frontier during an extended visit to his father's plantation near Hattiesburg, Mississippi; but despite his fascination with that region, by then he had cast his lot for a career at home, again rejecting his father's assurance of future wealth and prominence as an entrepreneur in a virgin land.

Upon returning to Charleston to pursue his law studies, Simms at twenty married Anna Giles, fathered a child and was admitted to the South Carolina bar the following year, tried unsuccessfully to edit his first literary journal, and by 1830 purchased half interest in a newspaper and published four more collections of poetry. But his father's death that year presaged a series of personal losses that would dramatically affect his subsequent career: in 1832 both his young wife and his grandmother died, as did his partner; and he was obliged to sell their shaky *City Gazette* at a great sacrifice. In despair Simms traveled north, taking with him the manuscript of another long poem, *Atalantis* (1832), and hoping to find success in Boston or New York among such leading literary figures as William Cullen Bryant, Evert Duyckinck, and Timothy Flint. When Harpers published the poem, Simms's entree among the nation's prominent writers was assured; the following year Harpers published his first short novel, *Martin Faber* (1833), and his first collection of stories, *The Book of My Lady*.[4]

Simms's Theory of *Romance*

Although these two works brought Simms a measure of attention among the fiction-reading public, he only became prominent during the next few years with the appearance, successively, of *Guy Rivers, The Yemassee,* and *The Partisan.* These three books achieved genuine popularity and, in a sense, set the pattern for virtually all the rest of his fiction, long and short; they also provided Simms with a basis for establishing his own theory of fiction, which, like Hawthorne's, drew a sharp distinction between the novel and the romance. "The Romance," he asserted in his preface to *The Yemassee* written some years later, "is of loftier origin than the Novel." Whereas the novel dealt with verifiably commonplace events and individuals, the romance concerned itself with heroic figures and adventures of epic grandeur. It was, in fact, the modern substitute for the ancient epic; as such, he added, "it seeks for its adventures among the wild and wonderful. It does not confine itself to what is known, or even what is probable. It grasps at the possible; and placing a human agent in hitherto untried situations, it exercises its ingenuity in extracting him from them, . . . according to such proprieties as are called for by the circumstances of the story."[5] *The Yemassee,* he argued, could therefore be defended as an *American* romance because even though extravagance might be charged against certain parts of the narrative, "the popular faith yields abundant authority for the wildest of its incidents." Simms's defense of the romance was not much different from Hawthorne's claim that so long as the romancer did not violate the truths of the human heart, it was permissible for him to inject into his narrative at least a moderate flavoring of the marvelous.

In virtually all the rest of his major fiction, Simms would indulge this privilege rather more lavishly than Hawthorne ever did in his. Yet his practice can be justified on the grounds that whether he was writing about the colonial South or the Revolutionary South or the frontier South of his own time, his subject was the emergence of a southern civilization, born out of a series of painful conflicts against a hostile environment composed, successively, of raw nature, savage Indians, invading British armies, and terrorist outlaw gangs. Thus his central theme was a heroic if not an epic one; his materials, either witnessed or absorbed through traditions and legends, were filled with wild and wonderful adventures. As a result, most of his best stories, long or short, are *"all* in a sense 'border' romances";[6] in depicting his native region, Simms's consistent aim as a creative artist was to serve as a prophetic voice, a visionary defender of the faith in a superior cultural hierarchy, an orderly tripartite society led by upper-class, landowning whites, serviced by middle-class white artisans, merchants, and professionals, both firmly based on the economic underpinnings of a benevolent slave system.

Scope of Simms's Short Fiction: The *Centennial Edition*

With equal earnestness and more or less equal artistic élan, Simms pursued this same sense of mission in the writing of short fiction from beginning to end of his career, though his defense of slavery per se did not become strident till the middle 1850s. By then virtually all upper-class southern slave owners, whether morally committed to their peculiar institution or not, had endured more than a quarter century of hostile abolitionist criticism from the North and bitterly resented what they considered to be such unfair attacks as Harriet Beecher Stowe's *Uncle Tom's Cabin.* As a landowner himself with twenty years of residence at the beautiful Woodlands plantation, which came with his second marriage in 1836 to Chevillette Roach, Simms had ample reason to share their resentment. With justice he felt that the southern planter's life as he lived it was an ideal one and accordingly deserved to be represented ideally in his stories. Hence the patriotic rationale for his best collection, *The Wigwam and the Cabin* (1845), as set forth in a dedicatory preface to a revised edition addressed to his father-in-law, Nash Roach, in 1856. The substance of these stories, he explained,

is local, sectional—and to be *national* in literature, one must needs be *sectional*. No one mind can fully or fairly illustrate the characteristics of any great country; and he who shall depict *one section* faithfully, has made his proper and sufficient contribution to the great work of *national* illustration. I can answer for it, confidently, that these legends represent, in large degree, the border history of the south. I can speak with confidence of the general truthfulness of its treatment. I have seen the life—have *lived* it—and much of my material is the result of a very early personal experience. The life of the planter, the squatter, the Indian, and the negro—the bold and hardy pioneer, the vigorous yeoman—these are the subjects . . . I need not apologize for the endeavor to cast over the actual that atmosphere from the realms of the ideal, which, while it constitutes the very element of fiction, is neither inconsistent with intellectual truthfulness, nor unfriendly to the great policies of human society.[7]

During the forty-five-year span of his career, Simms published about eighty short tales and sketches, "not including novelettes or stories of more than thirty-six thousand words," and left at his death in 1870 at least eight unfinished manuscripts of fiction, plus two finished but unpublished ones, which appeared in print for the first time in volume 5 of the new *Centennial Edition* (Introduction, xiii). The bulk of Simms's short fiction therefore equals that of Hawthorne and Poe, and although the artistry in most of his tales suffers by comparison with theirs, many of his tales were well thought of by contemporary artists and editors. Poe, for example, was not alone in praising the vigor, invention, suspense, and artistic management of themes in his review of the tales in *The Wigwam and the Cabin*.[8]

Besides the uncollected tales now available in *Centennial 5*, most of Simms's short fiction pieces appeared in one or more of the following collections: *The Book of My Lady: A Melange* (1833), *Martin Faber, & Other Tales* (1837), *Carl Werner, an Imaginative Story; With Other Tales of the Imagination* (1838), *The Wigwam and the Cabin* (1845), *The Lily and the Totem* (1850), *Marie de Berniere: A Tale of the Crescent City, etc. etc. etc.* (1853), *Southward Ho!* (1854), and *The Maroon; A Legend of the Caribbees, and Other Tales* (1855). Structurally, the first three collections above were clearly apprentice work: some of the pieces in them were reworked versions of earlier ones Simms had published separately four or five years before. With these he was still feeling his way into the literary market, trying his hand at a variety of subject matter and treatment in hopes of striking a popular and profitable vein to exploit.

His first volume—a mélange, indeed, consisting of some thirty scraps of essays, poems, and short narratives—was prefaced by an apologia lamenting the passing of the age of chivalry and appealing hopefully to the sentimental lady reader of annuals and giftbooks. Most of these tales and sketches, ranging in subject matter from the Egyptian festival of Isis to the activities of the Yemassees in the American Revolution, dealt with standard giftbook fare: romantic love frustrated by class lines, racial barriers, jealousy, pursuit, narrow escapes, and violence. Simms's second collection was equally undistinguished, except for its novella-length title piece, "Martin Faber," a highly melodramatic, self-confessed tale of seduction and murder, told by a typically Byronic figure in the waning moments of his life. Stylistically this tale exhibits some of Simms's most glaring faults—verbosity, sentimentality, overheated diction, and hackneyed gothic plot devices—yet, for an early American example of crime narrative associated with the psychology of sex, it does have occasional passages of exceptional power and vivacity.

Simms's third collection, however, showed that he was still experimenting with various types of fictional material. Actually two volumes in one, consisting of eight stories, two of which had appeared in his first collection, this too was a potpourri featuring the ancient Egyptian legend, the spectral, Faustian tale, steeped in *diablerie,* and the Indian legend, handed down from colonial times among the tribes of Carolina and Georgia. Simms's narrative methods were still amateurish, his situations implausible, his characterizations thin and improbable, and his style prolix and bombastic; nevertheless, several of these stories, notably "Conrade Weickhoff," "Logoochee," and "Jocassee," revealed once more some of the latent power and charm, as well as the vividly realistic detail, that Simms would later display more effectively.

Unfortunately, all three of his first collections were commercial failures, the result, he believed, of their having to buck the unfair competition of cheap reprints. As late as 1845, while Simms was negotiating for the publication of his fourth and best collection, *The Wigwam and the Cabin,* he complained about the meager returns a native author could now expect, whereas a decade earlier he had received as much as $200 "for one story in an annual, which cost me three or four sittings."[9] *Carl Werner,* he wrote Duyckinck, had "failed of circulation from the simple fact that it was an expensive book after the old time prices—say $2.00 just at the moment when the great revolution in cheap literature had begun."[10] To offset that loss, during these months Simms repeatedly urged publishers to reissue both his earlier and his more recent stories in new editions, which he confidently predicted would sell better than his first three collections. Throughout the 1840s, in fact, he strove energetically, but often futilely, to persuade various publishers that his short stories could be profitably marketed, in spite of cheap reprint competition.

Plight of the Professional Author: Risks and Rewards

Simms's proposals, like the efforts of Hawthorne and Poe, throw a grim light on the desperate plight of the professional writer, but especially the southern writer, of that day. In June 1843 he urged James Lawson, his New York agent, to interest Harpers in bringing out a cheap three-volume edition consisting of two of his novelettes, *Ellen Halsey* and *Castle Dismal,* plus five of the shorter tales that would appear later in *The Wigwam and the Cabin.*[11] A few months later he directed Lawson to peddle these first to Harpers either as a package deal or in separate thin volumes of about 150 pages at $125 each, and then to offer them on the same terms to Benjamin and Winchester, publishers of the *New World,* if Harpers rejected the deal.[12] Harper & Brothers did "decline taking them for reasons of their own";[13] whereupon Simms lowered his price to $100 for each of the novelettes, which were published late the following year by Burgess and Stringer.[14] As the sale of the novelettes soon appeared to be going reasonably well, Simms hoped to interest the same publisher in another small volume of tales.[15] But when E. A. Duyckinck became literary editor of both the *Democratic Review* and the publishing house of Wiley & Putnam, Simms approached this firm in hopes of extending the single volume into two and of securing a contract similar to the previous one, which would assure him a price of $400 for the two-volume edition of *The Wigwam and the Cabin.*[16]

Uncertain that he had on hand enough recent stories to fill two volumes, Simms assured Duyckinck that he planned to include in the collection several other stories not previously mentioned (though several had been published years before in his first collection), since these all logically belonged together.[17] Hoping to strike while the iron was hot, Simms avidly sought news of the critical response to *The Wigwam and the Cabin;* and when both Poe and W. A. Jones praised the book, comparing it favorably to Hawthorne's work, he again pressed Duyckinck to accept his proposal for a third volume of tales: "A collection which I hold to be far superior to those of the W. & C. of a purely imaginative kind."[18]

Whether or not Simms really believed these earlier stories to be among "the best specimens of [his] powers of creating and combining," as he assured Griswold shortly afterward,[19] he was in any case doomed to disappointment. Carey & Hart declined his proposal to bring out an illustrated edition of the stories in 1847,[20] and Simms was obliged to place them individually, for whatever meager sums they might bring, in magazines like *Graham's* and *Godey's*.[21] A few of them were finally republished in 1850 as filler material in *The Lily and the Totem,* a quasi-historical treatment of sixteenth-century Florida; and the rest, four year later in *Southward Ho!* Thus by 1854 many of the same stories had appeared in print three or four times under slightly changed titles; yet Simms was never to enjoy financial satisfaction from them, for even *The Wigwam and the Cabin,* which he had reluctantly agreed to bring out on a royalty basis of eight cents per copy, was on the remainder shelves at half price before 1850.[22]

It is not surprising, therefore, to find Simms during the next few years suffering from bouts of depression over the neglect shown his works everywhere (and especially in South Carolina), and threatening to leave his native state for good. He had worked hard during the preceding decade, having published most of the thirteen stories that appeared in *The Wigwam,* and at least half a dozen others as well as a volume of critical essays and several novels. Yet owing to the inefficiency and undependability of Charleston book sellers, publishers, and agents, he moaned, his works were left unbound to gather dust on the shelves.[23]

His good friend James H. Hammond's response to this cry of pain, occasioned by the ineptitude of the Charleston firm of Walker, Richards, & Company in handling the reissue of *The Wigwam,* expressed "the fullest most sincere sympathy with you in your troubles" and offered to do anything he could to alleviate them. But, Hammond added, Simms should know by now that authorship was a beggarly business and that the price of literary fame, especially for the southern writer, was the

sacrifice of present happiness, peace, & comfort. . . . However Authors may get on at the North—& I doubt if it is very comfortably, it is a settled fact I think— settled by your case that the south will not encourage & sustain them here. We are not & never—*never* will be a reading people. It is the same as to Publishers here, whether of books, periodicals or Newspapers. . . . Whatever you can get in exchange for the coinage of your brain, take it, close there, & let it go like bread upon the waters. If it can float, be not apprehensive; it will be picked up after many days & appreciated at its real value.[24]

Simms's Revisions: The Redfield Edition

This was perhaps just the sort of encouragement Simms needed, for within six more months he was confidently buying back from Harpers the copyrights on his earliest works so that a uniform edition could be issued by Redfield. He was gathering together his "scattered novellettes and tales," and looking forward to "other vols. of similar material; all of which [he assured Hammond] will yield me a little money."[25] Hammond's reply to this letter exposed one root cause of Simms's artistic weakness, though Simms would have found it difficult to act on his advice:

I hope all your new works & new editions prove profitable & of course you are assured they will or you would not venture. I cannot in my ignorance of such matters give you any advice on this head. But in revising use the knife freely & cut out every thing that impedes the action. I used even when a boy to curse Scott for his long twaddling scenes & you must not blame me if I say that you have caught the failing from him. Every body that I talked with concurred with me as to Scott & I have no doubt many would as to yourself. Ninety nine in every hundred read fiction for the Story & so it will be *always*. And the writer who has fine things to say must weave them so closely into his very framework that they will appear to belong necessarily to the tale or drop them sparingly & hastily for his hundredth reader so as not to annoy his ninety nine.[26]

Hammond revealed a sharp eye and a good memory for Simms's worst faults, pointing out that most readers would tire of some of the long conversations in even his best works. He also boggled at careless errors in names, time sequences, geographical measurements, and clichés. But if Hammond's advice made any impression on Simms, it was finessed in his frank admission several years later: ". . . if I could bring myself to the task I might improve and amend my shortcomings, and prune my excesses—I feel this—yet know not whether the value of the alteration would be sufficiently recognized to justify the labor."[27] By the middle of 1854 he was pleased to see that several of his early novels now appearing in Redfield's revised edition were getting good reviews from both northern and southern critics, some of whom were even calling him America's premier novelist.[28]

Toward the end of that year he was also seeking news of the success of *Southward Ho!,* which, he remarked, "ought to be a good book for the traveller & for the holidays," and confidently expecting larger sums from the magazines for "revised" single stories.[29] He would like to place one of them, Simms wrote Duyckinck, in either *Putnam's* or *Harper's,* "whichever shall pay best," for at least $150, though he would accept $100 for it;[30] and concerning another of his tales, "The Legend of the Happy Valley," recently published in the *Southern Literary Messenger,* he told John Esten Cooke that he expected to be paid at the rate of $1.00 per manuscript page for it, not "$1.00 per Messenger page." This story, however, turned out to be an expanded version of "Haiglar: A Story of the Catawbas," originally published in *The Book of My Lady* twenty years before; and since the later version filled eighteen of the *Messenger's* large, double-columned pages as against only eleven octavo pages in the original, it appears that Simms was padding out his old materials in refurbished formats rather than following Hammond's advice to use his knife freely.[31]

But with the publication of *Southward Ho!* he had virtually fulfilled his yearning to reissue his earlier short fiction in book form. His interests were now turning in other directions—toward politics and the South's increasing involvement in the coming hostilities, and toward his projected "uniform edition"—and references to his short stories seldom reappeared in his subsequent correspondence. Except for a few late strays, notably his extraordinary tall tale "How Sharp Snaffles Got His Capital and Wife," published posthumously in *Harper's,* his record as a short story artist would survive, at its best, largely on the work of one collection, *The Wigwam and the Cabin.*

Strengths and Weaknesses in Simms's Short Fiction

Of the thirteen stories making up *The Wigwam,* all but two had been published for the first time in magazines and annuals between 1840 and 1845, although Simms implied in his dedicatory letter to Nash Roach that most of them had been accumulating over many years dating back to the time of his early manhood.[32] This was partly the reason why he found it easier in 1856 "to acknowledge their faults than to amend or excuse them . . . [and] much easier to invent a new story than to repair the defects of an old one."[33] Whatever their defects, however, Simms felt confident that these stories could stand on their own merits as a fundamentally truthful treatment of the border history of the South.

The self-criticism in his dedicatory letter affirms both the strengths and the weaknesses of Simms's most impressive collection of stories. All but the last story, "Lucas De Ayllon"—a rambling, improbable "Historical Novellette"—bear the stamp of felt action. Simms perhaps witnessed the kind of events narrated in two or three of the stories; while the others are imaginatively retold versions of legends he had heard as a boy from his grandmother or as a youth during his sojourn in the interior with his father. Six of the stories have to do primarily with the activities of border whites; in five others the chief characters are Indians, and in the remaining two, Negroes. And in most of them the interrelationships between whites and red men or between whites and blacks are skillfully blended in highly suspenseful action involving violence, fraud, malice, deceit, and retribution. Though they are tales based on commonplace events, Simms recognized that the problem of the artist was to make these common events "appear in the right place, strike at the right time, and so adapt one fact to another, as to create mystery, awaken curiosity, inspire doubt as to the result, and bring about the catastrophe, by processes which shall be equally natural and unexpected."[34]

Simms met this problem most successfully in those stories for which he provided an eye-witness narrator, either named or implied, who could "breathe life" into the deeds recounted: for example, the grandmother in "Grayling"; the old pioneer, Dan Nelson, in "The Two Camps"; Rayner, the participant in "The Last Wager"; Col. Harris, the Mississippi planter, in "Oakatibbe"; Scipio, the slave, in "The Lazy Crow"; or the anonymous observer of events in "The Snake of the Cabin." He was less successful when, posing as a "historian," he felt obliged both to authenticate the truthfulness of his material and to assert his right as an artist to manipulate it to serve aesthetic ends. Thus, in "Sergeant Barnacle," "Caloya," and "Lucas De Ayllon," Simms virtually destroys the illusion of his story by pontificating in a long introductory chapter on the genuineness of his setting, characters, and action, as though he feared that otherwise the ensuing story might not be accepted. Yet, in partial extenuation of this practice, it should be quickly added that Simms's most powerful and realistic scenes were sometimes viciously criticized for being too coarse, vulgar, and degrading. A case in point is "Caloya," one of the most effective of all his stories, yet condemned as offensive by squeamish critics presumably because it dealt too explicitly with the attempted seduction of an Indian squaw by an aggressive black slave driver. When "Caloya" first appeared in the *Magnolia* in 1841, it soon aroused a controversy in which Simms felt compelled to defend both his own morality and that of the story itself. His diatribe against "very elegant people" who cannot stomach scenes of low life yet accept salacious innuendos in tales about "very fine and fashionable people in high life," is as stimulating an example of Swiftian irony as any criticism he ever wrote.[35]

But however cumbersome today's reader may find the opening paragraphs of stories like "Caloya," "The Two Camps," "The Last Wager," "The Giant's Coffin," or "Sergeant Barnacle," once past this rhetorical device Simms reveals considerable narrative power, achieving vivid effects even in poorly constructed tales and holding his reader spellbound through the playing out of some very dramatic scenes. There is, for example, the climactic retribution in "The Snake of the Cabin";[36] the entrapment scene in "The Giant's Coffin," describing the villain's frenzied efforts to free himself;[37] or the drunken brawling of Knuckles, the Indian husband, in "Caloya."[38] Equally noteworthy evidence of his creative ability can be seen in his realistic character portrayals, particularly those of Negroes and backwoodsmen, whose crude manners and speech are skillfully rendered in dialogue passages revealing both a sensitive eye and ear and a fund of comic gusto.[39] Simms's humor, in fact, ranging from the boisterous extravagance of a tall tale such as "Sharp Snaffles" or "Bald-Head Bill Bauldy" to the ironic whimsy of "The Armchair of Tustennuggee" and "Those Old Lunes," adds substantially to the narrative appeal of his stories. But for the modern reader these virtues, unfortunately, are too often diminished by a kind of Victorian sententiousness. Thus, prolixity and pontification march through his best stories; while editorial intrusions, irrelevant asides, and gratuitous ruminations on such matters as slavery and race relationships, motherhood and young love, or seduction and the sanctity of female honor, distort both their tone and point of view.

Whether Simms could have pruned these excesses, had he set his mind to the task, is debatable, since his tendency was always to expand rather than contract. But so too is his other assertion that it was easier for him to invent a new story than to repair the defects of an old one. In his later collections of stories the only evidence of newness immediately noticeable is the method he devised for incorporating them within successive pairs of hard covers. His aim in writing *The Lily and the Totem,* he said, was to produce a "Romance of History"; that is, to combine "in nearly equal degree, the picturesque and the historical."[40] Deliberately subordinating fiction to fact, Simms accordingly secured his basic narrative of the Huguenots in Florida from the writings of the French historian Charlevoix and filled out its picturesque elements with five highly romanticized tales of his own invention.[41] These, like the ones in *Southward Ho!,* had been previously published separately in the ladies' magazines; so that Simms's vaunted historical effort appears, at first blush, to be merely a device for assembling and republishing some of his earliest fictional pieces within a single volume.

The problem, however, is not that simple; for Simms had a genuine, deep-seated interest in both Spanish and French colonial history in America dating from the 1830s, when he began publishing romances like *Pelayo* (1838), *The Damsel of Darien* (1839), and *Count Julian* (1845). His interest in Spanish colonialism, in fact, grew apace throughout the 1840s as his splendid private library increased; so that even in the 1850s, while producing his finest Revolutionary romances—*Katharine Walton* (1851), *The Sword and the Distaff* (1852, retitled *Woodcraft* later on), *The Forayers* (1855), and *Eutaw* (1856)—he diverted his time and energies in turning out inferior works like *Vasconcelos* (1853) and refurbished versions of "The Maroon: A Legend of the Caribbees" (1850) and *Marie de Berniere: A Tale of the Crescent City* (1853 and 1855).[42] Simms's determination to make something viable out of all these historical romances has been labeled his "major weakness as a writer; a failure of his critical faculties to assert themselves and distinguish between what interested him historically and romantically and what made good literature."[43]

In *Southward Ho!* that weakness is all the more obvious, since the thirteen stories in this volume do not even develop a common theme. Dealing with such varied fare as French troubadours, Venetian doges, medieval crusades, Etruscan relics, South American liberators, Revolutionary pirates, and Pawnee Indians, all but a few of these were among his oldest productions. They were his "imaginative" stories, some of which he had managed to have republished two or three times in different magazines, and which now at last he succeeded in bundling together in one package. To unify its structure, he adapted Chaucer's scheme, inventing a cast of congenial traveling companions who, while sailing from New York to Charleston, entertain one another by retelling these thrice-told tales. But whereas the *Canterbury Tales* are admirably suited in style and content to the character of their individual narrators, Simms's stories in *Southward Ho!* are all too obviously his own, the artificiality of his mechanism revealing both his penchant for extending a tale as far as its limits can be stretched and his strategy for making the same story do double, even triple duty in a new context. An extreme example of this stratagem is "La Pola, the Maid of Bogota," which, over the course of twenty years after its original publication in the *Cosmopolitan* of Charleston, was reissued three more times in expanded versions before finally coming to rest in *Southward Ho!* If, indeed, it was easier for him "to invent a new story than to repair the defects of an old one," it seems to have been even easier at times to revise an old story by expanding its volume, if not by pruning its excesses.

Simms's Mastery of the Comic Mode: "Sharp Snaffles" and Others

Nevertheless, when Simms threw aside his self-imposed straitjacket of the romantic historical tale and shifted his imaginative vision toward the comic mode, he showed that even in the twilight of his career he still possessed energy and talent enough to compete with a new generation of tall-tale artists. So in a way it is fitting that his last three stories, none of which he was destined to see in print, would fulfill at last, in the twentieth century, the metaphoric prophecy of his friend Senator Hammond. Of the three, only "How Sharp Snaffles Got His Capital and Wife" was published shortly after his death; "Bald-Head Bill Bauldy" and "The Humours of the Manager" remained in manuscript until their appearance in the *Centennial Edition* of 1974. Together, these three narrative extravaganzas reveal evidence of Simms's yarn spinning technique, which, though heretofore not fully appreciated, placed him squarely in the forefront of the American tall-tale humor tradition.

"Sharp Snaffles" has justifiably been singled out as one of the finest literary examples of backwoods folk humor, combining dialect, gusty action and Munchausen exaggeration associated with hunting-camp activities. To dramatize the age-old theme of frustrated young lovers triumphant over parental disapproval, Simms expertly manipulates the framework device employed by the frontier yarn spinners, setting up at the outset the Saturday-night scene in the hunting camp, introducing the participants, and swiftly explaining the nature of their weekend festivities. Somewhat like Poe's scheme for the Folio Club sessions, the point of their entertainment is to conduct a "Lying Camp" in which one of the members is chosen to spin a yarn of extravagant invention and obvious yet artistic exaggeration. Thus, having selected Sam (alias Sharp alias Yaou) Snaffles to be the raconteur, Simms retires into the background simply to monitor Sam's wildly ludicrous tale of how he managed to overcome the hostility of his future father-in-law, Squire Hopson, by producing "capital" in the form of a mountainous supply of gold and silver coins—as well as the mortgage on the Squire's farm!—with which to secure the hand of his beloved Merry Ann. By giving Sam free rein to tell the entire tale in his own backwoods dialect, Simms steadily heightens and intensifies its effect down to Sam's final hilarious disclosure of his thirty-six offspring born to Merry Ann during the thirteen years of their marriage.

In some respects, "Bald-Head Bill Bauldy," the previously unpublished sequel to "Sharp Snaffles," is an even more impressive mock epic and thus doubles Simms's claim to the highest rank in this comic vein. It is longer than "Sharp Snaffles," sustaining a comic atmosphere through fifty-five pages; and by means of the same device of authentic backwoods dialect, it succeeds in getting across some highly suggestive sexual imagery couched in "language unacceptable in the polite literature of the time."[44] But, by attempting to overextend his satire of the traditional epic or captivity narrative, packing into the framework of "Bald-Head Bill Bauldy" the journey into battle motif—"fighting, capture, escape, journey, capture, descent into the underworld, and so forth"[45]—Simms loses much of the freshness of humorous gusto he achieved in "Sharp Snaffles." The reader grows a bit bored long before confirming his suspicion that Bauldy's vaunted exploits were all a dream. But Simms's other manuscript tale, "The Humours of the Manager," is deservedly characterized as "perhaps the best example of Simms's humor in a story of manners";[46] for while it deals with theatrical high jinks in New York City rather than with bilbulous backwoods behavior, it contains a wealth of skillfully contrived, well-controlled tongue-in-cheek humor bordering on satire.

Shortly after *The Wigwam and the Cabin* appeared, Poe reviewed the book by recalling that years earlier in *Martin Faber* Simms had displayed "evidence of genius, and that of no common order." He went on to suggest, as he had also asserted in commenting on the merits of another southerner's writing, that had Simms been "a Yankee, this genius would have been *immediately* manifest to his countrymen." But because he was a southerner, his book "therefore depended entirely upon its own intrinsic value and resources, but with these it made its way in the end. The 'intrinsic value' consisted first of a very vigorous imagination in the conception of the story; secondly, in artistic skill manifested in its conduct; thirdly, in general vigour, life, movement—the whole resulting in deep interest on the part of the reader. These high qualities Mr. Simms has carried with him in his subsequent books; and they are qualities which, above all others, the fresh and vigorous intellect of America should and does esteem."[47] Had Poe himself been granted another quarter century of life, there can be little doubt that in the 1870s he would have reiterated this critical judgment even more emphatically.

The Frontier Yarn Spinners and Porter's *Spirit of the Times*

Simms's "Sharp Snaffles" and its sequel, "Bald-Head Bill Bauldy," are, in a sense, anticlimactic spin-offs from a literary phenomenon that had become a tradition in the Old South, flourishing chiefly in small local newspapers since the 1820s. This phenomenon was the comic narrative or tall tale of the frontier. Originating as oral yarn spinning among backwoodsmen, boatmen, hunters, and campers who relieved the tedium of their labors after dark with wildly imaginative accounts of their exploits, these tales eventually achieved a recognizably standard form as they broke into print, first as anonymous or pseudonymous separate stories in the regional papers, but later as reprinted pieces in widely popular national media and anthologized collections.[48] Beginning in 1835 with the publication of Augustus Baldwin Longstreet's *Georgia Scenes,* the most important of these collections were William Tappan Thompson's *Major Jones's Courtship* (1843), Johnson Jones Hooper's *Some Adventures of Captain Simon Suggs* (1845), Thomas Bangs Thorpe's *Mysteries of the Backwoods* (1846) and his *Hive of "The Bee-Hunter"* (1854), Henry Clay Lewis's *Odd Leaves from the Life of a Louisiana "Swamp Doctor"* (1850), Joseph Glover Baldwin's *The Flush Times of Alabama and Mississippi* (1853), George Washington Harris's *Sut Lovingood's Yarns* (1867), and, without doubt, the two most influential of all, *The Big Bear of Arkansas, and Other Sketches* (1845) and *A Quarter Race in Kentucky, and Other Sketches* (1847), both of which were edited by William T. Porter.[49] Nearly all of the hundreds of tall-tale sketches in these and many other collections had appeared singly, either originally or as reprints, in Porter's famous New York weekly, the *Spirit of the Times,* a popular sporting journal enjoyed by leisured gentlemen throughout the nation from the early 1830s till Porter's death in 1858, but especially by well-to-do southern plantation owners, journalists, and politicians.[50]

The *Spirit*'s widespread appeal in the antebellum South was due primarily to the character and editorial acumen of Porter himself. His geniality and friendliness, reflected in countless small personal greetings, compliments, and services printed in the paper, endeared him to many planters whose estates he often visited on annual tours through the South. But his astuteness as editor endeared him to many more southerners who knew him only through the *Spirit*'s pages. Always on the lookout for racy anecdotes and sketches in small-town newspapers, Porter not only reprinted them with gusto and fanfare, giving full credit to their sources, but he also encouraged the authors of these pieces to send more of them directly to the *Spirit.* Thus, by filling its pages week after week with amusing yarns about bear, deer, and fox hunting, along with more sober data on cattle and horse breeding, fish culture, and horse racing, within a few years Porter had built up a small army of loyal correspondents who wrote extravagant tributes to the *Spirit*—which he was also delighted to print. Typical of hundreds of these were several he received in the 1840s from subscribers in Alabama who spoke of "the many weary hours which it has beguiled, and . . . the many pleasant moments which it has enlivened."[51]

More significant, however, by 1845 Porter could also boast that his paper had acquired a "circle of 'jolly good fellows' whose contributions to the columns of this journal have rendered it far more famous for original wit and humor than its being the 'chronicle of the Sporting World.'"[52] It was no idle boast, for he could name among these men such writers as Albert Pike, H. W. Herbert ("Frank Forrester"), N. P. Willis, C. F. M. Noland, T. B. Thorpe, and Washington Irving. And it was into this circle that he proposed to introduce another "choice spirit," recently discovered in an obscure East Alabama newspaper, J. J. Hooper, creator of the notorious Simon Suggs. Moreover, at this point in his career, Porter was busily negotiating with the firm of Carey & Hart for the publication of the first of his three highly successful anthologies, *The Big Bear of Arkansas, and Other Sketches*. For this and his second anthology, *A Quarter Race in Kentucky, and Other Sketches,* he had only to tap the rich files of the *Spirit* to come up with a total of fifty-four humorous sketches; yet in that horn of plenty there were still enough other choice pieces to fill the collections written by Thorpe, Hooper, and other *Spirit* contributors, which were being issued under the rubric of Carey & Hart's Library of Humorous American Writers.[53]

With impeccable taste, Porter had chosen the best of all the yarns in the *Spirit,* Thorpe's "Big Bear," for the title piece of his first anthology; the following year, he selected another extremely popular tale for the title piece of his second one. His editorial work on the *Spirit* and in assembling these two collections, now recognized as classics and available in expensive modern reprints, amply support his claim to be known as "one of the most important editors in America in the nineteenth century," for he had certainly been instrumental in bringing new zest and masculine vigor to American fiction.[54] Pioneering in the two fields of sporting and humor writing, he had literally enshrined a new class of writers and fathered a new style of American literature, which—as his friend Wilkes wrote after his death—"was not stewed in the closet, or fretted out at some pale pensioned laborer's desk, but sparkled from the cheerful leisure of the early scholar . . . and flowed from every mead, or lake, or mountain—in the land where the rifle or the rod was known."[55]

Porter's remarkable twofold achievement was thus the fulfillment of a lifelong dream, announced in the 1830s and restated periodically throughout his career. He had quickly noted that the broadest base for the *Spirit's* appeal lay in the humorous tall tales and sketches, especially those coming from the South and Southwest, which had been gaining increasing prominence in its pages during the early 1840s. And he had long since recognized that the adventurous life of the frontier, with its varied incidents and social types, its peculiarities of speech and manners, offered the most fruitful field in America for fresh, racy literary treatment. "Life at the West and

South," he observed in 1840, "is a teeming theme for Magazine writers; but the cleverest and most amusing have certainly been of a sporting nature. The curious and often rich provincialisms of dialect are here most appropriate."[56] By stimulating, publishing, and publicizing the creative efforts of those who could best furnish this sort of material, Porter established the literary reputation of at least a dozen southerners whose writings formed the nucleus of a tradition that would eventually reach an apex in the works of Mark Twain and William Faulkner. Besides the seven major figures discussed briefly below, others whose writings also appeared in the *Spirit* with some regularity were Thomas Kirkman, Alexander McNutt, George Wilkins Kendall, Charles F. M. Noland, Harden E. Taliaferro, and William C. Hall.[57]

Longstreet: *Georgia Scenes*

As a pioneering work in a new genre, the importance of Longstreet's *Georgia Scenes* (1835) may be appraised from two perspectives: its immediate appeal and its enduring literary influence. Though a modest little collection of nineteen brief sketches, identified only as "By a Native Georgian" and issued originally in book form from the office of Longstreet's Augusta newspaper, the *State Rights Sentinel,* the book quickly gained widespread popularity, both in the North and in the South. Poe's high praise in the *Southern Literary Messenger*—"Seriously, if this book were printed in England it would make the fortune of its author. . . . Seldom—perhaps never in our lives—have we laughed so immoderately over any book as over the one now before us"—was soon being echoed in New York, where the demand for new editions remained constant throughout the 1840s and 1850s.[58] And shortly after its author's identity became known, Longstreet was awarded an honorary degree by his alma mater, Yale University. Obviously the *Scenes* appealed to everybody as a fresh, amusing, yet authentic record of the lives of plain American folk on several different social levels.

From the outset, the key to Longstreet's enduring success lay in his disarmingly frank approach to his subject. His aim in writing the sketches, he said, was not merely to entertain, but "to supply a chasm in history which has always been overlooked—the manners, customs, amusements, wit, dialect, as they appear in all grades of society to an ear and eye witness to them." Thus the characters and incidents in the sketches, he insisted, were realistically portrayed; the antics and speech of these folk, as presented in their appearance, dress, remarks, "private games, quarrels, and fights," could be seen and heard in almost every county in Georgia "during the first fifty years of the Republic."[59] That was doubtless true enough, but Longstreet's triumphant rendering of the antics and speech of these yokels in his finest sketches was due largely to the artistic framework he prepared for them, as well as to the contrast in refinement between his genteel narrators, Hall and Baldwin,[60] and the rowdier characters themselves. The opening sketch, "Georgia Theatrics," for example, brilliantly sets the tone for all the remaining "Scenes" by presenting, from the viewpoint of an outraged clerical gentleman, a violent struggle with "loud, profane, and boisterous voices, which seemed to proceed from a thick covert of undergrowth about two hundred yards" ahead of him. But as he rushes forward, too late to prevent what appears to be a successful eye-gouging, he discovers wrathfully that only one combatant has been engaged in a dramatic rehearsal with himself—"jist seein' how I could 'a' *fout*" (*GS,* 3). The joke, it turns out, is just as much on the outraged moralist who jumped to a premature conclusion as it is on the embarrassed youth, "caught" in his play-acting.

Not all the sketches are handled so effectively. The six that focus primarily on women characters seem rather insipid to a modern taste, although Poe found "The Dance" an "inimitable farce" and had a good word for the satire in "The Charming Creature as a Wife" and the "sly humor" in "The Ball." In these three, however, as well as in "The Song," "The Mother and Her Child," and "A Sage Conversation," Longstreet's burlesquing of the excesses of feminine pretentiousness, frivolity, sentimentality, and credulity fails to generate more than an occasional wry grimace as compared with the hearty guffaws induced by several other sketches.

Possibly the finest of them all, "The Horse-Swap," for example, maintains a high level of hilarity from start to finish by pitting two con-men against each other in a stand-off exchange that leaves neither of them wholly satisfied. The "*Yellow* Blossom from Jasper," who prides himself on being "jist a *leetle* of the best man at a horse-swap that ever trod shoe leather," succeeds in palming off poor Bullet, cavorting with a painful six-by-four-inch sore concealed beneath his saddle blanket. But Blossom's triumph is cut short by the dismal news that he has been outfoxed: "His back's mighty bad off," cries old Peter Ketch's little son; "but dod drot my soul if he's put it to daddy as bad as he thinks he has, for old Kit's both blind and *deef,* I'll be dod drot if he eint" (*GS,* 15, 21). As in the best of Poe's hoaxes, the magic of Longstreet's genius here can be sensed in the economy of the treatment: characterization, description, dialogue, and action all function neatly together while leading toward a brilliant denouement. Small wonder that Faulkner found inspiration in this sketch for one of the most uproarious sequences in his Snopes trilogy, the Pat Stamper–Ab Snopes horse-trading episode told by Ratliff, the sewing machine salesman, in *The Hamlet*.

Other obvious literary forebears of the Snopes clan are also present in several more of Longstreet's better sketches. In "The Fight," for example, there is Ransy Sniffle, surely Longstreet's most memorable degenerate, who maneuvers the town's two strongest young men into a no-holds-barred conflict for the sheer joy of watching them nearly destroy each other. But Sniffle, the depraved dirt-eater, is not alone in providing the picturesque comedy in this drama of violent fisticuffs, for the conflict between the two champions, Bob Durham and Bill Stallions, is matched by the prior altercation between their two wives, and counterpointed by the comments of interested onlookers in the community and the owlish predictions of Squire Loggins regarding the outcome of the fight.

Community entertainment of a style slightly less uproarious is also picturesquely described in "The Gander Pulling," "The Character of a Native Georgian," and "The Shooting Match"; but the situations and characters developed in these three "scenes" are less vividly drawn than those of "The Horse-Swap" and "The Fight." Interest in "The Gander Pulling" is focused primarily on the primitive barbarism of a contest among horseback riders who attempt to snatch the head off the greased neck of a goose suspended by the legs above a circular path, the successful snatcher winning the entire pot of coins contributed individually by each. Longstreet affirmed that such sport actually occurred in Augusta exactly as he described it, and the repartee he ascribed to the participants does indeed make the whole engagement sound authentic. It is in fact the repartee among contestants that enlivens the scene in the other two sketches as well, though modern readers may find them less hilarious than Longstreet's contemporaries did.[61]

Thompson: Major Jones of Pineville

The first of Longstreet's contemporaries to profit from his exemplary artistry was William Tappan Thompson, a native of Ohio who as a youth of eighteen arrived in the South in 1830 and spent the remainder of his life in Georgia. He began reading law under Longstreet at about the same time that *Georgia Scenes* appeared. Shortly thereafter he founded his own literary periodical, the *Augusta Mirror,* which he subsequently merged with another journal in Macon, the *Family Companion and Ladies Mirror.* The first of his Major Joseph Jones letters appeared in this publication in June 1842;

but most of the twenty-eight letters Thompson eventually collected under the title *Major Jones's Courtship* (1843) were first published in the *Southern Miscellany,* another small weekly he edited in Madison, Georgia, from August 1842 to February 1844.

Like the *Georgia Scenes, Major Jones's Courtship* enjoyed nationwide popularity shortly after Carey & Hart published a second edition; and the book retained its appeal through many reprintings by other publishers long after the Civil War, though Thompson gained little financial profit from them. *Major Jones's Courtship,* however, was quite different from *Georgia Scenes* in form and substance: organized as a series of consecutive letters written by the same imaginary figure, Joseph Jones of Pineville, to the editor of the *Miscellany,* it was more decorous in tone than the antics and speech of Longstreet's yokels; but the Major Jones persona was decidedly less literate than Longstreet's genteel narrators. Hence the comic appeal of the Major's approach, especially for a middle-class audience, lay in the amusing situations he encounters and in the genial naïveté with which he later reports them, often ungrammatically, to the editor. His bashful method of proposing to the blushing Mary Stallions, for instance, was to offer himself as a surprise Christmas present concealed in a large meal sack hanging from a beam on her back porch. Nearly frozen stiff from the night's exposure, when the bag was lowered to the floor on Christmas morning before the astonished Mary and her sisters, he writes:

". . . I tumbled out all covered with corn meal, from hed to foot. 'Goodness gracious!' ses Miss Mary, 'if it aint the Majer himself!' 'Yes,' ses I, 'and you know you promised to keep my Crismas present as long as you lived.'

"The galls laughed themselves almost to deth and went to brushin off the meal as fast as they could, saying they was gwine to hang that bag up every Crismas till they got husbands too. Miss Mary—bless her bright eyes—she blushed as butiful as a morninglory, and sed she'd stick to her word. She was rite out o' bed, and her hair wasn't comed, and her dress wasn't fixt at all, but the way she looked pretty was rale distractin. I do blieve if I was froze stif, one look at her charmin face, as she stood lookin down to the floor with her rogish eyes, and her bright curls fallin all over her snowy neck, would fotch'd me too. I tell you what, it was worth hangin in a meal bag from one Crismas to another to feel as happy as I have ever since."[62]

Most of the other Major Jones letters are done in a similar manner, with the same folksy language imparting a characteristic tang to the Major's predictable observations on such familiar topics as family life, parlor games, and women's fashions; school commencements, coon hunting, and local politics. Unlike the raw frontier, the Major's Pineville, it has been said, "is a world where nice young ladies blush at the word 'stocking.' There are practical jokes and good-natured high-jinks . . . but not an eye-gouging in his county."[63]

To capitalize on the continuing popularity of these Pineville vignettes, however, Thompson broadened their scope in another collection of stories entitled *Chronicles of Pineville* (1845). Frankly patterned after Longstreet's earlier volume, the narrative form and humorous dialogue in these sketches offer a more realistic view of provincial southern village life, including some of its less attractive features, than do the Major's letters. But later still, Thompson, abandoning the domestic flavor of Pineville altogether, carried the Major farther afield in a series entitled *Major Jones' Sketches of Travel, Comprising the Scenes, Incidents, and Adventures in His Tour from Georgia to Canada* (1848). These enabled him to comment in typically home-spun terms on such vagaries of urban cultural phenomena as the grand opera in Philadelphia and the con-artists in New York. But, we are re-minded, "his transfer to a Northern scene also allowed the Major to com-ment satirically on national politics—whacking at abolitionists and free blacks, and cheering the virtues of the slavocracy back home."[64] Though gentler by far than his fellow Southwest yarn spinners in depicting the rural southern scene, Thompson's short fiction in the early Major Jones letters and the Pineville sketches fills an important if modest niche in the history of American literature because of its faithful record of the manners and customs of middle-class family life in antebellum Georgia.

Johnson Jones Hooper: Captain Simon Suggs

Johnson Jones Hooper, a more colorful disciple of Longstreet than Thompson, owes his literary fame chiefly to the creation of a supremely disreputable rogue named Simon Suggs, whose motto—"It's good to be shifty in a new country"—has become a byword in the literature of South-west humor. A native of North Carolina, Hooper as a youth of twenty in 1835 came to join his eldest brother, a practicing lawyer, in the frontier community of LaFayette, Chambers County, Alabama. Within a few years "Jonce" had acquired enough legal knowledge to be admitted to the bar in the neighboring Tallapoosa County, where he was appointed notary public in 1839 and census taker from the county early the next year. After com-pleting the census in 1841, Hooper became associated with and presently editor of the *East Alabamian,* a small weekly newspaper in LaFayette. His writings in that obscure paper soon led to his nationwide popularity through the pages of Porter's *Spirit of the Times*.[65]

Hooper's debut in the *Spirit* occurred in September 1843 with the appearance of an amusing sketch entitled "Taking the Census in Alabama" and signed "By a Chicken Man of 1840." Based on his own harrowing experiences as a census taker among the suspicious farmers of the county and first printed in the *East Alabamian* only a few weeks before, the sketch caught Porter's sharp editorial eye at once, reminding him "forcibly of the late Judge Longstreet's 'Georgia Scenes,'" as well as of the wisdom of enlisting its clever but still unknown author "among the correspondents of the Spirit."[66] Naturally pleased by such recognition from the editor of the prominent New York weekly, Hooper responded warmly to Porter's genial overtures and the two men soon became fast friends, though little more of Hooper's work was to be reprinted in the *Spirit* until the following year.

In December 1844, however, came the spurt of creative effort destined to catapult Hooper into the national limelight; for when the first of the Captain Suggs stories appeared in his LaFayette paper, Porter delightedly reprinted it beneath a laudatory preface in the next issue of the *Spirit* and clamored for more, crying that it would be a pity for such a gifted writer to hide "his light under a bushel."[67] This time Porter's urging brought results: within rapid succession during the next few weeks further installments of the saga of the Shifty Man were picked up from the *East Alabamian* and reprinted in the *Spirit;* and presently Porter could proudly announce that Hooper had agreed to send him original stories written expressly for the *Spirit*.[68] That Hooper's career as a nationally known writer of hilarious Alabama yarns was securely launched can be quickly seen in the praises that came pouring into the *Spirit* from all directions.[69]

Porter's aid in furthering Hooper's career was crucial, though not wholly altruistic. During the early months of 1845, while assembling his first anthology, *The Big Bear of Arkansas,* he recognized Hooper's potential as a drawing card and not only altered his original plan so as to include the first of the Suggs yarns in the collection but also urged Carey & Hart to approach Hooper with a proposal for bringing out a separate volume of Suggs pieces in their projected *Library of Humorous American Writers*. Then, when the publishers did sign a contract with Hooper for the first edition of *Some Adventures of Simon Suggs, Late Captain of the Tallapoosa Volunteers,* Porter cannily persuaded the firm to let him print advance chapters of the new work in the *Spirit,* which thus served as both an advertising medium for the two forthcoming volumes as well as a further means of extending both

Hooper's fame and the *Spirit*'s.[70] At one stroke Porter benefited Hooper, himself, and the firm of Carey & Hart, for he let no opportunity slip in reminding his subscribers of the delights in store for them when the two books should appear. And, when the *Adventures of Captain Simon Suggs* was published, several months after the solid success of *The Big Bear,* Porter assured his readers that it was "the best half dollars worth of genuine humor, ever enclosed between two covers."[71] The nation obviously agreed. Within a year, three editions of the book were issued, three more were published by 1850, and at least five more came out during the next six years. A twelfth edition was published in 1881, a thirteenth in 1928, and the most recent, a scholarly edition, in 1969.[72]

Hooper's success, during his own lifetime and ever since, is due almost entirely to the consummate artistry with which he conceived and executed his rascally hero and the successive exploits that test Suggs's capacity for cunning deceit. They begin when, as a quick-thinking adolescent, he escapes his father's wrathful punishment for card playing by persuading the simple-minded old man to let him cut a stacked deck for a buried Jack; and, leaping over years of undisclosed adventures in the wilds of western Georgia, they next reveal his propensities for self-protection as a fifty-year-old "sort of he-Pallas, ready to cope with his kind . . . in all the arts by which men *'get along'* in the world" (9). Like Longstreet's Peter Ketch, he outfoxes a desperate landseeker in a rigged horse trade (31–37); flim-flams a gullible stranger out of twenty dollars on his way to Tuscaloosa, where despite bankruptcy from "fighting the tiger" at faro, he recoups his losses by posing as a wealthy hog-breeder from Kentucky (38–64); pulls another fast land deal among the Creek Indians in Tallapoosa County (65–76); and, thanks to the false rumors of a Creek uprising, gets himself elected captain of the "Tallapoosy Vollantares" (84). The episodes surrounding Suggs's investiture as captain and his imposition of martial law at Fort Suggs are among the most hilarious in the saga, the comedy enlivened considerably by the presence of Yellow-legs, a sardonic replica of Longstreet's gadfly, Ransy Sniffle, the only one capable of ruffling Suggs's composure.

But the apex of Suggs's triumphant progress toward immortality occurs in a later episode entitled "The Captain Attends a Camp-Meeting" (111–26). In this sketch Hooper drew such a graphic picture of crowd hysteria at a frontier religious revival orchestrated by a group of hell-fire preachers that he felt obliged to assure his readers in a footnote that "the scenes described in this chapter are not *now* to be witnessed" (115). True or not, though implying that they might have been seen eight or ten years before, this self-protective disclaimer that he intended no disrespect to "any denomination of Christians" did not abate his enthusiasm for witnessing through Suggs's crafty dissimulation the conversion techniques required to turn the basic fraudulence of the operation to one's own advantage. As Suggs rides off triumphantly into the swamp with the fattened collection plate, one can safely assume that his avatar will survive and reappear, as indeed he does in Mark Twain's swindling King and Faulkner's Flem Snopes.

Joseph Glover Baldwin:
The Flush Times of Alabama and Mississippi

By an odd quirk of fate, the literary reputation of Joseph Glover Baldwin, Hooper's friend and fellow Alabamian, has survived through the pages of one book that he and his closest associates regarded as the least of his intellectual accomplishments: *The Flush Times of Alabama and Mississippi* (1853). A collection of twenty-six sketches, brief biographies, and humorous anecdotes, *Flush Times* is a vivid record of the same turbulent period that Simms and Hooper had experienced as young men on the Alabama frontier. But it differs from their writings in a number of ways as a result of its predominantly legalistic and judicial viewpoint. Like Hooper, Baldwin also came to Alabama from his native Virginia in 1836—". . . that golden era, when shin-plasters were the sole currency; when bank-bills were 'thick as Autumn leaves in Vallambrosa,' and credit was a franchise"—but instead of turning to journalism, he stuck to the law and prospered.[73] But instead of settling on the eastern edge of the state, he made his home in the western Alabama towns of Gainesville and Livingston, where he became a prominent criminal lawyer and eventually a judge and a successful candidate for the Alabama House of Representatives.

Within the eighteen years between his arrival and departure from Alabama, Baldwin's imagination was stirred by the chicanery and wild speculation in banking and land deals that produced a chaos of litigation in that area. Thus, under a thinly disguised fictional cloak, he began reminiscing jovially about specific lawsuits and individuals entangled in them in a series of sketches published originally in the *Southern Literary Messenger* in 1852. When these were expanded into book form the following year, *The Flush Times* became an immediate best-seller, rivaling the *Adventures of Captain Simon Suggs* in popularity and reprinted editions during the forthcoming century. But, although he was pleased with the success of *Flush Times*, by 1854 Baldwin had turned his attention—and his pen—to more serious concerns. That year he not only completed his second book, *Party Leaders,* a collection of sober biographical sketches, but also left Alabama for California, where he soon established a brilliant record as both trial lawyer and associate justice of the California Supreme Court.[74] On the basis of that record, he could honestly feel that he had but reached the threshold of a great career as a historian when death cut short his ambition in 1864 at age forty-nine.

Tributes paid to Baldwin's memory by ranking members of the California bench and bar support the view that he possessed a great legal mind and an extraordinary capacity for sustained, serious effort. They were less impressed with the modest literary fame he had brought to California in 1854 than with the immense labors he had performed as a Supreme Court justice between 1858 and 1862—more than 400 court opinions dealing with intricate judicial problems, which, they said, were "models of clear and logical perception . . . characterized by grace of style, and scholarly learning."[75] Accordingly, to these jurists who knew Baldwin intimately at the height of his intellectual power, he deserved to be remembered not merely "with the rollicking humorists of the school to which Johnson J. Hooper . . . and Judge Longstreet belonged," but as a political theorist whose keen mind, had he lived another decade, would have produced a "philosophic history" of California. He might not have become the modern Thucydides of the War Between the States, as his wife hoped and urged, but neither would he have been relegated to the anthologies of frontier humor.

Ironically, however, Baldwin's reputation has suffered the fate his fellow justices lamented. His *Party Leaders* and judicial opinions have been forgotten, while his creative abilities, judged almost exclusively on the merits of *Flush Times,* are less highly valued than those of his fellow yarn spinners Hooper, Longstreet, Thorpe, and Thompson. Nevertheless, despite the urbane, essayistic style of the book, and despite its scarcity of direct discourse, primitive frontier rough-and-tumble behavior, and ring-tailed, roaring braggarts, some of the sketches are like the best of Irving's—still fresh and entertaining. And some of Baldwin's fictive characters are as vividly realized as the best of Hooper's: for example, Ovid Bolus, the consummate liar; Caesar ("Sar") Kasm, the wily old defense lawyer; Simon Suggs, Jr., a greater rogue than even his own father; and Sam Hele, Esq., a Johnsonian misogynist who rids his community of the undesirable Yankee schoolmarm, Miss Charity Woodley, by assuring her that the place is a veritable Sodom of total depravity. There are many laughs in the encounters ascribed to these distinctive individuals.

Thomas Bangs Thorpe: "The Big Bear of Arkansas"

Thomas Bangs Thorpe probably worked harder than any other writer of his time to publicize the life of the antebellum southwestern frontier. A native Yankee, Thorpe had gone south for his health in 1837 and established himself in Louisiana; he remained there for seventeen years, carrying on a threefold career as artist, newspaper publisher, and essayist, devoting both his brush and pen to the depiction of scenes and activities in the lush virgin territory of the Mississippi Delta. With his artist's eye keyed to the romantic tradition of Thomas Cole and John James Audubon—and with enthusiasm equal to theirs—Thorpe sought to record the wonders and terrors of nature in a section of America still wild and primitive; and in his numerous tales and sketches he strove to illustrate the impact upon the settler of its trackless forests and teeming wildlife. Beginning in July 1839 with his first sketch, "Tom Owen, the Bee-Hunter," published in Porter's *Spirit of the Times,* Thorpe wrote nearly fifty others during the next six years, most of which also appeared first in the *Spirit,* though a few were published in the *Knickerbocker Magazine.* Included among the former was the most famous of all his writings, "The Big Bear of Arkansas," which Porter promptly recognized as a masterpiece and subsequently used with great success as the title story in his own first collection of Southwest frontier yarns in 1845.[76]

Although Thorpe's writings about the backwoods did not begin to attract nationwide attention until after Porter's anthology appeared, his sketches had become familiar to readers of the *Spirit* throughout the early 1840s because virtually every time another of them turned up, Porter informed his readers that it was from the author of "Tom Owen, the Bee-Hunter" and "The Big Bear of Arkansas." Thus, within the two-year span following the original publication of "The Big Bear," at least fifteen more of Thorpe's pieces appeared in the *Spirit,* several of which were also destined to be anthologized repeatedly in later collections.[77] Later in 1843 Thorpe began an excellent series of twelve burlesques entitled "Letters from the Far West," which appeared originally in his own Louisiana newspaper, the *Concordia Intelligencer.* These were also quickly picked up by Porter and reprinted in the *Spirit.* Actually parodies of another writer's sobersided reports of a fantastic hunting expedition financed by a wealthy Scotsman, Sir William Drummond Steward, the "Letters" were written in a typically tall-tale manner, poking fun at the expedition through the untutored speech of a naive Irishman.[78]

Shortly after the resounding success of *The Big Bear of Arkansas, and Other Sketches* and of Hooper's Simon Suggs collection, the Philadelphia publishers Carey & Hart, largely through Porter's urging, agreed to publish Thorpe's first book, *Mysteries of the Backwoods* (1846). A collection of sixteen of his sketches drawn from the *Spirit's* files, the book was favorably reviewed by both northern and southern critics; but unfortunately, since it lacked all but three of Thorpe's more amusing character studies, it was far less successful than either Porter's or Hooper's collections. [79]

Disappointed with the slow sales of his *Mysteries*, Thorpe next hoped to capitalize on the outbreak of the Mexican War by writing stirring firsthand accounts of General Zachary Taylor's campaign on the Rio Grande. He persuaded Carey & Hart to publish these, along with his own drawings, in two small books entitled *Our Army on the Rio Grande* (1846) and *Our Army at Monterey* (1847). But to Thorpe's dismay these proved to be even less successful than his first book, so that when Carey & Hart refused to handle a third projected work on Zachary Taylor, he was obliged to turn to another publisher, D. Appleton & Company, whom he found more receptive. Under his old pen name, Tom Owen, the Bee-Hunter, Appleton published *The Taylor Anecdote Book: Anecdotes and Letters of Zachary Taylor* (1848), an undistinguished little miscellany containing a biographical sketch of Taylor and a grab-bag collection of very short but amusing war anecdotes, the whole thing clearly intended to enhance Taylor's image as a presidential candidate. Though highly praised in New York, the book added little to Thorpe's literary prestige or his hopes for political preferment. [80]

After 1848 Thorpe's writings about the Southwest virtually ceased until he returned to New York with his family in 1854, but now at last he attained the literary success he had sought so long. Beginning in the early 1850s he regularly published articles and short humor tales in the newly established *Harper's Magazine*, as well as in *Godey's, Graham's, Appleton's, Baldwin's Monthly,* and the *Spirit,* of which he became a part owner in 1859. [81] But Thorpe enjoyed his "finest achievement" in 1854 when, with the publication of his second collection, *The Hive of "The Bee-Hunter,"* he finally succeeded in bringing together under his own name the best of his sketches and magazine writings on the Southwest, including "The Big Bear of Arkansas." Carefully revised and with a renewed emphasis upon both the romantic wonders of nature and the realistic peculiarities of western characters, the book immediately placed its author among the nation's foremost literary figures of the period—"a bright and captivating American humorist, an effective stylist, and a discerning and truly creative reporter of scenery, social customs, and character in the Southwest." [82] *The Hive* was not only widely acclaimed in leading literary journals, but representative samples from it were included in such prestigious anthologies as

Thomas Halliburton's *Traits of American Humor* and the Duyckincks' *Cyclopaedia of American Literature.*[83] Later in 1854 Thorpe also published his only long work of fiction, *The Master's House; A Tale of Southern Life.* It too was well received in the North as an honest effort at a reform novel in a manner reminiscent of Stowe's *Uncle Tom's Cabin,* but its literary quality was clearly seen to be far inferior to that of Thorpe's humorous sketches.[84]

The critical judgment of that day has been sustained through nearly 150 years of America's literary development. Scholars now recognize "The Big Bear of Arkansas" not only as "the high point" of Thorpe's long career, but also as a literary masterpiece comparable to the best of Boccaccio's and Chaucer's tales. Despite its brevity and seeming artlessness, this story has become a literary touchstone; its title is the source of an entire group of humorists now called "The Big Bear School."[85] What gives "The Big Bear" such unique status is its extraordinary blending of contrasting styles, narrators, and characterization. It is a story within a story, introduced in the staid, almost pompous language of a gentleman passenger aboard a Mississippi River steamboat, who sets the stage for the appearance of Jim Doggett, the Big Bear himself. But once Jim announces his presence, he is allowed to take over.

Relating at his own pace and in his own colorful vernacular, Doggett tells his entranced auditors the saga of a great "unhuntable bear" that he had pursued for years and finally shot from a squatting position while engaged in his habitual morning defecation. A combination of the earthy and the fantastic, the story is perfectly told; for as scholarly critics are quick to point out, embedded at the heart of Thorpe's "wild, free narrative," yet so artfully concealed, is "the oldest joke in the world—the joke of being caught with one's britches down."[86] Small wonder that the original narrator, captivated by the mystery associated with Doggett's account of the great bear's death, concludes the tale in a tone of reverential awe. Nor should we wonder why, on the basis of this story alone, Thorpe's works, complex and artistic, are placed "among the finest productions of the frontier humorists and realists."[87]

Henry Clay Lewis: Louisiana "Swamp Doctor"

Henry Clay Lewis, youngest of the Southwest frontier humorists, remained a shadowy figure until the 1960s, his real identity concealed beneath the alias "Madison Tensas, M.D.," and his complete literary achievement only partially explored. Credit for the discovery of Lewis's significance as both a medical practitioner and frontier humorist belongs to John Q. Anderson, whose book *Louisiana Swamp Doctor* (1962) combines the known facts of Lewis's brief life with twenty-five of the sketches and one of the five poems he is known to have written and published. Many of the sketches, published originally in the *Spirit,* reappeared in Lewis's single book, *Odd Leaves from the Life of a Louisiana Swamp Doctor,* which was published in March 1850, just four months before his death. The book was favorably reviewed by the *Spirit* and several other national periodicals, though without disclosing its author's real name.[88]

Despite the brevity of his career and the paucity of his published writings, Lewis is now recognized, along with Thorpe, Hooper, and Longstreet, as one of the foremost contributors to the genre of virile frontier humor. Avowedly, says a recent scholar: "Even to begin to appreciate Lewis's work is to know what American literature may have suffered with his death by drowning when he was only twenty-five."[89] Such tribute is well deserved. For although the whole of Lewis's literary career is enclosed within the five-year span from 16 August 1845, when his first sketch, "Cupping on the Sternum," appeared in Porter's *Spirit,* to his unfortunate death in a bayou near his home in Richmond, Louisiana, on 5 August 1850, in the uniqueness of that brief career there is reflected all the volatility of his equally exciting career as a medical practitioner.

Born in 1825 and orphaned at six, Lewis became initiated in the world's way at the tender age of ten, when he ran away from his oldest brother's home in Cincinnati and drifted as a riverboat cabinboy as far as New Orleans. He lived for a while with another brother in Yazoo City, Mississippi, where he learned the hardship of cotton-field labor during the boom-and-bust period of the "flush times" before becoming apprenticed to a practicing physician in 1842 "for the purpose of studying medicine and eventually becoming a doctor himself."[90] During the next four years young Lewis, intensely ambitious, learned much more about human affairs, both as a medical apprentice in Yazoo City and as a student of medicine at the Louisville (Kentucky) Medical Institute, where he earned his M.D. at the age of twenty in March 1846.

He learned not only how to cope professionally with human ailments but also how to transform creatively into some very durable and funny writing what he had learned—or failed to learn—about the human psyche during the course of his medical training and subsequent brief practicing career. His most frequently anthologized sketch, written and sent to the *Spirit* while Lewis was still a medical student, quickly gained wide popularity when Porter included it in his anthology *A Quarter Race in Kentucky* the following year. "Cupping on the Sternum," still regarded as "surely one of the finest pieces of humor in all Southwestern writing,"[91] tells a hilarious but rather grotesque tale of the young medical apprentice whose inadequate knowledge of the Latin anatomical designation "sternum" (breastbone) results in an embarrassing misapplication of his preceptor's instructions "to cup and blister [a] Negro girl Chaney very freely over the *sternum;* . . . as she has inflammation of the lungs."[92]

Although this sketch was not included in Lewis's collection *Odd Leaves,* in several important ways it set the pattern and tone for most of the ones that followed it. First, it established the persona of the narrator, Lewis's most original artistic concept, a pseudoautobiographical figure, "Madison Tensas, M.D., the Louisiana Swamp Doctor." Unlike his youthful creator, the Swamp Doctor is skillfully characterized in every sketch as the remembering "I," a worldly, sophisticated old bachelor, fiftyish perhaps, who enjoys recalling some of the more hair-raising escapades and adventures of his early career. Lewis's artistry in maintaining the authenticity of this persona enables him to project, along with other frontier type characters, their ludicrous predicaments, and their realistic vernacular dialect, in an astonishing series of grotesque and savage encounters with an air of verisimilitude that would have satisfied Poe himself. Indeed, both the content and form of these sketches often call to mind the horrendous jokes and hoaxes in the more famous of Poe's tales; for much of the humor in them is associated with cruelty, violence, physical pain, and chaos—a foreshadowing, as it were, of the surrealistic "black" humor of the present.[93]

In "Stealing a Baby" (151–58), for example, the old bachelor sadly recalls the time when, as a medical student, his theft of a dead black infant he planned to dissect caused him to lose his girlfriend Lucy forever when the corpse slipped from beneath his cloak on a rain-soaked street. Similarly, he recalls in "The Curious Widow," (116–21) how he and his fellow students drove their nosy landlady to hysteria by surreptitiously trapping her with a "gift" package containing the deformed face carved from an albino Negro's cadaver; while in "Valerian and the Panther" (125–38) he recalls the occasion when, returning from his first case in the swamp to attend a young boy whose sleeping father had bitten off three fingers, he almost became a corpse himself. In this tale the grisly joke of the boy's injury, sustained while trying to steal a quid of tobacco from the father's open mouth, is topped by the grislier climax of the narrator's narrow escape from the panther's teeth. Death or the threat of death as a hideous joke is also the subject of "Cupping an Irishman" (158–64), in which a lazy patient is set afire; of "The Day of Judgment"(102–7), wherein a mule is set afire; of "A Rattlesnake on a Steamboat" (145–51), wherein a boastful sailor nearly drowns; and it is treated even more dramatically in "A Struggle for Life" (244–56), the last of the *Odd Leaves,* which tells of the narrator's nearly fatal encounter with a drunken and maddened Negro dwarf.

Even though cruelty and physical pain are prominent in these and other sketches, their treatment is nevertheless—in varying degrees—genuinely humorous. And owing to the relish with which Lewis's spokesman retells them, the best of his tales are, like Chaucer's, very funny indeed. Two more that have deservedly earned such high ranking are "A Tight Race Considerin" (91–102) and "The Indefatigable Bear Hunter" (233–44); both are superb examples of the mock-oral, framed story. In "A Tight Race" Lewis creates the background for an explosively bawdy climax by having his narrator call to mind the Hibbs family, whose only son he had once inadvertently shot in the rear while on a bear hunt. The accident prompted the young man to tell, in his own vernacular, all about his unconquerable mother's wild horseback race with the parson to the meeting-house—almost a dead heat, which she won, however, by stripping off all her clothing and being tossed naked "like a lam for the sacryfise, plum through the winder 'mongst the mourners" (102). Whereas bear hunting plays a minor strain in this story, in "The Indefatigable Bear Hunter," as in Thorpe's masterpiece, it is the entire dramatic saga of an indomitable hunter—Mik-hoo-tah—who, having lost one leg to a grizzly bear, slew another in hand-to-hand combat with the very wooden leg the Swamp Doctor had made for him. It is hardly surprising that these two tales, along with "Cupping on the Sternum," have reappeared in many anthologies since the 1850s.

George Washington Harris: Sut Lovingood

George Washington Harris, perhaps the most gifted of the southern frontier yarn spinners, also lived to publish, in 1867, only a single collection of his tales; it bore the rather cumbersome and confusing title *Sut Lovingood. Yarns Spun by a "Nat'ral Born Durn'd Fool*["]. *Warped and Wove for Public Wear.* But in the 1840s and early 1850s he published numerous others, which remained uncollected until nearly a century after his death.[94] Thanks largely to the superb characterization of his central figure, the twenty-four pieces in the *Sut Lovingood Yarns* have by now established Harris's literary reputation as first among his peers in the writing of antebellum comic fiction. And even though the critic Edmund Wilson once disparaged the *Yarns*—not altogether unjustly—as "by far the most repellent book of any real literary merit in American literature"[95]—it has been much admired by Mark Twain, William Faulkner, Robert Penn Warren, and Flannery O'Connor for the obvious reason that "Sut Lovingood is one of the liveliest vernacular characters in American literature before Huckleberry Finn."[96]

Like many of his contemporary yarnspinners, Harris first gained national attention in Porter's *Spirit of the Times* when his four short "Sporting Epistles from East Tennessee" appeared between January and September 1843.[97] Written in a conventional epistolary manner, these described such local activities as coon hunting, quarter racing, log rolling, and quilting, but with less originality than Hooper's "Chicken Man" yarn published the same year. Two years later, however, Harris's writing again appeared in the *Spirit,* this time in a form that prefigured his eventual mastery of the mock-oral tale: in "The Knob Dance—a Tennessee Frolic" he created a fictional narrator, Dick Harlan, to express in his own racy vernacular the sights and activities of the regional experience.

As a mélange of frenzied dancing, shouting, fighting, flirting, and drinking, "The Knob Dance" contained in embryo the basic elements that Harris would subsequently develop with more controlled artistry. Not surprisingly, Porter included this piece under the title "Dick Harlan's Tennessee Frolic" in his second anthology, *A Quarter Race in Kentucky,* published in 1846. Porter at that time hoped that Harris would become "a more regular correspondent of the *Spirit,*" but little more of his writing appeared in print until 1854, the year Sut Lovingood appeared, though in 1848 Porter rejected one of Harris's yarns because he found it "too highly seasoned to be published as it is."[98]

Sut first appeared to readers of the *Spirit* in a fantastic yarn entitled "Sut Lovingood's Daddy, Acting Horse," which tells of a mountain family so poor that the father, after the death of his horse Tickytail, has himself strapped to the plow in a futile effort to work the family corn patch. When he clumsily destroys a hornets' nest, the angry insects, Sut gloats, "kiver'd 'im es quick es yu cud kiver a sick pup wif a saddil blanket"(*Yarns,* 24); so poor Dad winds up nearly naked in the creek fighting them off. Told in Sut's own dialect, this yarn set the tone and pattern for the creation of a bizarre community of beings. During the next few years Harris rounded out his characterization of Sut in a series of hilarious escapades, employing him sometimes as a thinly disguised mouthpiece for satire against specific persons and institutions Harris himself disapproved of, but oftener and more successfully as a comic observer and recorder of his own and others' general follies and frailties. With more than a dozen new Sut yarns finished by the end of 1858, Harris was vainly seeking a publisher to bring them out in book form but had to wait nearly another full decade before he succeeded.

Of the forty-odd yarns devoted to Sut, all but a few of the best are contained in the 1867 collection, which opens with "Sut Lovingood's Daddy, Acting Horse" and closes with "Dad's Dog-School." Within the twenty-four yarns in the volume Harris creates a fantastically comic world, dominated by Sut the traditional fool, who serves as both narrator and hero (sometimes victim) of a crescendo of outrageous pranks and practical jokes contrived to evoke both snickers and guffaws. Sut's motive as prankster in most of the yarns is to discomfort his victims and to disrupt the community by avenging himself against a number of preachers, sheriffs, school commissioners, and other "depressing symbols of propriety, power, and authority."[99] In "Parson Bullen's Lizards," for example, Sut's method of revenge upon the hypocritical cleric effectively strips him of both his dignity and his clothing in the midst of his hell-fire sermon; while in "Bart Davis's Dance" another hard-shelled preacher suffers a well-deserved pummeling for casting gloom on the gaiety of the occasion. Again in "Sicily Burns's Wedding" angry bees from an overturned hive attack a blindfolded bull, turning a marriage feast into chaos: Sut's self-justified retribution for the loss of his luscious girl friend to the circuit-riding preacher, Ole Clapshaw. The sheer pranksterism in these and other yarns would be tedious were it not for the rich characterization of Sut and the relish in his manner of relating them.

Thus a recurrent theme, the joys and agonies of sexual incontinence, provides much of the comedy in Sut's ribald account of his escapades. Variations on the sexual theme, its physical attributes, appetites, and frustrations, flower in Sut's imagery, not only as he describes Sicily's charms and trickery in "Blown Up With Soda," but also in the social commentary he reserves for the role of women in general. As he warms up to his analysis of the values of quilting parties in "Mrs. Yardley's Quilting," his comments on the physical appeal of free dancing, fighting, and lovemaking—especially among old maids and widows—persuade the reader to share his gusto for stolen kisses in dark corners, the aroma of warm bodies, the taste of "mountain dew," and for the sounds of bare shuffling feet. Dancing, drinking, fighting, and lovemaking on the sly also figure prominently in "Bart Davis's Dance." In both of these yarns the sense of plenitude, fertility, and exuberance is repeatedly evoked through imagery suggesting unrestrained sexual potency and satisfaction. Yet Harris achieved his most ambitious—and funniest—treatment of these urges while developing his favorite antiauthoritarian theme in the last four of the *Yarns*. Entitled successively "Rare Ripe Garden Seed," "Contempt of Court—Almost," "Trapping a Sheriff," and "Dad's Dog School," the first three develop an elaborate account of cuckoldry and revenge, while the fourth provides a fitting climax to the destruction of Sut's father, surpassing in antic suggestiveness the opening tale of the book.

To reflect upon the impact of the *Yarns* is to recognize the Shakespearean flavor of action and folk. Old and young, ugly and handsome, mean and lovable, repellent and attractive are brought to life through Harris's tumbling metaphors and similes. And if one masters Sut's initially puzzling dialect in the process of hearing his voice, one cannot but appreciate also his highly sophisticated point of view and cool detachment. His ironic contemplation of the wolfish world in which pain and bitter disappointment are the human lot is at least partially offset by his self-indulgent but persistent quest for pleasures of the flesh. Sut's behavior, like that of Hooper's Simon Suggs and Lewis's Swamp Doctor, is set forth in terms of such uncouth speech and blithe unconcern, one scholar has noted, "as to seem a deliberate challenge to current tastes. . . . Sut Lovingood stands off in defiance of the genteel in literature."[100]

This, in fact, may well be the major contribution the Old Southwest humorists made to the renewed vitality of modern American literature, as Simms himself probably recognized when, cautiously reviewing some of their writings, he suggested that although they were "full of fun and spirit," the humor in them was of the sort that "the less we say the better."[101] Compared to Poe and Hawthorne, they added few if any significant innovations to the form of the short story; but in terms of content, action, characterization, and especially language, they opened vast new areas for realistic exploration.

SHIFTING TRENDS TOWARD REALISM IN FICTION

By the 1850s many other American writers beside the Southwest yarn spinners were producing short fiction for the magazines and newspapers; but the short story itself, as a distinct literary form, still lacked independent status and respectability. Few besides Poe, Hawthorne, and Simms had tried to define its aesthetic significance or grappled with its formal requirements. Even such terms as *tale, sketch, story,* and *short story* were being used interchangeably with little conscious concern for the principles of unity and brevity laid down by Poe. Nevertheless, as the magazines proliferated and their circulations expanded, they depended more and more on short fiction to keep their readers happy. Scarcely a popular weekly or monthly periodical failed to include four or five tales in each issue—a steady stream of short fiction, most of it written by women, which could be casually dismissed as "the sentimental Godey type."[1] Typical titles, selected at random from hundreds like them by a recent scholar, suggest the accuracy of Hawthorne's scornful reference to "a damned mob of scribbling women": "'A Gift From Heaven,' 'An Old Maid's First Love,' . . . 'Kissing With a Moustache,' 'Two Scenes in the Life of a City Belle.'"[2] But critical reaction to this type of fiction, expressed with growing concern throughout the decade of the "feminine fifties," presaged an important change in the development of the short-story form. A new genre, foreshadowing the realistic short story of the twentieth century, was slowly evolving from the decaying remnants of the type of tales and sketches perfected by Irving, Hawthorne, and Poe.[3]

The central weakness noted in most of this popular fiction was its sacrifice of aesthetic honesty for the sake of a spurious "message" of either oversimplified wish-fulfillment or chastening retribution. For the sake of extracting the reader's precious tear of feeling, characters and situations were exaggerated and diluted, and the resolutions of their problems were miraculously achieved. Thus, however seemingly realistic the setting of the conventional story, there was a serious flaw in its contradiction between

119

real dilemmas and false solutions, a contradiction that sacrificed unity to doctrine and destroyed its effectiveness. Hawthorne's scorn was directed toward precisely this sort of empty commercialism, and Melville's reaction to it while he was struggling to complete *Moby-Dick* was even more graphically recorded in one of his famous letters to his friend: "Dollars damn me," he cried. ". . . What I feel most moved to write, that is banned,— it will not pay. Yet, altogether, write the *other* way, I cannot. So the product is a final hash, and all my books are botches."[4]

Despite a continuing market demand for the conventional melodramatic, sentimental, or sensational type of story—a demand that would survive long years into the twentieth century in sleazy pulps such as *True Romances*—its popularity did not go unchallenged. Throughout the 1850s critics repeatedly deplored the excesses of romanticized tales and called for a species of fiction that would deal more convincingly with issues of contemporary life. They wished to see stories that would not only truthfully mirror the surface features of the actual world but would also probe beneath the surface and explore the mysteries and ambiguities of human behavior. They were demanding a type of fiction that would convey an undercurrent of genuine significance, a basic theme or meaning reflecting what Hawthorne had called "truths of the human heart." Stories that derived their effects simply from cleverly contrived plots, implausible situations, and pasteboard characters would no longer suffice, though authors might still have to soften or conceal their harshest meanings within an acceptably genteel style.

Melville had touched upon one aspect of this problem when, in his somewhat overenthusiastic review of *Mosses from an Old Manse,* he drew a striking analogy between Shakespeare's and Hawthorne's alleged techniques of concealment. Readers who regarded Shakespeare "as a mere man of Richard-the-Third humps and Macbeth daggers," he wrote, were very much mistaken; for "it is those deep far-away things in him; short, quick probings at the very axis of reality;—those are the things that make Shakspeare, Shakspeare. Through the mouths of the dark characters of Hamlet, Timon, Lear, and Iago, he craftily says, or sometimes insinuates the things which we feel to be so terrifically true, that it were all but madness for any good man, in his own proper character, to utter, or even hint of them."[5] Hawthorne shared this ability to deceive "the superficial skimmer of pages," Melville declared, as was evident in his skillful method of masking a dark concern with original sin beneath such innocent titles as "Young Goodman Brown" and "A Select Party," which careless readers simply found quaint. Yet, for all their subtlety, even Hawthorne's best tales and sketches, Melville wrote on another occasion, lacked a sufficient roundness and solidity—"a plump sphericity."[6]

Melville's dissatisfaction with the thinness of characterization in Hawthorne's tales is another sign of shifting values in the creation of fiction at midcentury. By that time Hawthorne himself, as we have seen, disparaged the pallid tameness and lack of solid substance in his early tales. They reminded him of pale-tinted flowers "that blossomed in too retired a shade"; even those in which he had intended to draw pictures of actual life, he said, turned out to be allegories bereft of flesh and blood, passion, pathos, and humor. His harsh self-criticism was evidently not altogether ironic, for only the year before while composing a reminiscence of his Salem Custom-House experiences as an introduction to *The Scarlet Letter,* he spoke wistfully of his inability to exploit the rich "materiality of this daily life pressing so intrusively upon me," instead of trying feebly to evoke "the semblance of a world out of airy matter." It would have been wiser, he felt, to attempt to transform the living present into viable fiction, but his "brain wanted the insight and [his] hand the cunning to transcribe it."[7] And not many years later, after three more moderately successful longer works, Hawthorne underscored this shifting of taste by confessing that the kind of fiction he admired most, though unable to write it himself, could be seen in Anthony Trollope's novels: "solid and substantial, written on the strength of beef and through the inspiration of ale, and just as real as if some giant had hewn a great lump out of the earth and put it under a glass case, with all its inhabitants going about their daily business."[8]

This earthiness and solidity had been gradually gaining respectability during the preceding decade, partly as a result of the spreading popularity of the humorous tall tales featured at first in Porter's *Spirit of the Times* and later reissued in separate collections published by Carey & Hart, and partly as a result of changing literary fashions from abroad. Stories such as Thorpe's "Big Bear of Arkansas" and the escapades of Hooper's Simon Suggs marked a trend toward realism because, notwithstanding the obvious exaggeration of characters and action, they did suggest the actual locus of a specific culture. The contrast between the colloquial speech of a Jim Doggett or a Suggs and the drier, more urbane expression of the frame narrator sounded authentic and true to life. As opposed to the self-assurance of the omniscient author in the typical sentimental tale, allowing for the most implausible reversals of fortune, the denouement in a well-told Southwest humor tale oftener seemed to be a model of consistency, the logical culmination of developments within the structure of the narrative. Thus, in a short notice of Hooper's second volume, *The Widow Rugby's*

Husband: A Sight of the Ugly Man & Other Tales of Alabama, one critic could praise it as being among the best of "a singularly numerous collection of volumes of humorous literature of the South, . . . a series of very lively stories, roughly and adroitly told, and certainly compelling the broad grin of the reader."[9] No matter how ludicrous or outrageous the speech and actions of primitive folk in these yarns, the narratives themselves appealed strongly to many readers and critics alike because they seemed "natural," a term now showing up with increasing frequency in critical parlance.

On a more serious level, the naturalness this critic praised in Hooper's tales and sketches was also found noteworthy in the fiction of the British novelist Thackeray. The writer of an essay published a few months earlier in the same journal gratefully observed in Thackeray's novels a sign "that really preposterous works of fiction are rapidly going out of date." Stressing the point that characters and action in *Vanity Fair* and *Pendennis,* for example, are "natural," recognizable, not forced, he asked rhetorically: "What can be more natural . . . than that we should joy in meeting upon paper, men, women and children like those we know, and are familiar with, in everyday life."[10] Such approval of Thackeray's literary skill calls to mind Hawthorne's fondness for Trollope's fiction, though Hawthorne's simile of the giant potter's lump of earth under a glass case also suggests Melville's subtler requirement that in works of fiction one should "look not only for more entertainment, but, at bottom, even for more reality, than real life itself can show."[11]

Uttered in 1857, Melville's plea merely echoes what other critics of the decade had been demanding: fiction that would embody both the recognizable surface features of everyday life and basic themes faithfully depicting human motives and action. Implicitly or explicitly, these critics had been urging repeatedly two of Poe's critical principles: his concept of the "single effect"—not just as an artificial device for achieving a tightly unified, conventional plot, but rather as a means toward evoking from the reader a dominant impression based on the tale's undercurrent of significance; and the element that Poe had often designated as "vraisemblance"—that is, verisimilitude, the ability to make extraordinary events seem convincing by depicting them within a recognizable context of actual life. Consciously or not, accordingly, the critics were gradually establishing norms for the new variety of short fiction: "while simultaneously retaining the single-effect concept and the necessity of implied significance, [they] were encouraging the modification of the conventional tale. If they also advocated a realistic world of fiction, then they had, more or less unintentionally, established basic conditions suitable for the development of the new genre."[12]

That Melville could accommodate his fiction to this new set of conditions in the 1850s should not surprise anyone familiar with his frustrating career as a writer of long philosophical romances of the sea in the 1840s. Beginning with *Typee* (1846) and *Omoo* (1847), his first commercial successes, Melville had tried in vain to win the endorsement of a wide range of readers, but his risqué passages involving sexual encounters, as well as his blatant criticism of such cherished institutions as the Protestant missionary societies, flouted prevailing canons of taste and drew fire from some prominent critics. Horace Greeley, for example, asserted that Melville's tone was bad, if not morally diseased; and eventually this hostile attitude became a "majority opinion about Melville" as he strove futilely in successive books to impose his views of the creative process upon an apathetic public. The harder he tried to elevate a simple episodic narrative of adventure into a vehicle for digressive reflection and commentary, the more he alienated his readers. As he openly and repeatedly challenged their capacity to apprehend imaginative truth or to accept other than conventional, platitudinous beliefs, hostility toward his writings intensified.[13] Thus, to counteract such hostility, well before 1850 Melville began experimenting with a technique of concealment similar to Poe's and Hawthorne's—disguising the real inner meanings in his fiction beneath a surface layer of exciting adventure.

Melville's most remarkable achievement in the welding together of factual and fictitious material would be unveiled in his great masterpiece, *Moby-Dick,* which has inspired more intensive critical study during this century than any other single American narrative. And among its many brilliant foreshadowings of future literary developments, one in particular that points directly to the realistic short story of the next generation is a seventeen-page narrative entitled "The Town-Ho's Story" (chapter 54). In substance a tale of hatred and vengeance between two strong-willed characters, Steelkit and Radney, "The Town-Ho's Story" fits neatly into the overall structure of *Moby-Dick* as one of the many terrifying adventures brought to a climax by the violent might of the great white whale. But in the manner of its telling, the narrative is clearly a modification, perhaps even a parody, of the tall-tale form seen in "The Big Bear of Arkansas," a form called "the told story," which achieves a subtly heightened second climax through the narrator's recapitulation of events surrounding his original telling of the tale in a different setting many years before. Melville's craftsmanship in "The Town-Ho's Story" is thus all the more remarkable in that "submitting his talent for the first time to the conventions of as well-established and technically advanced a literary genre as then existed for his use, [he] for the first time produced a technically finished and self-contained work of narrative invention. In structure it conforms to the popular 'frame' technique of story-telling, the occasion of the telling being used at the beginning and end to set off the main line of action."[14]

The artistry that Melville displayed in "The Town-Ho's Story" and in numerous scenes in *White-Jacket* at the outset of the 1850s was a portent of the still more impressive techniques he would apply to the writing of the short fiction later in the decade. His mimetic characterizations and uncanny manipulation of factual details as a means of probing beneath the surface of everyday reality marked a further shifting toward modern realism in the art of fiction, just as Hawthorne's effort to explore a "neutral territory . . . where the Actual and the Imaginary may meet" represented an advance over Poe's more exotic concept of verisimilitude. But toward the end of the 1840s and even more noticeably by the middle 1850s the same shifting of values can be seen accelerating in the writings of less prominent writers, particularly in New England and New York. Writers like Fitz-James O'-Brien and Fitz-Hugh Ludlow were beginning to exploit the hazards and pitfalls of urban life by relying on recognizably specific events and localities while others like Harriet Beecher Stowe and Rose Terry Cooke were launching into the realm of local-color regionalism, a movement that would flourish briskly throughout the nation during the next three decades. By the 1850s the modern realistic short story as an independent genre in the United States had clearly begun to emerge.

Notes and References

Types of Magazine Short Fiction before 1820

1. *Monthly Miscellany and Vermont Magazine* 1, no. 2 (May 1794):64–65; no. 3 (June 1794):133–35. The heading indicates that the story was reprinted from the *American Museum,* which is characterized by Frank Luther Mott as "the first successful American magazine." see *A History of American Magazines* (Cambridge, Mass., 1939), 1:100–103. Other data on "Azakia" appear in Jack B. Moore, *Native Elements in American Magazine Short Fiction: 1741–1800* (Chapel Hill, 1963), pp. 21–25, 255.

2. Quoted in Mott, *History,* 1:23.

3. For samples of these see ibid., pp. 42–44, 96, 109.

4. Lyle H. Wright, "A Statistical Survey of American Fiction, 1774–1850," *Huntington Library Quarterly* 2 (April 1939):311; cited in Alexander Cowie, *The Rise of the American Novel* (New York: American Book Co., 1951), pp. 4, 755.

5. Mott, *History,* 1:24.

6. Ibid., pp. 41–44, 120–24, 173–75. See also Moore, *Native Elements,* pp. 27, 245–54.

7. Quoted in Mott, *History,* 1:174. Mott shows, however, that after 1825 some American critics were defending "moral fiction" as "one of the most important vehicles through which good and virtuous sentiments can be diffused."

8. These were published respectively in the *Gentleman and Ladies Town & Country Magazine* 1 (August, September, December 1784):135–36, 138–42, 183–84, 596–99; *Columbian Museum* 3 (December 1789):736–39; *Massachusetts Magazine* 1 (September 1789):536–38; 3 (June, July, August 1791):353–55, 425–26, 471–72; *New York Magazine* 1 (January 1790):22–23; and *New York Weekly Magazine* 1 (April 1796):315.

9. Moore, *Native Elements,* pp. 253–54.

10. "The Custom House," in *The Scarlet Letter,* Norton Critical Edition, ed. Sculley Bradley et al. (New York: Norton, 1978), p. 31.

11. William Charvat, *Origins of American Critical Thought: 1810–1835* (Philadelphia: University of Pennsylvania, 1936), pp. 160–61.

12. *Boston Magazine* 1 (February 1784): 127–29.

13. Ibid., 3 (May 1786):211–13.

14. *Gentleman and Lady's Town and Country Magazine* 6 (June 1789):251–52.

15. *Massachusetts Magazine* 7 (November 1795):467–73. Half a dozen more tales of the same sort appeared in other New York and Philadelphia magazines within the next two years.

16. *Boston Magazine* 3 (June 1786):235–37, and see "Florio," *Massachusetts Magazine* 2 (January 1790): 44–46.

17. *Gentleman and Lady's Town and Country Magazine* 1 (September 1784):144–46; 6 (February 1789):19–21; 6 (April 1789):115–18; 6 (October and November 1789):483–85, 520–21; and *Massachusetts Magazine* 4 (December 1792):718–19.

18. The literary values of both these stories are discussed at some length in Moore, *Native Elements,* pp. 84–88, 213–15. A more detailed analysis of "The Captain's Wife" may also be found in Moore's later article, "'The Captain's Wife': A Native Short Story Before Irving," *Studies in Short Fiction* 1, no. 2 (Winter 1964):103–6.

19. Moore, "A Native Story" p. 106. For a dissenting view that takes strong issue with both Moore's interpretation and mine, the reader may consult a later article in the same journal by John Merren entitled "The Resolute Wife, or a Hazard of New Criticism," *Studies in Short Fiction* 15, no. 3 (Summer 1978):291–300. Merren contends that "Ruricolla's contributions to this story are minimal."

20. Moore demonstrates that many of the stories in each of the six categories mentioned in his study made more than a merely incidental use of native elements, and that at least a few of them, like "The Captain's Wife," were reasonably well constructed. Among the scores of Indian tales he examined, even the sentimentalized or comic ones, he found "a core of work . . . that in some way makes real and effective use of the Indian." Similarly, many of the stories involving Negroes presented facts and tendencies common to relationships between whites and blacks and also "recorded the tragedy of Negro experience . . . in its violence and injustice." Even the most popular types of sentimental stories often combined foreign plots and stereotypes "with American materials and experiences to create a kind of native fiction." The key phrase here is "a kind of native fiction," since the authentic American origin of most of these stories has yet to be established. See *Native Elements,* pp. 41, 71, 80–81, 103, 150, 160, 176, 225–28.

21. "Azakia" was first published in *American Museum* 6 (September 1789):193–98; it was later reprinted in *Vermont Magazine* 2 (May 1794):62–63, and (June 1794):134–36; still later it was again reprinted in *New York Weekly Magazine* (January 1797):31–37. Clearly one of the more popular tales of the period, "Azakia" is summarized in Moore, *Native Elements,* pp. 21–25, and is treated at greater length by him in a more recent article, "Making Indians Early: The Worth of 'Azakia,'" *Studies in Short Fiction* 13, no. 1 (Winter 1976):51–60. Further comment on his interpretation appears below in note 24.

22. These three stories, respectively, appeared in *Theologica Magazine* 2 (September-October 1796): 17–20; *Gentleman and Lady's Town and Country Magazine* 1 (June 1789–January 1790):227–29, 286–87, 349–52, 418–21, 467–78, 585–89, 626–30; and *New York Magazine* 3 (January-April 1792):36–39, 92–95, 169–72, 228–31.

23. Moore, *Native Elements,* p. 21.

24. *Vermont Magazine* 2 (June 1794):135. It is now known that the skillful development of Azakia as "one of the most interesting young women in early fiction" was the work of an eighteenth-century French writer, whose original story was published in 1765, later translated into English, and twice reprinted in England's *Universal Magazine.* Thus "it seems likely that this was the source of the American reprintings." See Edward W. Pitcher, "A Note on 'Azakia': Jack B. Moore's 'Early American Story,'" *Studies in Short Fiction* 14, no. 4 (Fall 1977):395–96. Pitcher's disclosures underscore the difficulties of trying to establish an exact canon of early original American stories. As he points out, this cannot be done until all the reprinted stories from British and other European magazines have been accounted for.

25. An extended discussion of this story and its theological background in New England appears in Moore, *Native Elements,* pp. 88–101.

26. See Percy Boynton, *Literature in American Life* (Boston: Ginn, 1936), p. 195; also Moore, *Native Elements,* pp. 114–27. Many similar tales are discussed in Herbert Ross Brown's *The Sentimental Novel in America, 1789–1860* (Durham, N.C.: Duke University Press, 1940).

27. Moore, *Native Elements,* p. 252.

28. C. Hugh Holman, *A Handbook to Literature* (New York: Odyssey, 1972), p. 514.

29. For brief but trustworthy discussions of romanticism and the development of short fiction in France, see Albert Joseph George, *The Development of French Romanticism* (Syracuse, N.Y., 1955) and *Short Fiction in France, 1800–1850* (Syracuse, N.Y., 1964). Further information on Russian writers of the period may be found in Janko Larvin, *Russian Writers: Their Lives and Literature* (New York: Van Nostrand, 1954). The most helpful brief study of German literary influence in America is available in Henry A. Pochman, *German Culture in America* (Madison, 1961). His two chapters on "Early American Fiction" and "Germanic Materials and Motifs in the Short Story," pp. 358–408, are of particular interest.

30. *Boston Weekly* 1 (3 and 10 November 1802):9, 14; (4 December 1802):22–23; (22 January and 5, 12, 19 February 1803):53–54, 64, 68, 72; and (22 October 1803):209.

31. Ibid., 1, 3d series (March 1813):239.

32. For example, "Emily Hammond," *Port Folio* 3 (10 and 17 January 1807):19–21, 39–41; "The Story of Amelia Howard," *Port Folio* 3, 2d series (May 1810):365-70; "Hamet, A Tale," *Port Folio* 8, 2d series (August 1812):184–89; and "Tales of a Parrot," *Port Folio* 8 (November 1812):499–515.

33. Ibid., 4; 3d series (November and December 1814):466–80; 5 (January 1815):38–55.

34. "Observations on English and American Literature," ibid., pp. 38–55.

35. See ibid., p. 101; also "Gambling and Dissipation," ibid., pp. 162–65; "The Starling: A Novel in Miniature," *Port Folio* 3, 5th series (February 1817):147–52; "Fashion: an Allegory," ibid., pp. 159–62; and "The Adventures of a One Dollar Note," ibid., pp. 242–47.

36. *Baltimore Repertory* 4, 5th series (November 1817): 395–99.

37. The original publication of this sketch, if prior to its appearance in the *Baltimore Repertory* 1, no. 1 (January 1811): 35–41, is apparently shrouded in mystery. Many other variant versions may be found in John Donald Wade's *Augustus Baldwin Longstreet* (Athens: University of Georgia Press, 1969), pp. 178–80; and also in B. R. McElderry's introduction to his edition of *Georgia Scenes* (New York: Sagamore Press, 1957).

38. *Port Folio* 11, no. 1 (March 1821):131–36.

39. The full title of this feature is "Devoted to Politicks and Belles Lettres"; the magazine ran from January 1814 to February 1815.

40. *Boston Weekly Magazine* 1 (8, 15, 22 March):87, 90, 94; (19, 26 April):109, 113; (3, 10 May):117, 121.

41. *Weekly Magazine and Ladies Miscellany* 1, no. 35 (14 November 1824):135–36. Other interesting titles in this periodical included "Selden and Edwina," "Alonzo and Maria," "Caleb and Matilda: An American Tale," and "The Dream of Love," a prize story for which the author, Charles Ludlow of Richmond, won $20 (27 March, 3 April 1824):7, 9; (17, 24 April, 1 May):17, 19, 21–22; (27 November):144; and (18 December):156–57.

42. *Belles-Lettres Repository* 1, no. 1 (1 May 1819):226–30; 3 (15 May 1820):48–49; (15 June 1820):118–22.

43. *Western Review* 1 (May 1820):244–54.

44. Ibid., p. 314.

45. *New York Journal and Belles-Lettres Repository* 2 (1 March 1820):349–52. See also the *New England Galaxy* 1, no. 17 (6 February 1818):2–3.

46. *New England Galaxy* 7, 32 (10 September 1824). The full title of the story is "Some Account of Peter Rugg, the Missing Man, Late of Boston, New England. In a Letter to Mr. Herman Krauff." The "letter" was signed by "Jonathan Dunwell" and dated New York, 28 August 1824. A brief discussion of the story is given in F. L. Pattee, *The Development of the American Short Story* (New York, 1923), pp. 37–39.

Irving Sets the Pattern

1. Pattee, *Development of the Short Story in America*, p. 1.

2. William Charvat, *The Profession of Authorship in America* (Columbus, Ohio, 1968), p. 29.

3. S. T. Williams, *The Life of Washington Irving,* 2 vols. (New York, 1935), 1:160–91. See also Williams, *Irving's Sketch Book Notes* (New Haven: Yale University Press, 1927); Pochmann, *German Culture in America,* pp. 367–81, 696; and Pochmann, *Washington Irving: Representative Selections* (New York: American Book Company, 1934), pp. lx–lxxxiv.

4. Charvat, *Profession,* pp. 32–34. Charvat notes that the commercial boom for fiction writers had begun in England just a few years earlier when, with the publication of *Waverley* in 1814, Scott "had evolved a formula for successful fiction which had earned him an average of £10,000 for the next five years (in modern values totaling, possibly, a quarter of a million dollars)."

5. Ben Harris McClary, *Washington Irving and the House of Murray* (Knoxville, 1969), introduction and chapters 1 and 2, pp. xxi–xlv, 3–39. McClary points out that in August 1820 Irving sold to Murray the doubtfully valid British copyright to *The Sketch Book* for two hundred and fifty guineas (pp. 25, 215).

6. Ibid., p. 35.

7. Perry Miller, ed. *The Sketch Book* (New York, 1961), afterword, pp. 373–75.

8. See parallels worked out in Pochmann, *German Culture in America,* pp. 367–71, 697–98.

9. W. L. Hedges, *Washington Irving: An American Study* (Baltimore, 1965), p. 161. Hedges adds that the protagonists in all the sketches "tend to be variations of, or foils to, the personality of the Crayonesque observer of the author behind the story."

10. Thomas Moore, *Memoirs, Journal, and Correspondence,* ed. Lord John Russell, 8 vols. (London: Longman, Brown, Green & Longmans, 1853), 3:211. Quoted in McClary, *Washington Irving,* pp. 35–36.

11. See Williams's appendix in *Life,* 2:280–86, for details on Irving's sources.

12. "I would have it understood that I am not writing a novel, and have nothing of intricate plot or marvelous adventure to promise the reader." *Bracebridge Hall, The Complete Works of Washington Irving* (Boston: Twayne Publishers, 1977), 9:9. Further page references to this volume are given in parentheses in the text. For an analysis of the structure of *Bracebridge Hall* and of its relationship to *The Sketch Book* see Hedges, *Washington Irving,* pp. 164–70.

13. McClary, *Washington Irving,* pp. 41–45.

14. Williams, *Life,* 1:211–14.

15. Hedges, *Washington Irving,* pp. 171–74.

16. Ibid., p. 178. Hedges draws here an illuminating comparison between Irving's and de Tocqueville's views on the subject of gravity among free peoples.

17. On this point see ibid., p. 183.

18. Ibid., p. 186.

19. Ibid., p. 189.

20. For a detailed summary of these unfavorable criticisms see Williams, *Life,* 1:273–79, 2:294–96. Notable exceptions to these criticisms were Poe's and

Longfellow's, both of whom applauded *Tales of a Traveller,* as did a number of German critics. See Williams, *Life,* 2:295–96.

21. McClary, *Washington Irving,* pp. 55–67.

22. *Letters of Washington Irving to Henry Brevoort,* ed. George S. Helman, 2 vols. (New York: G. P. Putnam's Sons, 1918), 2:398–99.

23. Pierre M. Irving, *The Life and Letters of Washington Irving,* 3 vols. (New York: G. P. Putnam's Sons, 1869), 2:166.

24. *Letters to Brevoort,* 2:399.

25. Hedges, *Washington Irving,* p. 194.

26. Williams, *Life,* 1:274.

27. Hedges, *Washington Irving,* p. 195. Hedges argues convincingly that Poe's abortive "Tales of the Folio Club" might have been very similar in design to Irving's *Tales of a Traveller* if he had succeeded in publishing them as a book (pp. 200–204).

28. *The Works of Washington Irving* (New York: George P. Putnam, 1860), p. vii, x. Further page references to this volume are given in parentheses in the text.

29. Hedges, *Washington Irving,* p. 200.

30. Ibid., p. 199.

31. Ibid., p. 216.

32. In a long letter of 7 December 1824, written to his nephew Pierre after the disappointing reception of the *Tales,* Irving warned against the precarious career of the professional writer. Pierre M. Irving, *Life and Letters,* 2:59.

Hawthorne's Short Fiction

1. *The Snow Image And Uncollected Tales,* in *The Centenary Edition of the Works of Nathaniel Hawthorne,* ed. William Charvat et al. (Columbus: Ohio State University Press, 1963), 11:3–6. Further page references to the contents of this volume will appear in the text parenthetically as *Works,* 11.

2. The most recent and, in many respects, the clearest discussion of this complicated phase of Hawthorne's apprenticeship appears in Nina Baym, *The Shape of Hawthorne's Career* (Ithaca and London, 1976), pp. 19–52.

3. *Works,* 9:3–7.

4. See letters to Longfellow and Duyckinck quoted in J. Donald Crowley's article "The Unity of Hawthorne's Twice-Told Tales," *Studies in American Fiction* 1, no. 1 (Spring 1973):51, 58; also the concluding paragraph of Hawthorne's sketch "The Old Manse," in *Mosses,* in *Works,* 10:34–35.

5. Baym, *Shape,* p. 46. Her detailed account of the presumed makeup of the collection differs slightly from earlier accounts by Adkins and Weber, both of whom she cites, pp. 25, 40.

6. Crowley, "Unity," p. 50.

7. Crowley, "The Artist as Mediator: The Rationale of Hawthorne's Large-scale Revisions in His Collected Tales and Sketches," in *Melville and Hawthorne in the Berkshires* (Kent, Ohio, 1968), pp. 79–87. Crowley concludes that Hawthorne "habitually viewed his work 'rhetorically': that is to say, in relation to his audience, an audience with grave misgivings about fiction, some of them similar to his own. Nearly all of his large-scale revisions indicate his desire to mediate between his art and his audience, to guarantee the value of his fiction by virtue of his own reliability as narrator" (ibid., p. 87).

8. Cf. "Historical Commentary," in *Works*, 9:503–14.

9. Nina Baym's assertion that Hawthorne made too many concessions to an imaginary audience whose demands he misjudged finds support in her comparison of strengths and weaknesses in both the 1837 and the expanded 1842 editions of *Twice-Told Tales*. Only about four or five of the original eighteen tales reappear frequently in modern anthologies, while even fewer of those included in the later second volume are now noticed. Those that have survived the test of time most successfully are "The Gray Champion," "The Minister's Black Veil," "The May-Pole of Merry Mount," and "The Gentle Boy" from the first volume; and "The Ambitious Guest," "Peter Goldthwaite's Treasure," and "Endicott and the Red Cross" from the second group. See Baym, *Shape*, pp. 79–81.

10. Even Crowley admits that the collection of tales and sketches in this second volume of the *Twice-Told Tales* is demonstrably weaker and less successfully unified than that of the first volume. See Crowley, "Unity," pp. 53–55.

11. Baym, *Shape*, p. 81.

12. A strong case for the imaginative scope as well as the technical and stylistic mastery of this work is made by Baym. It is, she says, an "achievement of a very high order, marked by fluency, ease, and a successfully executed frame of considerable complexity that is organically tied to the narrative." See ibid., pp. 88–98.

13. John J. McDonald, "'The Old Manse' and Its Mosses: The Inception and Development of *Mosses from an Old Manse*," *Texas Studies in Language and Literature* 16, no. 1 (Spring 1974):82.

14. Quoted in ibid., p. 80.

15. Quoted in ibid., p. 91–92. See also pp. 91–98, and J. D. Crowley's "Historical Commentary" in *Works*, 10:501–10, for detailed data on Hawthorne's struggle to make ends meet during this period.

16. See McDonald, "'The Old Manse' and Its Mosses," pp. 86–87 for Hawthorne's own suggested table of contents as compared with the final selections.

17. Ibid., pp. 101, 103. When a second edition of the *Mosses* was published in 1854, three more pieces were added—"Feathertop," first published in 1852, to complete volume 1; and two sets of desultory sketches dating from the early 1830s entitled "Passages from a Relinquished Work" and "Sketches from Memory" to fill out volume 2—thus making the collection as a whole even less unified than the first edition.

18. In her detailed analysis of the changing Hawthorne persona through the later *Mosses* selections (pp. 98–116), Baym senses in the author himself a continuing uncertainty and lack of control over his material because, she feels, his "approach to the domain of imagination is as equivocal as ever" (p. 102). See, for example, her illuminating comparison between "Drowne's Wooden Image" and "The Artist of the Beautiful" (p. 112).

19. McDonald, "'The Old Manse' and Its Mosses," pp. 103, 108.

20. See, for example, *Studies in Short Fiction, College English, Nineteenth-Century Fiction, New England Quarterly, Modern Language Quarterly*.

21. Crowley, "Historical Commentary," in *Works*, 10:527. The remainder of this essay provides an excellent summary of contemporary critical reaction to specific tales and sketches in the collection as well as of the sharply contrasting opinions of their merits voiced by Poe and Melville (pp. 527–35). Poe's essay, entitled "Tale Writing—Nathaniel Hawthorne" appeared in *Godey's Lady's Book* in November 1847 and was in the main an updating of his review of *Twice-Told Tales*, which had appeared in *Graham's Magazine* in 1842. Melville's essay, entitled "Hawthorne and His Mosses," was published in two successive issues of the *Literary World*, 17 and 24 August 1850.

22. Quoted in ibid., p. 532.

23. A recent reprinting of Melville's essay can be found in the anthology *American Literature: The Makers and the Making* (New York: St. Martin's Press, 1973), 1:834–42. The anthology is edited by Cleanth Brooks, R. W. B. Lewis, and Robert Penn Warren. The quoted statements above appear on pp. 836–37 and 841.

24. Crowley, *Works*, 10:535–36.

25. Hawthorne's final short fiction effort, "Feathertop," a satirical exposé of the "stuffed shirt" written in the fall of 1851, was first published the following winter, in January 1852, hence too late to be included in *The Snow Image*. Crowley explains that the ordering of tales in this volume was due largely to the delay Hawthorne's publishers encountered in trying to locate some of his earliest anonymous pieces, which had appeared originally in the *Token* and other New England magazines. "Major Molineux" and "Wives of the Dead," both dating from 1832, were the last of the manuscripts delivered to the printer. See *Works*, 11:391–92.

26. Crowley, *Works*, 11:394. For a clarification of the problem of authenticating Hawthorne's unacknowledged tales and sketches, see ibid., pp. 400–409. Alphabetical and chronological listings of the complete tales are given on pp. 479–88.

27. *Works*, 11:4.

28. Terence Martin, *Nathaniel Hawthorne* (New York, 1965), p. 21.

29. *Works*, 11:279–80.

30. See Hyatt Waggoner, *Hawthorne: A Critical Study* (Cambridge, Mass, 1955), p. 82. Waggoner offers a brilliant critical analysis of both the structure and meaning of this story, as well as of its structural similarity to others among Haw-

thorne's renowned early tales, in his third chapter, "The Discovery of Meaning," pp. 78–92.

31. For two perceptive readings of this tale, see Daniel Hoffman's "Yankee Bumpkin and Scapegoat King," in *Form and Fable in American Fiction* (New York, 1961), pp. 113–25; and R. W. B. Lewis's in *American Literature: The Makers and the Making,* 1:440–44.

32. Herman Melville, "Hawthorne and His Mosses," reprinted in *American Literature: The Makers and the Making,* 1:841.

33. Henry James, *Hawthorne,* (Ithaca: Cornell University Press reprint, 1963), p. 81. Mark Van Doren observed that this remarkable statement "illuminates James more than it does Hawthorne." See *The Best of Hawthorne* (New York: Ronald Press, 1951), p. 416.

34. *Works,* 10:74, 75, 86–89 passim.

35. Michael J. Colacurcio, "Visible Sanctity and Specter Evidence: The Moral World of Hawthorne's 'Young Goodman Brown,'" *Essex Institute Historical Collections* 110 (1974):298. Besides listing and comparing the views of more than a dozen other critical commentaries on "Young Goodman Brown," this analysis scrutinizes not only the language but also every meaningful detail in the course of Brown's progress from beginning to end of the tale, relating each of them to prevailing beliefs of the period. The essay provides an excellent insight into Hawthorne's artistic grasp of his subject and helps to show why the story is one of his greatest.

36. For an admirable discussion of the literary background and implications of this tale, see Hoffman's *Form and Fable in American Fiction,* chapter 7: "The Maypole of Merry Mount and the Folklore of Love," pp. 126–48.

37. *Works,* 9:62–67 passim.

38. Ibid., p. 67.

39. Ibid., p. 52.

40. Ibid., 10:268–83.

41. Ibid., 11:161–69.

42. Ibid., 10:56.

43. Ibid., pp. 91–93.

44. Baym, *Shape,* pp. 105–6. In "The Birth-mark," "Hawthorne examines more specifically than he had done before the sexual problems that underlie the protagonist's social alienation, as well as the sexual reasons for his inability to take the help offered by the woman. Critics have found adumbrations of the motif of rejection of the female in such stories as 'Roger Malvin's Burial,' 'Young Goodman Brown,' and 'The Minister's Black Veil,' but this is the first instance in which Hawthorne identifies the male obsession overtly with a revulsion against women and specifically with a revulsion against her [*sic*] physical nature. 'Rappaccini's Daughter' was written almost two years after 'The Birth-mark'; its treatment of the sexual theme is more ambiguous because the earlier story states simply that sex is good and that Aylmer's revulsion is perverse. His idealism is nothing more

than a rationalized distaste for sexuality." Ibid., pp. 109–10. Baym sees Owen Warland, artist of the beautiful, in much the same light.

45. *Works*, 11:94. Baym, incidentally, sees less merit in this tale than in any of the others in this group: *Shape*, pp. 117–18.

46. Lewis, *American Literature: The Makers and the Making*, 1:460–61.

Poe's Short Fiction

1. Facsimile reproductions of the title pages of these three collections of tales appear in Volume 2 of the late Thomas O. Mabbott's edition, *Collected Works of Edgar Allan Poe* (Cambridge, Mass.: Harvard University Press, 1978), at the frontispiece and between pp. 474 and 477. Tables of contents and other bibliographical data concerning the three collections and the first edition of Poe's complete works are given in volume 3 of Mabbott's edition, pp. 1396–1400. Apparently all but one of Poe's known tales and sketches, arranged chronologically in the order of their source backgrounds, are included in these two volumes of Mabbott's edition. Since this work when completed is likely to become the definitive edition, superseding Harrison's "Virginia Edition" of the complete works, it will be used for all further reference to individual tales discussed in this chapter and will be designated as *Works*.

2. Whereas Fred Lewis Pattee, in his pioneering work on the American short story, confidently listed a total of seventy tales by Poe, together with the dates of their original publication and the magazines or newspapers in which they first appeared, Mabbott's recent edition increases the total to seventy-eight. See Pattee, *Development of the American Short Story* pp. 141–44, and *Works*, 2:ix–xii.

3. *Works*, 2:xv. For a clear, succinct, and authoritative discussion of all significant aspects of Poe's tales, Mabbott's introduction (pp. xv–xxxii) is indispensable. See also his separate introductions to each of the tales throughout volumes 2 and 3.

4. Quoted in *Works*, 2:xvii. Mabbott promptly notes that Poe himself wrote in his essay "The Philosophy of Composition" that he preferred to begin "with the consideration of an *effect*. Keeping originality *always* in view. . . ."

5. See *Works*, 2:13–255, for complete details, with texts and notes, on the initial publication, revisions, and republication of each of these tales.

6. Extensively revised and retitled "Loss of Breath," this story was reprinted in the *Southern Literary Messenger* in 1835 after Poe became editor of that periodical. Each of the other stories listed above likewise reappeared in the *Messenger*, as did "The Bargain Lost," which was retitled "Bon-Bon."

7. Others in this early group of retitled and republished stories were "The Visionary," later retitled "The Assignation" and published originally but anonymously in the *Lady's Book* and republished in the *Messenger;* and "Lion-izing," a humorous literary satire that first appeared in the *Messenger* (May 1835) and was reprinted with various revisions in both *Tales of the Grotesque and Arabesque* and the

Broadway Journal, as well as in Poe's last collection, *Tales.* Finally, "Berenice," "Morella," "Hans Pfaall," and "King Pest," all four of which appeared originally in the *Southern Literary Messenger* in 1835, were reprinted in *Tales of the Grotesque and Arabesque,* as well as in other magazines during Poe's lifetime. It is interesting to note that "Berenice," one of the most bizarre among Poe's earliest horror stories, was also reprinted from the *Broadway Journal* by the *Spirit of the Times* in April 1845. See *Works,* 2:208, 224, 239.

    8. Quoted in *Works,* 2:201. Evidently this proposal was promptly reject-ed, for the following month Poe submitted to the *Baltimore Saturday Visitor* a hand-written manuscript volume entitled "The Tales of the Folio Club." It contained six stories, including the "Ms. Found in a Bottle," for which he received the fifty-dollar prize. Two years later a notice in the *Southern Literary Messenger* (August 1835) stated that "the *Tales of the Folio Club* are sixteen in all, and we believe it is the author's intention to publish them in the autumn." A year after that Poe wrote another publisher that he was prepared to republish in book form seventeen tales that, he said, had "appeared in the *Messenger.*" Ibid., p. 202.

    9. The complete text of this *jeu d'esprit,* which remained in manuscript form until 1902, is given in *Works,* 2:203–7, together with Mabbott's notes ex-plaining whom among Poe's contemporary writers some of these names probably stood for and which of the eleven stories each was presumably responsible for. A much more detailed treatment of the whole problem of the Folio Club tales, how-ever, is to be found in G. R. Thompson's brilliant study, *Poe's Fiction: Romantic Irony in the Gothic Tales* (Madison, 1973), chapter 3, pp. 39–67.

    10. See Thompson, *Poe's Fiction,* pp. 42–51, for detailed analyses of all these tales. Concerning the clever use of bawdry in "Lion-izing," particularly the innuendo in its references to "noses" and "nosology," students might be interested to consult an amusing pair of articles entitled "Poe's 'Lion-izing': A Quiz on Wil-lis and Lady Blessington" by Richard P. Benton in *Studies in Short Fiction* 5 (Spring 1968):239–44; and "On the Nose—Further Speculations on the Sources and Meaning of Poe's 'Lion-izing'" by G. R. Thompson in volume 6 of the same jour-nal (Fall 1968):94–97.

    11. Quoted in Thompson, *Poe's Fiction,* p. 43. It is interesting to note that Mabbott includes Poe's apology but omits mention of this defense in his reference to "Berenice" (*Works,* 2:208), possibly because he could not agree that this tale was simply another of Poe's literary parodies, though of a different sort from the hoaxing he was pulling in "Lion-izing."

    12. Thompson, *Poe's Fiction,* pp. 9, 10, 12–13. Thompson distinguishes between an ordinary hoax and a literary hoax by noting that in the latter a writer attempts to persuade his readers "not merely of the reality of false events but of the reality of false literary intentions or circumstances—that a work is by a certain writer or of a certain age when it is not, or that one is writing a serious Gothic story when one is not." Thompson thus sees a strong affinity between Poe's aes-thetic theory and that of the romantic irony prevalent among many of his German

and French contemporaries whose "Romantic artist-hero held the world together by the force of his own mind—or . . . watched the world and his own mind crumble under the stress of dark contrary forces. The result, in the works of these writers, is an ambivalent pessimism: a kind of black humor, or black irony, and as well a skepticism engendered by the self-awareness of the subjective human mind insistently reaching out toward an illusive certainty."

13. For an exhaustive list of works by these and other critics bearing on Poe's relationship to the European romantic ironists, see Thompson's notes in his *Poe's Fiction*, pp. 200–215.

14. Ibid., p. 43.

15. Ibid., p. 14.

16. Ibid., p. 54.

17. Mabbott, however, considers this "one of the great stories in Poe's early Arabesque manner." Noting that in 1835 Poe himself called it his best tale, Mabbott also explains that its central theme received parallel treatment in such later tales as "Ligeia," "The Black Cat," and "Eleanora." He includes two of the seven different versions of the story extant during Poe's lifetime: *Works,* 2:221–37.

18. Mabbott refers to "King Pest" as "one of the least valuable of Poe's stories" and cites four probable sources for it; but he does not seem to have been aware of the contemporary political implications in it (*Works,* 2:238–39).

19. Mabbott points out that this satiric tale as originally published in 1838 "was designed as one story including another." But when the publishers Lea and Blanchard brought out Poe's first collection, *Tales of the Grotesque and Arabesque* (1840), "The narratives were treated as separate units—Poe in his preface said there were twenty-five tales, counting these as two. Griswold's and most subsequent collections have followed that pattern." Mabbott's full commentary and notes on this, perhaps the funniest of all Poe's takeoffs, are well worth the student's attention (*Works,* 2:334–62).

20. *Works,* 2:472–74.

21. Cf. *Works,* 2:422–25, for a detailed explanation of Irving's article and Poe's response to it. Mabbott's notes indicate that Poe also used several other minor sources in fleshing out this tale.

22. Thompson, *Poe's Fiction,* p. 138.

23. For a thorough discussion of this review and its sequel, see Robert D. Jacobs, *Poe: Journalist and Critic* (Baton Rouge: Louisiana State University Press, 1969), pp. 317–28, 391–94. And concerning possible hoaxing in the same review, see also Robert Regan, "Hawthorne's 'Plagiary'; Poe's Duplicity," a fascinating speculation in *Nineteenth Century Fiction* 25 (1970):281–98.

24. Quoted in Eric W. Carlson, *Introduction to Poe* (Glenview, Ill., 1967), pp. 487, 498. It is interesting to compare the illustrative details Poe used to support his central idea in the two essays. In both cases he cited Irving's *Tales of a Traveller* as favorable examples of skillfully constructed tales; yet none of them, he felt, could be commended "as a whole" because "in many of them the interest is

subdivided and frittered away, and their conclusions are insufficiently climactic." So too with the stories of John Neal and W. G. Simms. Ibid., p. 498.

25. See *Works,* 2:474–75, for a facsimile of Poe's handwritten title page and table of contents. Two of the stories originally planned for his collection, "The Pit and the Pendulum" and "The Mystery of Marie Roget," were for some reason crossed out; and Poe instructed the printer to "preserve the order of the Table of Contents" as he had listed them.

26. Quoted in *Works,* 3:1397.

27. Mabbott points out that in "Usher" alone Poe made more than fifty changes: *Works,* 3:1397–98.

28. See *Works,* 3:1217–43, 1252–65, 1343–55.

29. A detailed account of the genesis and development of Poe's work on "The Mystery of Marie Roget," including his attempt to sell the story to two different publishers at the same time, appears in *Works,* 3:715–22, 774–88.

30. For further details on the publication and reception of the story see *Works,* 3:799–805.

31. G. R. Thompson, "Edgar Allan Poe," in *Dictionary of Literary Biography,* (Detroit: Gale Research, 1979), p. 275.

32. A number of these differing interpretations are summarized in *Works,* 2:661. But see also Thompson, *Poe's Fiction,* pp. 132–36.

33. Cf. *Works,* 2:667–69. It has even been argued recently that in this tale Poe was deceiving his readers by "out-Hawthorning Hawthorne" without their knowing. See also Regan, "Hawthorne's 'Plagiary'; Poe's Duplicity," pp. 291–98.

34. Source materials for "The Tell-Tale Heart" are summarized in *Works,* 3:789–91.

35. The titles of these seven tales are "The Spectacles," "The Premature Burial," "The System of Doctor Tarr and Professor Feather," "Mesmeric Revelation," "The Balloon Hoax," "The Angel of the Odd," and "The Literary Life of Thingum Bob, Esq." During the next two years Poe added four more tales of varying effectiveness to this expanding catalog of comic satires. Most impressive of the group, perhaps, is "The Facts in the Case of M. Valdemar," another ludicrously grotesque narrative of a dead man kept in suspended animation through a mesmeric trance until, at the climax, his body dissolves into "a nearly liquid mass of loathsome—of detestable putridity" (*Works,* 3:1243). Detailed analyses of the implications of this tale and "Mesmeric Revelation" are presented in Thompson, *Poe's Fiction,* pp. 153–60.

36. For the involved relationship between this satire and Poe's ostensibly serious philosophical essay *Eureka,* published the year before, readers may consult *Works,* 3:1289–90, 1305–19. See also Harold Beaver, ed., *The Science Fiction of Edgar Allan Poe* (New York: Penguin Books, 1977), pp. 395–442.

37. In addition to the ongoing definitive edition of the *Collected Works,* edited by T. O. Mabbott, several of the most useful full-length studies that pro-

vide stimulating insights into both Poe's cultural environment and his artistic
reaction to it are listed in the Bibliography under Poe.
  38. Patrick F. Quinn, *The French Face of Poe* (Carbondale, Ill., 1957), pp.
10–11.
  39. Stuart and Susan Levine, eds., *The Short Fiction of Edgar Allan Poe* (Indianapolis, 1976), p. xv.
  40. See Carlson's review in *PSA Newsletter* 10, no. 2 (Fall 1982):2–3.
  41. Quoted in Carlson, *Introduction to Poe*, p. 441.

Simms and the Southern Frontier Humorists

  1. See Mott, *History of American Magazines,* 1:796–809, for a chronological list of all magazines started during the period.
  2. The most ambitious scholarly project devoted to the Simms revival is
the ongoing Centennial Edition, entitled *The Writings of William Gilmore Simms,*
which is being published under the auspices of the University of South Carolina.
To date only four volumes of this massive undertaking have appeared, the most
recent in 1975, under the general editorship of John Caldwell Guilds. Guilds also
edited with introductions and explanatory notes the third volume in this group,
which appeared in 1974 as volume 5 and bearing the title *Stories and Tales.* Further
reference to this volume will be cited in the text as *Centennial 5.* Besides the Centennial Edition, other significant scholarly interpretation of Simms's fiction may
be found in J. V. Ridgely, *William Gilmore Simms* (New York, 1962); C. Hugh
Holman, *The Roots of Southern Writing* (Athens: University of Georgia Press, 1972),
pp. 16–86; Lewis P. Simpson, *The Dispossessed Garden* (Athens: University of
Georgia Press, 1975), pp. 34–64; and Keen Butterworth, "William Gilmore
Simms," in the *Dictionary of Literary Biography,* 3:306–18.
  3. *The Letters of William Gilmore Simms,* ed. Mary C. Simms Oliphant, A.
T. Odell, and T. C. Duncan Eaves (Columbia, 1952–1956), 5:55. Hereafter cited
in the text as *Letters.*
  4. For further biographical details see Butterworth, "Simms," pp. 306–
18.
  5. *The Yemassee,* ed. Joseph V. Ridgely (New Haven, Conn.: College &
University Publishers, 1964), p. 24.
  6. Ibid., p. 10.
  7. "To Nash Roach, Esq. of South Carolina," in *The Wigwam and the Cabin,* new and revised edition (New York: Redfield, 1856), pp. 4–5.
  8. *Broadway Journal* 2 (4 October 1845):190. Cited in *Centennial 5,* p.
xii.
  9. *Letters,* 2:54 (10 April 1845).
  10. Ibid., 2:98 (8 August 1845); see also ibid., 2:79 (25 June 1845).

11. Ibid., 1:352. The other five stories were "Barnacle Sam," "The Last Wager," "Murder Will Out," "The Armchair of Tustennuggee," and "The Lazy Crow."

12. Ibid., 1:368–70 (29 September 1843); 1:374–77 (16 October 1843); 1:381–84 (31 October 1843).

13. Ibid., 1:390–91 (22 November 1843).

14. Ibid., 1:435–37 (15 November 1844).

15. Ibid., 1:443–45 (19 November 1844).

16. Ibid., 1:438–39 (15 November 1844); 2:20 (19 January 1845); 2:53–56 (10 April 1845).

17. Simms also tried to interest Duyckinck in still another "collection in one vol. of things purely imaginative, some of which appeared in a couple of vols. published by Adlard, which did not take because of the sudden rush, at that time, into cheap literature." His reference was to the stories in *Carl Werner,* which he continued to urge Duyckinck to consider because, he insisted, they "contain as adequate proofs as I have ever seen of the imaginative and inventive power. A volume of Imaginative Stories—purely such . . . indeed, as have no resemblance in American Literature, unless in the writings of Poe, and partially of Hawthorne—are to be collated out of my materials" (*Letters,* 2:79, 98–99).

18. Ibid., 2:144 (9 February 1846); 2:106 (19 October 1845); 2:146–47 (20 February 1846); 2:198 (24 October 1846).

19. Ibid., 2:224 (6 December 1846).

20. Ibid., 2:379–82 (13 December 1847). "I should be perfectly satisfied to take my pay out of the profits. What say you? The Tales might bear illustration admirably in the style of your ghost book" (ibid., p. 381).

21. Concerning "The Pilgrim of Love," Simms authorized Lawson to "sell it to any publisher who will give you $25 (cash) for it. It is worth more" (ibid., 2:346–47 [5 September 1847]). He was glad to get $20 for this story from Israel Post, publisher of the *Union Magazine,* and he urged Lawson to see whether Post would take any others at the same price (ibid., 2:364 [3 November 1847]). *Graham's* began publishing these "other articles," a total of five stories between October 1847 and December 1849, at a slightly higher rate (ibid., 2:347, footnote; 2:432, footnote 115).

22. Ibid., 2:97 (8 August 1845); 3:50–52 (19 June 1850).

23. Ibid., 3:210–15 (24 November 1852).

24. Ibid., pp. 213–14.

25. Ibid., 3:236–38 (letter to Lawson, 20 June 1853); 3:240–41 (letter to Hammond, same date; see footnote 59, p. 241, indicating that this may have been a reference to *Southward Ho!,* to be published by Redfield the following year).

26. Ibid., 3:242–43, footnote 63.

27. *The Wigwam and the Cabin* (New York: Redfield, 1856), in dedicatory epistle to Nash Roach, pp. 3–4.

28. *Letters,* 3:315–16 (17 July 1854), footnote 152.

29. Ibid., 3:340 (6 December 1854). Footnote 249 shows that *Southward Ho!* was reviewed in *Harper's, Putnam's,* and *Graham's* successively from January to March 1855. But before Christmas Simms again wrote Duyckinck that he was "anxious to hear from you how you folks speak of it in your quarter" (ibid., 3:351 [20 December 1854]).

30. Ibid., 3:339 (6 December 1854). Footnote 247 shows that both *Putnam's* and *Harper's* turned down this story, "The Pirate's Hoard," which ran to about thirty pages; and that it was finally published in *Graham's* from January to April 1856.

31. Ibid., 3:355–56 (24 December 1854), footnote 307.

32. The two exceptions, "Oakatibbe" and "Jocassee," had been published at least twice before, as early as 1828. The other eleven stories appeared originally as follows: "The Lazy Crow," "Grayling: Or Murder Will Out," "The Two Camps," "The Last Wager," and "The Giant's Coffin" in the *Gift* for 1840, 1842, 1843, and 1845; "The Armchair of Tustenuggee" in *Godey's* in 1840; "The Snake in the Cabin" and "Those Old Lunes" in the *Southern and Western Monthly* in 1845; "Sergeant Barnacle" in *Graham's* in 1845; "Caloya: Or the Loves of a Driver" in the *Magnolia* in 1841; and "Lucas De Ayllon" in the *Ladies' Companion* in 1842.

33. *Wigwam and the Cabin* (1856), p. 4.

34. "The Two Camps. A Legend of the Old North State," ibid., pp. 37–38.

35. *Letters,* 1:190–91, 254–66.

36. *Wigwam and the Cabin,* pp. 166–67.

37. Ibid., pp. 273–75.

38. Ibid., pp. 419–25.

39. See the following passages in "The Lazy Crow" and "Caloya," ibid., pp. 345–52, 336–70, 384–88.

40. *The Lily and the Totem; or, The Huguenots in Florida* (Charleston: Walker, Evans & Cogswell, 1871); dedicatory epistle to J. H. Hammond, p. iv.

41. Their titles are "The Legend of Guernache," "Lachane, the Deliverer," "The Conspiracy of LeGenre," "Narrative of LeBarbu: The Bearded Man of Calos," and "Iracana: The Eden of the Floridians."

42. The tangled publication record of those last two works is discussed in *Centennial 5,* pp. 704–61.

43. Butterworth, "Simms," p. 311.

44. *Centennial 5,* p. 804

45. Ibid.

46. Ibid., p. 828.

47. Quoted in Jay B. Hubbell, *The South in American Literature* (Durham, N.C.: Duke University Press, 1954), p. 600.

48. Some idea of the prevalence of these newspaper reprints may be found in my article "Newspaper Humor in the Old South, 1835–1855," *Alabama Review* 3 (April 1949):102–12.

49. The scholarship on most of these men and their works is now fairly extensive, but concise, up-to-date biographical and bibliographical data on all of them are available in volume 3 of the *Dictionary of Literary Biography.*

50. The most comprehensive treatment of Porter's career as editor of the *Spirit* is to be found in Norris Yates, *William T. Porter and the "Spirit of the Times": A Study of the "Big Bear" School of Humor* (Baton Rouge: Louisiana State University Press, 1957).

51. "The Fastest Duel on Record," *Spirit* 15, no. 441 (15 November 1845). For many other similar encomiums, see my articles "Alabama Writers in the *Spirit*," *Alabama Review* 10 (October 1957):243–69, and "'York's Tall Son' and his Southern Correspondents," *American Quarterly* 7 (Winter 1955):371–84.

52. *Spirit* 14, no. 547 (11 January 1854). "Aside from a host of correspondents among breeders and turfmen of the highest intellectual merit," he added, "of writers on purely literary themes, we believe that our correspondents at this moment comprise more men of genius—disciples of Momus, we mean, than any newspaper or magazine ever had." Ibid.

53. Specific details on the makeup of Porter's anthologies are discussed in my article "'Mr. Spirit' and *The Big Bear of Arkansas*," *American Literature* 27, no. 3 (November 1955):332–46. His third anthology, also quite successful, was an American adaptation of a famous British work, Hawker's *Instructions to Young Sportsmen*, which Porter dedicated to the wealthy South Carolina planter Colonel Wade Hampton, Jr.

54. Thomas E. Dasher, "William Trotter Porter," in *DLB*, 3:299. Facsimile reprints of the two collections, including all the original Darley illustrations, were issued by the AMS Press of New York in 1973.

55. *Porter's Spirit of the Times* 4 (24 July 1858):328. Porter relinquished the editorship of the original *Spirit* in 1856 and then joined forces with George Wilkes as senior editor of an ill-fated new journal bearing his name (see Mott, *History of American Magazines*, 1:480 n.). The quotation above is part of the full-page obituary on Porter written by Wilkes. After Porter's death this magazine, like its predecessor, went downhill rapidly and expired in the throes of a legal squabble over ownership and management.

56. *Spirit* 9 (1 February 1840):565.

57. Representative yarns written by all these southerners, together with biographical, critical, and bibliographical data, are included in *Humor of the Old Southwest*, 2d ed., ed. Hennig Cohen and William B. Dillingham (Athens, Ga., 1975).

58. Poe's review of *Georgia Scenes*, published in March 1836, is quoted at some length in John Donald Wade's excellent biography, *Augustus Baldwin Longstreet: A Study in the Development of Culture in the South* (Athens: University of Georgia Press, 1969), pp. 152–53, 170–71, 175, 177, 182. In all, eight new editions of the book were brought out by Harpers between 1840 and 1860; three more were published in 1884, 1894, and 1897 (ibid., p. 156); and at least two more

have appeared in this century, the most recent in 1957, edited with an introduction by B. R. McElderry, Jr. (New York: Sagamore Press).

59. Quoted in Walter Blair, *Native American Humor* (New York, 1937), pp. 65–66. See also Wade, *Longstreet*, pp. 157–58.

60. Of the nineteen sketches, twelve were purported to be told by Hall and six by Baldwin. The extra one, signed by "Timothy Crabshaw," was "The Militia Company Drill," actually the work of Longstreet's friend Oliver H. Prince. As Wade points out, "all of the sketches with women as their chief characters were signed 'Baldwin,' and all of those with men as their chief characters were signed 'Hall.' Now Lyman Hall and Abraham Baldwin were two of the early Georgia patriots. Hall had signed the Declaration of Independence, while Baldwin had signed the Constitution, and also had been the state's first influential man in Congress" (*Longstreet*, p. 150.).

61. Fuller discussions of these and the remaining sketches in *Georgia Scenes* are developed in Wade, *Longstreet*, pp. 169–86.

62. Letter 12 from *Major Jones's Courtship,* quoted in *Humor of the Old Southwest,* p. 125.

63. Walter Blair and Hamlin Hill, *America's Humor* (New York, 1978), p. 184.

64. Ibid., p. 186.

65. Hooper's rise to prominence among antebellum southern humorists is most fully treated in W. Stanley Hoole's biography, *Alias Simon Suggs: The Life and Times of Johnson Jones Hooper* (University, Ala: University of Alabama Press, 1952). For a succinct recent account, see Robert Bain, "Johnson Jones Hooper," in *DLB,* 3:161–63.

66. *Spirit* 13 (9 September 1843):326. See Hoole, *Suggs,* p. 46.

67. "Captain Suggs of Tallapoosa," ibid., 14 (11 January 1845):547.

68. Ibid., 14 (25 January 1845):571; 14 (1 February 1845):583.

69. Ibid., 15 (8 March 1845):9; 15 (15 March 1845):21–27; 15 (22 March 1845):38; 15 (5 April 1845):57; 15 (16 August 1845):296. See also Hoole, *Suggs,* pp. 55–56.

70. Letters to Carey and Hart, 3 March and 10 April 1845 (in New York Historical Society Library). See also Hoole, *Suggs,* pp. 56–59.

71. *Spirit* 15 (20 September 1845):356. Advance notices of the book appeared on 19 July (15:246), 16 August (15:296), and 13 September (15:333).

72. Edited with an introduction by Manly Wade Wellman (Chapel Hill: University of North Carolina Press), this edition also includes an excellent bibliography, together with Hooper's genuine dedication to Porter, the original Felix Darley illustrations, two of the later Suggs stories ("The Muscadine Story" and "The Widow Rugby's Husband"), and the parody written by Joseph Glover Baldwin entitled "Simon Suggs, Jr., Esq.," which was published in his *Flush Times of Alabama and Mississippi.* Page references to this edition will be cited in the text.

73. The quoted passage is from the opening of Baldwin's best-known

sketch, "Ovid Bolus, Esq., Attorney at Law and Solicitor in Chancery," in *The Flush Times of Alabama and Mississippi*, edited with introduction by William A. Owens (New York, 1957), p. 1. Page references to this edition are cited hereafter in the text.

74. The full title of Baldwin's second book was *Party Leaders; Sketches of Thomas Jefferson, Alexander Hamilton, Andrew Jackson, Henry Clay, John Randolph of Roanoke, Including Notices of Many Other Distinguished American Statesmen* (New York: D. Appleton & Co., 1855).

75. *Sacramento Daily Union* 5 October 1864. This and numerous other contemporary accounts of Baldwin's career in California are included in the Lester Gray Collections of memorabilia housed in the New York Public Library. Fuller details on these documents are treated in my article "Joseph Glover Baldwin: Humorist or Moralist?," *Alabama Review* 5 (April 1952):122–41.

76. The most comprehensive biography of Thorpe is Milton Rickels's *Thomas Bangs Thorpe: Humorist of the Old Southwest* (Baton Rouge: Louisiana State University Press, 1962); see his bibliography of Thorpe's writings, pp. 258–66. A more recent, succinct account of Thorpe's career is Robert Bains, "Thomas Bangs Thorpe," in *DLB*, 3:335–39.

77. Besides "The Big Bear of Arkansas," Porter included in his first collection another "original character" from Thorpe named Stoke Stout of Louisiana; and in his second collection, *A Quarter Race in Kentucky*, Porter reprinted Thorpe's second-best bear story "Bob Herring, the Arkansas Bear Hunter." Thorpe also reprinted from the *Spirit* in his own collections—*Mysteries of the Backwoods* (1846) and *The Hive of the Bee-Hunter* (1854)—two of his other amusing pieces, which are still in print in Cohen and Dillingham's *Humor of the Old Southwest*, pp. 279–95. These are "A Piano in Arkansas" and "The Disgraced Scalp-Lock."

78. Rickels, *Thorpe*, pp. 78–86.

79. Ibid., pp. 101–7.

80. Ibid., pp. 153–59.

81. Over a hundred titles of these magazine pieces, including many having to do with art and artists, are listed in Thorpe's bibliography for the years from 1853 till his death in 1878. See ibid., pp. 259–66.

82. Ibid., p. 180. The full title of Thorpe's second collection was *The Hive of "The Bee-Hunter," A Repository of Sketches, Including Peculiar American Character, Scenery, and Rural Sports. By T. B. Thorpe, of Louisiana. Author of "Tom Owen, the Bee-Hunter"; "Mysteries of the Backwoods," etc. etc. Illustrated by Sketches from Nature. New York: D. Appleton and Company, M.DCCC.LIV.*

83. Rickels, *Thorpe*, pp. 133–35.

84. See ibid., pp. 180–90, for a full discussion of this novel.

85. Blair and Hill, *America's Humor*, p. 203. This recent study provides a thorough critical analysis of the artistry in Thorpe's tale, a discussion almost as long as "The Big Bear" itself: pp. 200–212. Another excellent discussion of the story appears in Rickels, *Thorpe*, pp. 49–61.

86. James M. Cox, "Humor of the Old Southwest," in *The Comic Imagination in American Literature,* ed. Louis D. Rubin, Jr. (New Brunswick, N.J., 1973), p. 109.

87. Rickels, *Thorpe,* p. 190.

88. John Q. Anderson, *Louisiana Swamp Doctor: The Life and Writings of Henry Clay Lewis, alias "Madison Tensas, M.D."* (Baton Rouge, 1962), pp. 53–55.

89. Cox, "Humor," pp. 110–11.

90. Anderson, *Louisiana Swamp Doctor,* p. 13.

91. Cox, "Humor" p. 110. The sketch is also included in Cohen and Dillingham, *Humor of the Old Southwest,* together with two others of Lewis's more famous pieces, "A Tight Race Considerin'" and "The Indefatigable Bear Hunter," pp. 336–54.

92. Anderson, *Louisiana Swamp Doctor,* p. 89. Further page references to other sketches included in this work are parenthetically indicated in the text.

93. See, for instance, a recent study by Charles Israel, "Henry Clay Lewis's *Odd Leaves:* Studies in the Surreal and Grotesque," *Mississippi Quarterly* 28 (Winter 1974–75):61–69; also Alan H. Rose, "The Image of the Negro in the Writings of Henry Clay Lewis," *American Literature* 41 (May 1969): 255–63.

94. The most complete edition of these previously uncollected tales and sketches is M. Thomas Inge's *High Times and Hard Times: Sketches and Tales by George Washington Harris* (Kingsport, Tenn., 1967). Together with scholarly introductions and bibliographical data, this volume contains nearly fifty additional sketches, yarns, and satires that were not included among the original collections of Sut Lovingood's *Yarns.* Mr. Inge has also edited "for the Modern Reader" the most recent volume of *Sut Lovingood's Yarns* (New Haven, Conn., 1966).

95. *Patriotic Gore* (New York: Oxford University Press, 1962), p. 509. Wilson's strictures had appeared several years earlier in a long essay-review of Brom Weber's 1954 edition of *Sut Lovingood,* published by Grove Press. Wilson's essay, entitled "Poisoned!," was printed in the *New Yorker* 31 (7 May 1955):150–154+ . Perceptive analyses of the weaknesses in Wilson's criticism may be found in Brom Weber, "A Note on Edmund Wilson and George Washington Harris," in *The Lovingood Papers* (1962), pp. 47–53; and in Milton Rickels, *George Washington Harris* (New York, 1965), pp. 128–29. Rickels's book is the definitive biography.

96. Robert Bain, "George Washington Harris," in *Dictionary of Literary Biography* (1979), 3:138.

97. See Inge, *High Times and Hard Times,* pp. 10–31. References to quotations from this work appear in parentheses in the text.

98. Quoted in Rickels, *Harris,* p. 26.

99. Ibid., p. 77.

100. Arlin Turner, "Seeds of Literary Revolt in the Humor of the Old Southwest," *Louisiana Historical Quarterly* 39 (1956):149.

101. Quoted in ibid., p. 143.

Shifting Trends toward Realism in Fiction

1. Mott, *A History of American Magazines,* 2:173. Mott notes that although Melville, Simms, Curtis, and Fitz-James O'Brien were among the short-fiction writers of the period, "most of the best as well as the worst work was done by women."

2. Robert F. Marler, "From Tale to Short Story: The Emergence of a New Genre in the 1850s," *American Literature* 46, no. 2 (May 1974):155.

3. Ibid. Marler notes that the legacies of Irving, Hawthorne, and Poe can be seen in the mass of this undistinguished fiction, "where the comparatively balanced effects of Irving's sentimentalism, Poe's sensationalism, and Hawthorne's moralism were so heavily emphasized, distorted, and unconsciously parodied that the decay of the tale is unmistakable."

4. *The Letters of Herman Melville,* ed. Merrell R. Davis and William H. Gilman (New Haven: Yale University Press, 1960), p. 128. In the same letter Melville assured Hawthorne that if any writer tried to earn a living by writing the truth, he would have to join a bread line; indeed, "Though I wrote the Gospels in this century, I should die in the gutter" (ibid., p. 129).

5. "Hawthorne and His Mosses," quoted in *Herman Melville, Representative Selections,* ed. with introduction by Willard Thorpe, (New York: American Book Company, 1938), p. 334.

6. See letter to Evert Duyckinck, 12 February 1851, ibid., p. 386.

7. "The Custom House," in *The Scarlet Letter,* Norton Critical Edition, p. 32.

8. Quoted in the "Historical Commentary" to centenary *Mosses from an Old Manse,* p. 536.

9. *Southern Quarterly Review* 20 (July 1851):272. The same section of critical notices carried a very favorable review of Hawthorne's *House of the Seven Gables* (pp. 265–66) and a shorter one of another humorous volume, *Polly Peablossom's Wedding and Other Tales,* which the critic also judged favorably: "A collection of broad grin Southern & Western exaggeration—comicalities of the woods & wayside; such as will compel laughter if not reflection. Just the volume to snatch up in railway & steamboat, & put out of sight in all other places" (ibid., p. 272).

10. Ibid., 19 (January 1851):79–80.

11. *The Confidence Man,* Norton Critical Edition (New York: Norton, 1971), p. 158. Melville was, of course, defending himself here against the bitter censures his earlier books *Moby-Dick* and *Pierre* had suffered at the critics' hands.

12. Marler, "Tale to Short Story," p. 162.

13. See Charvat, *Profession of Authorship in America* pp. 217–231.

14. Warner Berthoff, *The Example of Melville* (New York: Norton, 1972), p. 135. Berthoff makes a detailed and thoroughly convincing case for Melville's mastery of short-fiction technique in his analysis of "The Town-Ho's Story" (ibid., pp. 133–38).

Bibliography

Selected Bibliography of Articles of General Interest

Austin, Mary. "The Folk Story in America." *South Atlantic Quarterly* 33 (January 1934):10–19.

Baldeshwiler, Eileen. "The Lyric Short Story: The Sketch of a History." *Studies in Short Fiction* 6, no. 4 (1969):443–53.

Beck, Warren. "Art and Formula in the Short Story." *College English* 5 (November 1943):55–62.

Blair, Walter. "'A Man's Voice, Speaking': A Continuum in American Humor." In *Veins of Humor*. Edited by Harry Levin. Cambridge, Mass.: Harvard University Press, 1972, pp. 185–204.

Boyce, Benjamin. "English Short Fiction in the Eighteenth Century: A Preliminary View." *Studies in Short Fiction* 5, no. 1 (1968):95–112.

Cohen, Hennig. "A Comic Mode of the Romantic Imagination: Poe, Hawthorne, Mellville." In *The Comic Imagination in American Literature*. Edited by Louis D. Rubin, Jr. New Brunswick, N.J.: Rutgers University Press, 1973, pp. 85–99.

Cox, James M. "Humor of the Old Southwest," In *The Comic Imagination in American Literature*, pp. 101–12.

Current-García, Eugene, "Alabama Writers in the *Spirit*." *The Alabama Review*, 10, no. 3 (1957):243–69.

————. "'Mr. Spirit' and 'The Big Bear of Arkansas.'" *American Literature* 27, no. 3 (1955):332–46.

————. "Newspaper Humor in the Old South, 1835–1855." *Alabama Review* 3, no. 2 (1949):102–12.

————. "'York's Tall Son' and His Southern Correspondents." *American Quarterly* 7, no. 4 (1955):371–84.

Dasher, Thomas E. "William Trotter Porter." In *Dictionary of Literary Biography*. Detroit: Gale Research, 1979, 3:298–300.

Dillingham, William B. "Days of the Tall Tale." *Southern Review*, n.s.4 (1968):569–77.

Ellison, George R. "William Tappan Thompson and the *Southern Miscellany,* 1842–1844." *Mississippi Quarterly* 13 (1969):47–57.

Engstrom, A. G. "The Formal Short Story in France and Its Development Before 1850." *Studies in Philology* 42 (July 1945):627–39.

Farrell, James T. "Nonsense and the Short Story" and "The Short Story." In *The League of Frightened Philistines and Other Papers.* New York: Vanguard Press, 1945, pp. 72–81, 136–48.

Fitz Gerald, Gregory. "The Satiric Short Story: A Definition." *Studies in Short Fiction* 5, no. 3 (1968):349–54.

Friedman, Norman. "What Makes a Short Story Short?" *Modern Fiction Studies* 4 (Summer 1958):103–17.

Gullason, Thomas A. "Revelation and Evolution: A Neglected Dimension of the Short Story." *Studies in Short Fiction* 10, no. 4 (1973):347–56.

———. "The Short Story: An Underrated Art." *Studies in Short Fiction* 2, no. 1 (1964):13–31.

Harris, Wendell V. "English Short Fiction in the 19th Century." *Studies in Short Fiction* 6, no. 1 (1968):1–93.

Hartley, L. P. "In Defence of the Short Story." In *The Novelist's Responsibility.* London: Hamish Hamilton, 1967, pp. 157–59.

Janeway, Elizabeth, et al. "Is the Short Story Necessary?" In *The Writer's World.* Edited by Elizabeth Janeway. New York: McGraw-Hill, 1969, pp. 251–73.

Kennedy, J. Gerald. "The Magazine Tales of the 1830's." *American Transcendental Quarterly,* no. 24, supplement two (1974):23–28.

Marler, Robert F. "From Tale to Short Story: The Emergence of a New Genre in the 1850's." *American Literature* 46, no. 2 (1974):153–69.

May, Charles M. "The Unique Effect of the Short Story: A Reconsideration and an Example." *Studies in Short Fiction* 13, no. 3 (1976):289–97.

Mayo, Robert D. "The Gothic Short Story in the Magazines." *Modern Language Review* 37, no. 4 (1942):448–54.

Merren, John. "The Resolute Wife, Or a Hazard of New Criticism." *Studies in Short Fiction* 15, no. 3 (1978):291–300.

Moore, Jack B. "Images of the Negro in Early American Short Fiction." *Mississippi Quarterly* 22, no. 1 (1969):47–57.

———. "Making Indians Early: The Worth of 'Azakia'." *Studies in Short Fiction* 13, no. 1 (1976):51–60.

———. "'The Captain's Wife': A Native Short Story Before Irving." *Studies in Short Fiction* 1, no. 2 (1964):103–6.

Parks, Edd Winfield. "The Intent of the Ante-Bellum Southern Humorists." *Mississippi Quarterly* 13, no. 2 (1960):163–68.

Pitcher, Edward W. "A Note on 'Azakia': Jack B. Moore's 'Early American Story.'" *Studies in Short Fiction* 14, no. 4 (1977):395–96.

Pochmann, Henry A. "Germanic Materials and Motifs in the Short Story." In *German Culture in America: Philosophical and Literary Influences: 1600–1900.* Madison: University of Wisconsin Press, 1957, pp. 367–408.

Rickels, Milton. "Inexpressibles in Southwestern Humor." *Studies in American Humor* 3, no. 2 (1976):76–83.

Schlauch, Margaret. "English Short Fiction in the 15th and 16th Centuries." *Studies in Short Fiction* 3, no. 4 (1966):393–434.

Stead, Christina, et al. "The International Symposium on the Short Story." *Kenyon Review* 30, no. 4 (1968:443–90; part 2, 31, no. 1 (1969):58–94; part 3, 31, no. 4 (1969):450–503.

Turner, Arlin. "Realism and Fantasy in Southern Humor." *Georgia Review* 12, no. 4 (1958):451–57.

———. "Seeds of Literary Revolt in the Humor of the Old Southwest." *Louisiana Historical Quarterly* 39, no. 2 (1956):143–51.

———. "The Many Sides of Southern Humor." *Mississippi Quarterly*, 13, no. 4 (1960):155–56.

Thorp, Willard. "Suggs and Sut in Modern Dress: The Latest Chapter in Southern Humor." *Mississippi Quarterly* 13, no. 4 (1960):169–75.

Wright, Lyle H. "A Statistical Survey of American Fiction, 1774–1850." *Huntington Library Quarterly* 2, no. 3 (April 1939):309–18.

Selected Bibliography of Books of General Interest

Bates, H. E. *The Modern Short Story: A Critical Survey.* Boston: The Writer, 1972.

Blair, Walter. *Native American Humor.* New York: American Book Company, 1937.

————, and Hamlin Hill. *American Humor.* New York: Oxford University Press, 1978.

Charvat, William. *Literary Publishing in America, 1790–1850.* Philadelphia: University of Pennsylvania Press, 1959.

————. *The Profession of Authorship in America, 1800–1870: The Papers of William Charvat.* Edited by Matthew J. Bruccoli. Columbus: Ohio State University Press, 1968.

Cohen, Hennig, and William B. Dillingham, eds. *Humor of the Old Southwest.* 2d ed. Athens: Universitiy of Georgia Press, 1964; rev. 1975.

Current-García, Eugene, and Patrick, Walton R., eds. *What Is the Short Story?* Chicago: Scott, Foresman, 1961: rev. 1974.

George Albert J. *The Development of French Romanticism.* Syracuse, N.Y.: Syracuse University Press, 1955.

————. *Short Fiction in France: 1800–1850.* Syracuse, N.Y.: Syracuse University Press, 1964.

Hoffman, Daniel. *Form and Fable in American Fiction.* New York: Oxford University Press, 1961; Norton, 1973.

Klinkowitz, Jerome. *The Practice of Fiction in America. Writers from Hawthorne to the Present.* Ames: Iowa State Universtiy Press, 1980.

May, Charles E., ed. *Short Story Theories.* Athens: Ohio University Press, 1976.

Moore, Jack B. *Native Elements in American Magazine Short Fiction, 1741–1800.* Chapel Hill: University of North Carolina Press, 1963.

Mott, Frank Luther. *A History of American Magazines.* 5 vols. Cambridge: Harvard University Press, 1939–1968.

Pattee, Fred Lewis. *The Development of the American Short Story: An Historical Survey.* New York: Harper & Brothers, 1923.

Pochmann, Henry A. *German Culture in America.* Madison: University of Wisconsin Press, 1961.

Slotkin, Richard. *Regeneration through Violence: The Mythology of the American Frontier, 1600–1860.* Middletown Conn.: Wesleyan University Press, 1973.

Thompson, G. R., and Locke, Virgil L., eds. *Ruined Eden of the Present: Hawthorne, Melville, and Poe*. West Lafayette, Ind.: Purdue University Press, 1981.

Thurston, Jarvis, et al. *Short Fiction Criticism—A Checklist of Interpretations Since 1925 of Stories and Novelettes (American, British, Continental), 1800–1958*. Denver: Swallow Press, 1960.

Voss, Arthur. *The American Short Story: A Critical Survey*. Norman: University of Oklahoma Press, 1973.

Walker, Warren S. *Twentieth-Century Short Fiction Explication: Interpretations, 1900–1975, of Short Fiction Since 1800*, 3d ed. Hamden, Conn.: Shoe String Press, 1977.

Weixlmann, Joe. *American Short Fiction Criticism and Scholarship, 1959–1977: A Checklist*. Chicago, Athens (Ohio), London: Swallow Press, 1982.

Articles and Books Devoted to Specific Authors

Joseph Glover Baldwin

Current-García, Eugene. "Joseph Glover Baldwin: Humorist or Moralist?" *Alabama Review* 5, no. 2 (1952):122–41.

Owens, William A. "Introduction." *The Flush Times of Alabama and Mississippi.* By Joseph Glover Baldwin. New York: Hill & Wang, 1957, pp. v–ix.

Rubin, Louis D., Jr. "The Great American Joke." *South Atlantic Quarterly* 72 (1973):82–94.

George Washington Harris

Current-García, Eugene. "Sut Lovingood's Rare Ripe Southern Garden." *Studies in Short Fiction* 9 (1972):117–29.

Inge, M. Thomas. "Introduction." *In High Times and Hard Times: Sketches and Tales By George Washington Harris.* Nashville: Vanderbilt University Press, 1967, pp. 3–8.

———. "Introduction." *Sut Lovingood's Yarns.* By George Washington Harris. New Haven, Conn.: College and University Press, 1966, pp. 9–24.

Rickels, Milton. *George Washington Harris.* New York: Twayne, 1965.

———. "The Imagery of George Washington Harris." *American Literature* 31 (1959):173–87.

Nathaniel Hawthorne

Abel, Darrel. "Black Glove and Pink Ribbon: Hawthorne's Metonymic Symbols." *New England Quarterly* 42 (1969):163–80.

Abrams, Robert E. "The Psychology of Cognition in 'My Kinsman, Major Molineux.'" *Philological Quarterly* 58 (1979):336–47.

Adama, Richard P. "Hawthorne: The Old Manse Period." *Tulane Studies in English* 8 (1958):115–51.

Allen, Mary. "Smiles and Laughter in Hawthorne." *Philological Quarterly* 52 (1973):119–28.

Allison, Alexander W. "The Literary Contexts of 'My Kinsman, Major Molineux.'" *Nineteenth-Century Fiction* 23 (1968):304–11.

Alson, Eberhard. "Poe's Theory of Hawthorne's Indebtedness to Tieck." *Anglia* 91 (1973):342–56.

Baym, Nina. "Hawthorne's Myths for Children: The Author versus His Audience." *Studies in Short Fiction* 10 (1973):35–46.

––––––. "Hawthorne's Women: The Tyranny of Social Myths." *Centennial Review* 15 (1971):250–72.

––––––. "The Head, the Heart, and the Unpardonable Sin." *New England Quarterly* 40 (1967):31–47.

––––––. *The Shape of Hawthorne's Career.* Ithaca, N.Y.: Cornell University Press, 1976.

Becker, Isidore H. *The Ironic Dimension in Hawthorne's Short Fiction.* New York: Carlton Press, 1971.

Bell, Millicent. *Hawthorne's View of the Artist.* New York: State University of New York, 1962.

Benoit, Raymond. "Hawthorne's Psychology of Death: 'The Minister's Black Veil.'" *Studies in Short Fiction* 8 (1971):553–60.

Bercovitch, Sacvan. "Endicott's Breastplate: Symbolism and Typology in 'Endicott and the Red Cross.'" *Studies in Short Fiction* 4 (1967):289–99.

Bland, R. Luman. "William Austin's 'The Man with the Clocks: A Vermont Legend': An American Influence on Hawthorne's 'The Man of Adamant.'" *Nathaniel Hawthorne Journal,* 1977, pp. 139–45.

Boswell, Jeanetta. *Nathaniel Hawthorne And The Critics: A Checklist of Criticism, 1900–1978.* Metuchen, N.J.: Scarecrow Press, 1982.

Brenzo, Richard. "Beatrice Rappaccini: A Victim of Male Love and Horror." *American Literature* 48 (1976):152–64.

Brill, Lesley W. "Conflict and Accommodation in Hawthorne's 'The Artist of the Beautiful.'" *Studies in Short Fiction* 12 (1975):381–86.

Brodwin, Stanley. "Hawthorne and the Function of History: A Reading of 'Alice Doane's Appeal.'" *Nathaniel Hawthorne Journal,* 1974, pp. 116–28.

Broes, Arthur T. "Journey into Moral Darkness: 'My Kinsman, Major Molineux,' as Allegory." *Nineteenth-Century Fiction* 19 (1964):171–84.

Brown, Dennis. "Literature and Existential Psychoanalysis: 'My Kinsman, Major Molineux' and 'Young Goodman Brown.'" *Canadian Review of American Studies* 4 (1973):65–73.

Burhans, Clinton S., Jr. "Hawthorne's Mind and Art in 'The Hollow of the Three Hills.'" *Journal of English and Germanic Philosophy* 60 (1961):286–95.

Burns, Shannon. "Alchemy and 'The Birth-mark.'" *American Transcendental Quarterly,* no. 42 (1979):147–58.

––––––. "Hawthorne's Literary Theory in the Tales." *Nathaniel Hawthorne Journal,* 1977, pp. 261–77.

Canaday, Nicholas, Jr. "Hawthorne's Minister and the Veiling Deceptions of Self." *Studies in Short Fiction* 4 (1967):135–42.

Carnochan, W. B. "'The Minister's Black Veil': Symbol, Meaning, and the Context of Hawthorne's Art." *Nineteenth-Century Fiction* 24 (1969):182–92.

Carpenter, Richard C. "Hawthorne's Polar Explorations: 'Young Goodman

Brown' and 'My Kinsman, Major Molineux.'" *Nineteenth-Century Fiction* 24 1969):45–56.

Clark, C. E. Frazer, Jr. "New Light on the Editing of the 1842 Edition of *Twice-Told Tales*." *Nathaniel Hawthorne Journal,* 1972, pp. 91–139.

Coffey, Dennis G. "Hawthorne's 'Alice Doane's Appeal': The Artist Absolved." *ESQ* 2 (1975):230–40.

Colacurcio, Michael J. "Parson Hooper's Power of Blackness: Sin and Self in 'The Minister's Black Veil.'" *Prospects* 5 (1980):331–411.

————. "Visible Sanctity and Specter Evidence: The Moral World of Hawthorne's 'Young Goodman Brown.'" *Essex Institute Historical Collections* 110 (1974):259–99.

Crews, Frederick. "Giovanni's Garden." *American Quarterly* 16 (1964):402–18.

Crowley, J. Donald. "The Artist as Mediator: The Rationale of Hawthorne's Large-scale Revisions in His Collected Tales and Sketches." In *Melville and Hawthorne in the Berkshires: A Symposium.* Edited by Howard P Vincent. Kent, Ohio: Kent State University Press, 1968, pp. 79–88.

————. *Nathaniel Hawthorne.* London: Routledge & Kegan Paul, 1971.

————. "The Unity of Hawthorne's *Twice-Told Tales*." *Studies in American Fiction* 1 (1973):35–61.

Curran, Ronald T. "Irony: Another Thematic Dimension to 'The Artist of the Beautiful.'" *Studies in Romanticism* 6 (1966):34–45.

D'Avanzo, Mario L. "The Literary Sources of 'My Kinsman, Major Molineux': Shakespeare, Coleridge, and Milton," *Studies in Short Fiction* 10 (1973):121–36.

Davis, Joseph A. "The Oldest Puritan: A Study of the Angel of Hadley Legend in Hawthorne's 'The Gray Champion.'" *Rackham Literary Studies,* no. 4 (1973):25–43.

Dennis, Carl. "How to Live in Hell: The Bleak Vision of Hawthorne's 'My Kinsman, Major Molineux.'" *University Review* (Kansas City) 37 (1971):250–58.

Doubleday, Neal F. *Hawthorne's Early Tales: A Critical Study.* Durham, N.C.: Duke University Press, 1972.

Dryden, Edgar A. *Nathaniel Hawthorne: The Poetics of Enchantment.* Ithaca, N.Y.: Cornell University Press, 1977.

Durban, James. "Hawthorne's Debt to Edmund Spenser and Charles Chauncy in 'The Gentle Boy.'" *Nathaniel Hawthorne Journal,* 1976, pp. 189–95.

England, A. B. "Robin Molineux and the Young Ben Franklin: A Reconsideration." *Journal of American Studies* 6 (1972):181–88.

Erlich, Gloria Chasson. "Guilt and Expiation in 'Roger Malvin's Burial.'" *Nineteenth-Century Fiction* 26 (1972):377–89.

Feeney, Joseph H., S.J. "The Structure of Ambiguity in Hawthorne's 'The Maypole of Merry Mount.'" *Studies in American Fiction* 3 (1975):211–16.

Fishman, Burton J. "Imagined Redemption in 'Roger Malvin's Burial'" *Studies in American Fiction* 5 (1977):257–62.

Fogle, Richard Harter. *Hawthorne's Fiction: The Light and the Dark*. Rev. ed. Norman: University of Oklahoma Press, 1964.

Gupta, R. K. "Hawthorne's Theory of Art." *American Literature* 40 (1968):309–24.

———. "Hawthorne's Treatment of the Artist." *New England Quarterly* 45 (1972):65–80.

Hurley, Paul J. "Young Goodman Brown's 'Heart of Darkness.'" *American Literature* 37 (1966):410–19.

Jones, Buford. "*The Faery Land* of Hawthorne's Romances." *Emerson Society Quarterly*, no. 48 (1967):106–24.

Liebmann, Sheldon W. "Ethan Brand and the Unpardonable Sin," *American Transcendental Quarterly*, no. 24, supplement two (1974):9–14.

———. "Hawthorne and Milton: The Second Fall in 'Rappaccini's Daughter.'" *New England Quarterly* 41 (1968):521–35.

———. "Hawthorne's Romanticism: 'The Art of the Beautiful.'" *ESQ* 22 (1976):85–95.

———. "Moral Choice in 'The Maypole of Merry Mount.'" *Studies in Short Fiction* 11 (1974):173–80.

———. "The Reader in 'Young Goodman Brown.'" *Nathaniel Hawthorne Journal*, 1975, pp. 156–69.

———. "Robin's Conversion: The Design of 'My Kinsman, Major Molineux.'" *Studies in Short Fiction* 8 (1971):443–57.

———. "'Roger Malvin's Burial': Hawthorne's Allegory of the Heart." *Studies in Short Fiction* 12 (1975):253–60.

Lynch, James J. "Structure and Allegory in 'The Great Stone Face.'" *Nineteenth-Century Fiction* 15 (1960):137–46.

Martin, Terence. "The Method of Hawthorne's Tales." In *Hawthorne Centenary Essays*. Edited by Roy Harvey Pearce. Columbus: Ohio State University Press, 1964, pp. 7–30.

———. *Nathaniel Hawthorne*. New York: Twayne, 1965; rev. ed. 1983.

McDonald, John J. "'The Old Manse' and Its Mosses: *The Inception and Development of Mosses from an Old Manse*." *Texas Studies in Literature and Language* 16 (1974):72–108.

McWilliams, John P., Jr. "Fictions of Merry Mount." *American Quarterly* 29 (1977):3–30.

———. "'Thorough-going Democrat' and 'Modern Tory': Hawthorne and the Puritan Revolution of 1776." *Studies in Romanticism* 15 (1976):549–71.

Monteiro, George "The Full Particulars of the Minister's Behavior—According to Hale." *Nathaniel Hawthorne Journal*, 1972, pp. 173–82.

———. "Hawthorne's Emblematic Serpent." *Nathaniel Hawthorne Journal*, 1973, pp. 134–42.

Morsberger, Robert E. "'The Minister's Black Veil': 'Shrouded in a Blackness, Ten Times Black.'" *New England Quarterly* 46 (1973):454–63.

Newberry, Frederick. "'The Gray Champion': Hawthorne's Ironic Criticism of Puritan Rebellion." *Studies in Short Fiction* 13 (1976):363–70.

Pandeya, Prabhat K. "The Drama of Evil in 'The Hollow of the Three Hills.'" *Nathaniel Hawthorne Journal,* 1975, pp. 177–81.

Reece, James B. "Mr. Hooper's Vow." *ESQ* 2 (1975):93–102.

Robinson, E. Arthur. "'Roger Malvin's Burial': Hawthorne and the American Environment." *Nathaniel Hawthorne Journal,* 1977, pp. 147–66.

Ross, Morton L. "What Happens in 'Rappaccini's Daughter.'" *American Literature* 43 (1971):336–45.

Rouse, Blair. "Hawthorne and the American Revolution: An Exploration." *Nathaniel Hawthorne Journal,* 1976, pp. 17–61.

Schultz, Dieter. "'Ethan Brand' and the Structure of the American Quest Romance." *Genre* 7 (1974):233–49.

St. Armand, Barton Levi. "Hawthorne's 'Haunted Mind': A Subterranean Drama of the Self." *Criticism* 13 (1971):1–25.

———. "'Young Goodman Brown' as Historical Allegory." *Nathaniel Hawthorne Journal,* 1973, pp. 183–97.

Shaw, Peter, "Fathers, Sons, and the Ambiguities of Revolution in 'My Kinsman, Major Molineux.'" *New England Quarterly* 49 (1976):559–76.

———. "Their Kinsman, Thomas Hutchinson: Hawthorne, the Boston Patriots, and His Majesty's Royal Governor." *Early American Literature* 11 (1976):183–90.

Simpson, Lewis P. "John Adams and Hawthorne: The Fiction of the Real American Revolution." *Studies in the Literary Imagination* 9, no. 2 (1976): 1–17.

Stern, Richard Clark. "Puritans at Merry Mount: Variations on a Theme." *American Quarterly* 22 (1970):846–58.

Stewart, Randall. *Nathaniel Hawthorne: A Biography.* New Haven: Yale University Press, 1948.

Stock, Ely. "History and the Bible in Hawthrone's 'Roger Malvin's Burial.'" *Essex Institute's Historical Collections* 100 (1964):279–96.

———. "The Biblical Context of 'Ethan Brand.'" *American Literature* 37 (1965):115–34.

Stoehr, Taylor. "Hawthorne and Mesmerism." *The Huntington Library Quarterly,* 33 (1969):33–60.

———. "'Young Goodman Brown' and Hawthorne's Theory of Mimesis." *Nineteenth-Century Fiction* 23 (1969):393–412.

Strandberg, Victor. "The Artist's Black Veil." *New England Quarterly* 41 (1968):567–74.

Swann, Charles. "'Alice Doane's Appeal': Or How to Tell a Story." *Literature and History,* no. 5 (1977):4–25.

Turner, Arlin. "Elizabeth Peabody Reviews Twice-Told Tales." *Nathaniel Hawthorne Journal,* 1974, pp. 75–84.

———. *Nathaniel Hawthorne: A Biography.* New York: Oxford University Press, 1980.

Waggoner, Hyatt H. *Hawthorne: A Critical Study.* Rev. ed. Cambridge, Mass.:

Harvard University Press, 1963.

Warren, Robert Penn. "Hawthorne Revisited: Some Remarks on Hellfiredness." *Sewanee Review* 81 (1973):75–111.

White, Peter. "The Monstrous Birth and 'The Gentle Boy': Hawthorne's Use of the Past." *Nathaniel Hawthorne Journal*, 1976, pp. 173–88.

Williamson, James L. "Vision and Revision in 'Alice Doane's Appeal.'" *American Transcendental Quarterly* 40 (1978):348–53.

————. "'Young Goodman Brown': Hawthorne's 'Devil Manuscript.'" *Studies in Short Fiction* 18 (1981):155–62.

Johnson Jones Hooper

Hoole, W. Stanley. *Alias Simon Suggs: The Life and Times of Johnson Jones Hopper.* University, Ala.; University of Alabama Press, 1952.

Smith, Winston. "*Simon Suggs* and the Satiric Tradition." In *Essays in Honor of Richebourg Caillard McWilliams.* Edited by Howard Creed. Birmingham, Ala.: Birmingham-Southern College, 1970, pp. 49–56.

Welman, Manly Wade. "Introduction." In *Adventures of Simon Suggs, Late of the Tallapoosa Volunteers.* By Johnson Jones Hooper. Chapel Hill: University of North Carolina Press, 1969, pp. ix–xxviii.

Washington Irving

Bone, Richard A. "Irving's Headless Hessian: Prosperity and the Inner Life." *American Quarterly* 15 (1963):167–75.

Dawson, William P. "'Rip Van Winkle' as Bawdy Satire: The Rascal and the Revolution." *ESQ: Journal of American Renaissance* 27 (1981):198–206.

Hedges, William L. *Washington Irving: An American Study, 1802–1832.* Baltimore: Johns Hopkins Press, 1965.

————. "Washington Irving: Nonsense, the Fat of the Land and the Dream of Indolence." In *The Chief Glory of Every People: Essays on Classic American Writers.* Edited by Matthew J. Bruccoli. Carbondale and Edwardsville: Southern Illinois University Press, 1973, pp. 141–60.

Martin, Terence. "Rip, Ichabod, and the American Imagination." *American Literature* 31 (1959):137–49.

McClary, Ben Harris, ed. *Washington Irving and the House of Murray: Geoffrey Crayon Charms the British, 1817–1856.* Knoxville: University of Tennessee Press, 1969.

Miller, Perry. "Afterword." In *The Sketch Book.* New York: New American Library, 1961, pp. 371–78.

Pochmann, Henry A. "Germanic Materials and Motifs in the Short Story: Washington Irving." In *German Culture in America.* Madison: University of Wisconsin Press, 1961, pp. 367–81, 696–705.

————. "Washington Irving: Amateur or Professional?" In *Essays on American Literature in Honor of Jay B. Hubbell.* Edited by Clarence Gohdes. Durham, N.C.: Duke University Press, 1967, pp. 63–76.

Ringe, Donald A. "Irving's Use of the Gothic Mode." *Studies in the Literary Imagination* 7, no. 1 (1974):51–65.

———. "New York and New England: Irving's Criticism of American Society." *American Literature* 38 (1967):445–67.

Roth, Martin. *Comedy and America: The Lost World of Washington Irving.* Port Washington, N.Y.: Kennikat, 1976.

Shear, Walter. "Time in 'Rip Van Winkle' and 'The Legend of Sleepy Hollow.'" *Midwest Quarterly* 17 (1976):158–72.

Smith, Herbert F. "Introduction." In *Bracebridge Hall, or The Humourists: A Medley, by Geoffrey Crayon, Gent.* By Washington Irving. Boston: Twayne, 1977, pp. xiii–xxxiii.

Wagenknecht, Edward. *Washington Irving: Moderation Displayed.* New York: Oxford University Press, 1962.

Williams, Stanley T. *The Life of Washington Irving.* 2 vols. New York: Oxford University Press, 1935.

Young, Philip. "Fallen from Time: The Mythic Rip Van Winkle." *Kenyon Review* 22 (1960):547–73.

Henry Clay Lewis

Anderson, John Q. "The Life of Henry Clay Lewis." In *Louisiana Swamp Doctor: The Life and Writings of Henry Clay Lewis, alias "Madison Tensas, M.D."* Baton Rouge: Louisiana State University Press, 1962.

Israel, Charles. "Henry Clay Lewis's Odd Leaves: Studies in the Surreal and Grotesque." *Mississippi Quarterly* 28 (1975):61–69.

Rose, Allen H. "The Image of the Negro in the Writings of Henry Clay Lewis." *American Literature* 41 (1969):255–63.

Augustus Baldwin Longstreet

Downs, Robert B. "Yarns of Frontier Life: Augustus Baldwin Longstreet's Georgia Scenes." In *Books That Changed the South.* Chapel Hill: University of North Carolina Press, 1977, pp. 74–81.

Edgar Allan Poe

Allen, Michael. *Poe and the British Magazine Tradition.* New York: Oxford University Press, 1969.

Autrey, Max L. "Edgar Allan Poe's Satiric View of Evolution." *Extrapolation* 18 (1977):186–99.

Bailey, J. O. "What Happens in 'The Fall of the House of Usher'?" *American Literature* 35 (1964):445–66.

Beebe, Maurice. "The Universe of Roderick Usher." *Personalist* 37 (1956):147–60.

Blair, Walter. "Poe's Conception of Incident and Tone in the Tale." *Modern Philology* 41 (1944):228–40.

Budick, E. Miller. "The Fall of the House: A Reappraisal of Poe's Attitudes toward Life and Death." *Southern Literary Journal* 9, no. 2 (1977):30–50.

———. "Poe's Gothic Idea: The Cosmic Geniture of Horror." *Essays in Literature* (Western Illinois Universtiy) 3 (1976):73–85.

Carlson, Eric W. "Introduction." In *Introduction to Poe: A Thematic Reader*. Glenview, Ill.: Scott, Foresman, 1967, pp. xv–xxxv.

———. *Poe on the Soul of Man*. Baltimore: Edgar Allan Poe Society and Enoch Pratt Free Library, 1973.

Carson, David L. "Ortolans and Geese: The Origin of Poe's *Duc De L'Omelette*." *CLA Journal* 8 (1965):227–83.

Cecil, L. M. "Poe's 'Arabesque.'" *Comparative Literature* 18 (1966):55–70.

Cox, James M. "Edgar Poe: Style as Pose." *Virginia Quarterly Review* 44 (1968):67–89.

Davidson, Edward H. *Poe: A Critical Study*. Cambridge: Harvard University Press, 1957.

De Portmartin, Armand. "The Storytellers." In *Affidavits of Genius: Edgar Allan Poe and the French Critics, 1847–1924*. Edited and translated by Jean Alexander. Port Washington, N.Y.: Kennikat, 1971, pp. 126–30.

Dowell, Richard W. "The Ironic History of Poe's 'Life in Death': A Literary Skeleton in the Closet." *American Literature* 42 (1971):478–86.

Drabeck, Bernard A. "'Tall and Fether'—Poe and Abolitionism." *American Transcendental Quarterly*, no. 14 (1972):177–84.

Eakin, Paul John. "Poe's Sense of an Ending." *American Literature* 45 (1973):1–22.

Etienne, Louis. "The American Storytellers—Edgar Allan Poe." In *Affidavits of Genius: Edgar Allan Poe and the French Critics, 1847–1924*. Edited and translated by Jean Alexander. Port Washington, N.Y.: Kennikat, 1971, pp. 132–44.

Fisher, Benjamin F. "Poe and the Art of the Well Wrought Tale." *Library Chronicle* 41 (1976):5–12.

———. "Poe's 'Metzengerstein': Not a Hoax." *American Literature* 42 (1971):487–94.

Fusco, Richard. "Poe's Revisions of 'The Mystery of Marie Roget'—A Hoax?" *Library Chronicle* 41 (1976):91–99.

Gargano, James W. *The Masquerade Vision in Poe's Short Stories*. Baltimore: Enoch Pratt Free Library, Edgar Allan Poe Society, and Library of the University of Baltimore, 1977.

———. "The Question of Poe's Narrators." *College English* 25 (1963):177–81.

Garrison, Joseph M., Jr. "The Function of Terror in the Work of Edgar Allan Poe." *American Quarterly* 18 (1966):136–50.

Griffith, Clark. "Poe and the Gothic." In *Papers on Poe: Essays in Honor of John Ward Ostrom*. Edited by Richard P. Veler. Springfield, Ohio: Chantry Music Press, Wittenberg University, 1972, pp. 21–27.

Hirsch, David H. "The Pit and the Apocalypse." *Sewanee Review* 76 (1968):632–52.

Hoffman, Daniel. "I Have Been Faithful to You In My Fashion: The Remarriage of Ligeia's Husband." *Southern Review,* n.s. 8 (1972):89–105.

Howarth, William L. "Introduction." In *Twentieth Century Interpretations of Poe's Tales.* Englewood Cliffs, N.J.: Prentice-Hall, 1971, pp. 1–32.

Hubbell, Jay B. "The Literary Apprenticeship of Edgar Allan Poe." *Southern Literary Journal* 2, no. 1 (1969):99–105.

———. "Poe and the Southern Literary Tradition." *Texas Studies in Literature and Language* 2 (1960):151–71.

Jacobs, Robert D. "Poe's Earthly Paradise." *American Quarterly* 12 (1960):404–13.

Jones, Buford, and Ljunquist, Kent. "Monsieur Dupin: Further Details on the Reality behind the Legend." *Southern Literary Journal* 9, no. 1 (1976):70–77.

Keller, Mark. "Dupin in the 'Rue Morgue': Another Form of Madness?" *Arizona Quarterly* 33 (1977):249–55.

Kennedy, J. Gerald. "The Limits of Reason: Poe's Deluded Detectives." *American Literature* 47 (1975):184–96.

Lawson, Lewis A. "Poe's Conception of the Grotesque." *Mississippi Quarterly* 19 (1966):200–205.

Levine, Stuart. *Edgar Poe: Seer and Craftsman.* Deland, Fla.: Everett/Edwards, 1972.

Levine, Stuart, and Levine, Susan. "History, Myth, Fable, and Satire: Poe's Use of Jacob Bryant." *ESQ* 21 (1975):197–214.

———, eds. *The Short Fiction of Edgar Allan Poe: An Annotated Edition.* Indianapolis: Bobbs-Merrill, 1976.

Liebman, Sheldon W. "Poe's Tales and His Theory of the Poetic Experience." *Studies in Short Fiction* 7 (1970):582–96.

Martin, Terence. "The Imagination at Play: Edgar Allan Poe." *Kenyon Review* 28 (1966):194–209.

McKeithan, D. M. "Poe and the Second Edition of Hawthorne's *Twice-Told Tales.*" *Nathaniel Hawthorne Journal,* 1974, pp. 257–69.

Mengeling, Marvin, and Mengeling, Frances. "From Fancy to Failure: A Study of the Narrators in the Tales of Edgar Allan Poe." *University Review* (Kansas City) 33 (1967):293–98; 34 (1967):31–37.

Moldenhauer, Joseph J. "Murder as a Fine Art: Basic Connections between Poe's Aesthetics, Psychology, and Moral Vision." *PMLA* 83 (1968):284–97.

Mooney, Stephen L. "The Comic in Poe's Fiction." *American Literature* 33 (1962):433–41.

———. "Poe's Gothic Waste Land." *Sewanee Review* 70 (1962):261–83.

Moss, Sidney P. "Poe's Apocalyptic Vision." In *Papers on Poe: Essays in Honor of John Ward Ostrom.* Edited by Richard P. Veler. Springfield, Ohio: Chantry Music Press, Wittenberg University Press, 1972, pp. 42–53.

————. *Poe's Literary Battles: The Critic in the Context of His Literary Milieu.* Durham, N.C.: Duke University Press, 1963.

Pitcher, Edward William. "Horological and Chronological Time in 'Masque of the Red Death.'" *American Transcendental Quarterly,* no. 29 (1976):71–75.

Pollin, Burton. *Discoveries in Poe.* Notre Dame, Ind.: University of Notre Dame Press, 1970.

————. *Poe, Creator of Words.* Baltimore: Enoch Pratt Free Library, Edgar Allan Poe Society, and Library of the University of Baltimore, 1974.

————. "Poe's 'Some Words with a Mummy' Reconsidered." *ESQ,* no. 60, supplement (1970):60–67.

————. "Poe's Tale of Psyche Zenobia: A Reading for Humor and Ingenious Construction." In *Papers on Poe: Essays in Honor of John Ward Ostrom.* Edited by Richard P. Veler. Springfield, Ohio: Chantry Music Press, Wittenberg University, 1972, pp. 92–103.

————. *Undine* in the Works of Poe." *Studies in Romanticism* 14 (1975):59–74.

Porte, Joel. "In the Hands of an Angry God: Religious Terror in Gothic Fiction." In *The Gothic Imagination: Essays in Dark Romanticism.* Edited by G. R. Thompson. Pullman: Washington State University Press, 1974, pp. 42–64.

Quinn, Patrick F. *The French Face of Edgar Poe.* Carbondale: Southern Illinois University Press, 1957.

Regan, Robert. "Hawthorne's 'Plagiary'; Poe's Duplicity." *Nineteenth-Century Fiction* 25 (1970):281–98.

Robinson, E. Arthur. "Poe's 'The Tell-Tale Heart.'" *Nineteenth-Century Fiction* 19 (1965):369–78.

St. Armand, Barton Levi. "The 'Mysteries' of Edgar Poe: The Quest for a Monomyth in Gothic Literature." In *The Gothic Imagination: Essays in Dark Romanticism.* Edited by G. R. Thompson. Pullman: Washington State University Press, 1974, pp. 65–93.

————. "Usher Unveiled: Poe and the Metaphysic of Gnosticism." *Poe Studies* 5 (1972):1–8.

Schroeter, James. "A Misreading of Poe's 'Ligeia.'" *PMLA* 76 (1961):397–406.

Seelye, John. "Edgar Allan Poe: *Tales of the Grotesque and Arabesque.*" In *Landmarks of American Writing.* Edited by Hennig Cohen. New York: Basic Books, 1969, pp. 101–110.

Shulman, Robert. "Poe and the Powers of the Mind." *ELH* 37 (1970):245–62.

Sippel, Erich W. "Bolting the Whole Shebang Together: Poe's Predicament." *Criticism* 15 (1973):289–308.

Smith, Allan. "The Psychological Context of Three Tales by Poe." *Journal of American Studies* 7 (1973):279–92.

Smith, Herbert. "Usher's Madness and Poe's Organicism: A Source." *American Literature* 39 (1967):379–89.

Spitzer, Leo. "A Reinterpretation of 'The Fall of the House of Usher.'" *Comparative Literature* 4 (1952):351–63.

Stauffer, Donald Barlow. "Poe's Views on the Nature and Function of Style." *ESQ*, no. 60 (1970):23–30.

———. "Style and Meaning in 'Ligeia' and 'William Wilson.'" *Studies in Short Fiction* 2 (1965):316–30.

———. "The Two Styles of Poe's 'MS. Found in a Bottle.'" *Style* 1 (1967):107–20.

Sullivan, Ruth. "William Wilson's Double." *Studies in Romanticism* 15 (1976):253–63.

Tate, Allen. "The Angelic Imagination: Poe as God." In *Collected Essays*. Denver: Swallow, 1959, pp. 432–54.

———. "Our Cousin, Mr. Poe." In *Collected Essays*. Denver: Swallow, 1959, pp. 455–71.

Thompson, G. R. "Dramatic Irony in 'The Oval Portrait': A Reconsideration of Poe's Revisions." *English Language Notes* 6 (1968):107–14.

———. "Is Poe's 'A Tale of the Ragged Mountains' a Hoax?" *Studies in Fiction* 6 (1969):454–60.

———. *Poe's Fiction: Romantic Irony in the Gothic Tales*. Madison: University of Wisconsin Press, 1973.

———. "Poe's 'Flawed' Gothic: Absurdist Techniques in 'Metzengerstein' and the *Courier* Satires." *ESQ*, no. 60, supplement (1970):38–58.

———. "'Proper Evidences of Madness': American Gothic and the Interpretation of 'Ligeia.'" *ESQ* 18 (1972):30–49.

Wagenknecht, Edward. *Edgar Allan Poe: The Man Behind the Legend*. New York: Oxford University Press, 1963.

Wilbur, Richard. "Edgar Allan Poe." In *Major Writers of America*. Edited by Perry Miller. 2 vols. New York: Harcourt Brace & World, 1962. 1:369–82.

———. "Introduction." In *Poe*. New York: Dell, 1959, pp. 7–39.

Woodson, Thomas, ed. *Twentieth-Century Interpretations of "The Fall of the House of Usher."* Englewood Cliffs, N.J.: Prentice-Hall, 1969.

William Gilmore Simms

Guilds, John C. "The Achievement of William Gilmore Simms: His Short Fiction." In *The Poetry of Community: Essays on the Southern Sensibility of History and Literature*. Edited by Lewis P. Simpson. Spectrum Monograph Series in the Arts and Sciences, vol. 2. Atlanta: School of Arts and Sciences, Georgia State University, 1972, pp. 25–35.

———. "Introduction." In *The Writings of William Gilmore Simms. Volume 5: Stories and Tales*. Columbia: University of South Carolina Press, 1974, pp. xi–xxiv.

———. "William Gilmore Simms and the *Southern Literary Gazette*." *Studies in Bibliography* 21 (1968):59–92.

Kibler, James E., Jr. "Simms's Indebtedness to Folk Tradition in 'Sharp Snaffles.'" *Southern Literary Journal* 4, no. 2 (1972):55–68.

Oliphant, Mary C., et al., eds. *The Letters of William Gilmore Simms.* 5 vols. Columbia: University of South Carolina Press, 1952–56.

Ridgely, J. V. *William Gilmore Simms.* New York: Twayne, 1962.

Wimsatt, Mary Ann. "Simms and Irving." *Mississippi Quarterly* 20 (1967):25–37.

————. "Simms's Early Short Stories." *Library Chronicle* 41 (1977):163–79.

William Tappan Thompson

Shippey, Herbert. "William Tappan Thompson." In *Antebellum Writers in New York and the South.* Edited by Joel Myerson. *Dictionary of Literary Biography,* vol. 3. Detroit: Gale Research, 1979, pp. 332–35.

Thomas Bangs Thorpe

Bain Robert. "Thomas Bangs Thorpe." In *Antebellum Writers in New York and the South.* Edited by Joel Myerson. *Dictionary of Literary Biography,* vol. 3. Detroit: Gale Research, 1979, pp. 335–39.

Current-García, Eugene. "Thomas Bangs Thorpe and the Literature of the Ante-Bellum Southwestern Frontier." *Louisiana Historical Quarterly* 39 (1956):199–222.

Lemay, J. A. Leo. "The Text, Tradition, and Themes of 'The Big Bear of Arkansas.'" *American Literature* 47 (1975):321–42.

Rickels, Milton. *Thomas Bangs Thorpe, Humorist of the Old Southwest.* Baton Rouge: Louisiana State University Press, 1962.

Index

About the Author

Eugene Current-García is Hargis Professor Emeritus of American Literature at Auburn University, where he taught courses in American fiction, poetry, and drama from 1947 until his retirement in 1978. After receiving the A.B. and M.A. degrees from Tulane University (1930–32), he continued graduate work in English and American studies at Harvard University, where he received the Ph. D. in 1947. Before then he taught consecutively for a number of years at the University of Nebraska and at Louisiana State University. He also served for a year in Nicaragua as director of the English-teaching program sponsored by the United States Department of State. During the year 1953–54 he attended Princeton University as a postdoctoral Ford Foundation Fellow, and from 1956 to 1958 he held the Chair of American Literature as Fulbright Lecturer at the University of Thessaloniki, Greece. At Auburn University he helped to found the *Southern Humanities Review* in 1967 and served as coeditor and editor of that journal until 1979. In 1974 he was awarded the title of First American Scholar by the honorary fraternity of Phi Kappa Phi.

Besides the present volume, Professor Current-García has published books on O. Henry (Twayne, 1965) and (with Dorothy B. Hatfield) on *The Papers of W. O. Tuggle* (1972). He has also edited (with Walton R. Patrick) the following textbooks on short fiction published by Scott, Foresman: *What Is the Short Story?* (1961), *Realism and Romanticism in Fiction* (1962), *Short Stories of the Western World* (1969), and *American Short Stories* (1952–1982), which is now in its fourth edition. Since the 1940s his articles and reviews have appeared in such journals as *American Literature, American Quarterly, Studies in Short Fiction*, the *Southern Review, Alabama Review, Mississippi Quarterly*, and others.

DATE DUE

NOV 2 1 '98			